Issues in Religion and Theology

4

Visionaries and their Apocalypses

Issues in Religion and Theology 4

Visionaries and their Apocalypses

Edited with an Introduction by

PAUL D. HANSON

FORTRESS PRESS | SPCK
Philadelphia | London

First published in Great Britain 1983
SPCK
Holy Trinity Church
Marylebone Road
London NW1 4DU

First published in the USA 1983
Fortress Press
2900 Queen Lane
Philadelphia
Pennsylvania 19129

Library of Congress Cataloging in Publication Data
Main entry under title:

Visionaries and their apocalypses.

(Issues in religion and theology; 2)
Bibliography: p.
1. Apocalyptic literature—History and criticism—
Addresses, essays, lectures. I. Hanson, Paul D. II. Series.
BS646.V57   1983   220.6   83–5488
ISBN 0–8006–1765–7

British Library Cataloguing in Publication Data

Visionaries and their apocalypses.—(Issues in religion and theology; 2)
1. Apocalyptic literature
I. Hanson, Paul D.   II. Series
236   BS646

ISBN 0–281–04057–5

Filmset in Monophoto Times by Northumberland Press Ltd, Gateshead
Printed in Great Britain by Richard Clay (The Chaucer Press) Ltd, Bungay, Suffolk

Contents

The Contributors

KLAUS KOCH is Professor of Old Testament and History of Ancient Near Eastern Religions at the University of Hamburg. Among his many works are *The Growth of the Biblical Tradition* and *The Prophets* (2 vols.).

PAUL D. HANSON is Bussey Professor of Divinity at Harvard University. He is the author of *The Dawn of Apocalyptic, Dynamic Transcendence*, and *The Diversity of Scripture*.

JOHN J. COLLINS is Professor of Religious Studies at DePaul University. He is the author of *The Apocalyptic Vision of the Book of Daniel* and *Between Athens and Jerusalem*. He also edited *Apocalypse: The Morphology of a Genre* (*Semeia* 14).

MICHAEL E. STONE is Professor of Armenian Studies and of Jewish Thought at the Hebrew University of Jerusalem. He is well known for his contributions to the history of Second-Temple Judaism and has co-authored, with G. W. E. Nickelsburg, *Faith and Piety in Early Judaism: Texts and Documents*.

JONATHAN Z. SMITH is the Robert O. Anderson Distinguished Service Professor of the Humanities and in the College at the University of Chicago. He is known for his essays in the history of religions, especially in *Map Is Not Territory: Studies in the History of Religions*.

NORMAN PERRIN (1921–76) was Professor of New Testament at the University of Chicago. He wrote such widely acclaimed works as *Rediscovering the Teaching of Jesus, What is Redaction Criticism?*, and *Jesus and the Language of the Kingdom*.

JOHN G. GAGER is Professor of Religious Studies at Princeton University and is the author of *Moses in Greco-Roman Paganism*.

Acknowledgements

Klaus Koch, "What is Apocalyptic? An Attempt at a Preliminary Definition" is reprinted by permission from *The Rediscovery of Apocalyptic* 18–35, 132–8. Copyright © 1972 by SCM Press, London.

Paul D. Hanson, "Old Testament Apocalyptic Reexamined" is reprinted by permission from *Interpretation: A Journal of Bible and Theology* 25 (1971) 454–79. Copyright © 1971 by Union Theological Seminary, Va.

John J. Collins, "Apocalyptic Eschatology as the Transcendence of Death" is reprinted from *Catholic Biblical Quarterly* 36 (1974) 21–43 by permission of the author and *CBQ*. Copyright © 1974 by John J. Collins.

Michael E. Stone, "New Light on the Third Century" and "Enoch and Apocalyptic Origins" are reprinted by permission from *Scriptures, Sects, and Visions: A Profile of Judaism from Ezra to the Jewish Revolts* (Philadelphia: Fortress Press, 1980; Oxford: Basil Blackwell, 1982) 27–47. Copyright © 1980 by Michael Edward Stone.

Jonathan Z. Smith, "Wisdom and Apocalyptic" is reprinted by permission from *Religious Syncretism in Antiquity: Essays in Conversation with Geo Windengren*, ed. Birger A. Pearson (Missoula, Mont.: Scholars Press, 1975) 131–56. Copyright © 1975 by University of California Institute of Religious Studies.

Norman Perrin, "Apocalyptic Christianity" is reprinted by permission from *The New Testament: An Introduction*, 65–85. Copyright © 1974 by Harcourt Brace Jovanovich Inc.

John G. Gager, "The Attainment of Millennial Bliss Through Myth: The Book of Revelation" is reprinted by permission from *Kingdom and Community: The Social World of Early Christianity*, 45–57, 64–5. Copyright © 1975 by Prentice-Hall, Inc., Englewood Cliffs, N. J.

Series Foreword

The "Issues in Religion and Theology" series intends to encompass a variety of topics within the general disciplines of religious and theological studies. Subjects are drawn from any of the component fields, such as biblical studies, systematic theology, ethics, history of Christian thought, and history of religion. The issues have all proved to be highly significant for their respective areas, and they are of similar interest to students, teachers, clergy, and general readers.

The series aims to address these issues by collecting and reproducing key studies, all previously published, which have contributed significantly to our present understandings. In each case, the volume editor introduces the discussion with an original essay which describes the subject and its treatment in religious and theological studies. To this editor has also fallen the responsibility of selecting items for inclusion – no easy task when one considers the vast number of possibilities. Together the essays are intended to present a balanced overview of the problem and various approaches to it. Each piece is important in the current debate, and any older publication included normally stands as a "classical" or seminal work which is still worth careful study. Readers unfamiliar with the issue should find that these discussions provide a good entrée, while more advanced students will appreciate having studies by some of the best specialists on the subject gathered together in one volume. The editor has, of course, faced certain constraints: analyses too lengthy or too technical could not be included, except perhaps in excerpt form; the bibliography is not exhaustive; and the volumes in this series are being kept to a reasonable, uniform length. On the other hand, the editor is able to overcome the real problem of inaccessibility. Much of the best literature on a subject is often not readily available to readers, whether because it was first published in journals or books not widely circulated or because it was originally written in a language not read by all who would benefit from it. By bringing these and other studies together in this series, we hope to contribute to the general understanding of these key topics.

The series editors and the publishers wish to express their gratitude to the authors and their original publishers whose works are reprinted or translated here, often with corrections from living authors.

We are also conscious of our debt to members of the editorial advisory board. They have shared our belief that the series will be useful on a wide scale, and they have therefore been prepared to spare much time and thought for the project.

DOUGLAS A. KNIGHT
ROBERT MORGAN

Abbreviations

ANET	J. B. Pritchard, *Ancient Near Eastern Texts* (1955², 1969³)
Apoc. Abr.	*Apocalypse of Abraham*
2 Apoc. Bar.	*Apocalypse of Baruch = 2 Bar.*
Apoc. of John	Apocalypse of John (= Revelation)
As. Mos.	*Assumption of Moses*
BASOR	*Bulletin of the American Schools of Oriental Research*
B.C.E	Before the Common Era
Bib	*Biblica*
BJRL	*Bulletin of the John Rylands Library*
BWANT	Beiträge zur Wissenschaft vom Alten und Neuen Testament
BZAW	Beihefte zur *ZAW*
CBQ	*Catholic Biblical Quarterly*
C.E.	The Common Era
EBib	Etudes bibliques
ET	English translation/English translator
FRLANT	Forschungen zur Religion und Literatur des Alten und Neuen Testaments
GCS	Griechische christliche Schriftsteller
HAT	Handbuch zum Alten Testament
HNT	Handbuch zum Neuen Testament
HR	*History of Religions*
HSM	Harvard Semitic Monographs
HTR	*Harvard Theological Review*
HTS	Harvard Theological Studies
HZ	*Historische Zeitschrift*
ICC	International Critical Commentary
IDB	G. A. Buttrick (ed.), *Interpreter's Dictionary of the Bible*
IDBSup	Supplementary volume to *IDB*

Int	*Interpretation*
JBL	*Journal of Biblical Literature*
JCS	*Journal of Cuneiform Studies*
JEA	*Journal of Egyptian Archeology*
JNES	*Journal of Near Eastern Studies*
JQR	*Jewish Quarterly Review*
JQRMS	Jewish Quarterly Review Monograph Series
JTC	*Journal for Theology and the Church*
JTS	*Journal of Theological Studies*
KAT	Kommentar zum Alten Testament
LXX	Septuagint
MT	Masoretic Test
NovT	*Novum Testamentum*
NRT	*La nouvelle revue théologique*
NTS	*New Testament Studies*
OTL	Old Testament Library
OTS	*Oudtestmentische Studiën*
1Q	Qumran, Cave 1 (= Dead Sea Scrolls)
1QH	*Hôdāyôt* (*Thanksgiving Hymns*)
1–2–5 QJN	*The New Jerusalem* (Fragments)
1QM	*Milḥāmāh* (*War Scroll*)
11Q	Qumran, Cave 11
11QMelch	*The Melchizedek Document*
1QMyst	*Book of the Mysteries*
1QpHab	*Commentary on Habakkuk*
1QpMic	*Commentary on Micah*
1QpNah	*Commentary on Nahum*
1QpPs 68	*Commentary on Psalm 68*
4Q	Qumran, Cave 4
4QPrNab	*The Prayer of Nabonidus*
4QpPs 37	*Commentary on Psalm 37*
4QPsDan	*Pseudo-Daniel*
1QpZeph	*Commentary on Zephaniah*
1QS	*Serek hayyaḥad* (*Rule of the Community, Manual of Discipline*)
1QSa	Appendix A (*Rule of the Congregation, The Messianic Rule*) to 1QS

RB	*Revue biblique*
RGG	*Religion in Geschichte und Gegenwart*
RQ	*Römische Quartalschrift für Christliche Altertumskunde und Kirchengeschichte*
SBLMS	Society of Biblical Literature Monograph Series
SUNT	Studien zur Umwelt des Neuen Testaments
Tr	*Theologische Rundschau*
VT	*Vetus Testamentum*
VTSup	Vetus Testamentum, Supplements
WUNT	Wissenschaftliche Monographien zum Alten und Neuen Testament
ZA	*Zeitschrift für Assyriologie*
ZAW	*Zeitschrift für die altestamentliche Wissenschaft*
ZNW	*Zeitschrift für die neutestamentliche Wissenschaft*
ZTK	*Zeitschrift für Theologie und Kirche*

Introduction

The Relevance of Apocalyptic Literature Today

Apocalyptic is a literature that is drawn and torn by contending forces. Within the crosscurrents and eddies of this material there comes to expression an ominous sense of final ending. The present order having plunged hopelessly into degenerateness and anomie, the structures once capable of sustaining life are at the point of rupture. Situated at this dread threshold, the apocalypticist looks in several directions in the effort to explain the prevailing doom. A backward glance, often in the form of a resumé of history, discerns patterns and trajectories which explain why it is that things have reached this nadir. Careful scrutiny of the present in turn focuses on signs of an imminent turning, a final collapse, and reduction to a state of chaos reminiscent of primordial formlessness. Finally, since the final cataclysm is interpreted as a catharsis, the seer peers into the future to describe a new order which will supplant the old, a supernatural order of unprecedented glory and blessing for those favored by the One directing this cosmic drama.

In the case of early Jewish and Christian apocalypticism (from the period of the Babylonian exile down to the Roman persecutions), this bleak world view has come to expression primarily in periods of crisis. Thus the early expressions of the apocalyptic vision in Isaiah 24—27, Isaiah 56—66, and Zechariah 9—14 stem from the turmoil of the late sixth and fifth centuries B.C.E. Persecutions at the hands of the Seleucids and the threat posed by Hellenization to the Jewish faith in the second century B.C.E. gave rise to apocalyptic sections found in *1 Enoch* and the Book of Daniel, as well as to the apocalyptic writings of the Qumran community (the Dead Sea Scrolls). And from the Roman persecutions came Mark 13, the Book of Revelation (the Apocalypse of John), and a considerable number of extrabiblical writings like 4 Ezra and the Syriac *Book of Baruch*, as well as later parts of *1 Enoch* and of the *Testaments of the Twelve Patriarchs*.

1

As in the case of any mythology, the question arises, why read such expressions of the bizarre and the fantastic? Indeed, there have been periods in which apocalyptic literature has been rejected out of hand by the educated and culturally enriched elite. The refined, rational mind, after all, discerned order and harmony at the core of the universe, and disdained the mentality which described the world in terms of tension and impending doom as perverted and not to be taken seriously. For the intelligentsia of the Enlightenment, for the idealistic philosophers and liberal theologians of the nineteenth century, and for sober scholars and thinkers at the beginning of this century, apocalypticism, with few exceptions, was ignored or repudiated with loathing.

Post WWII interest

Then, in a flash, the world mood changed. The optimism of a strident civilization succumbed to grave self-doubts in a world engulfed by war. This led to the rediscovery of an ancient literature which described the world as torn by opposing forces, forces larger than human in stature and battling for supremacy. Apocalypticism once again seemed relevant, and passed quickly from eclipse into the light of renewed scholarly scrutiny.

In the aftermath of the First World War, an answer began to take shape to the question, why read a literature interpreting reality in terms of conflict and tension and replete with bizarre symbols and mythical figures? That answer arose among inhabitants of a ravaged and broken planet, to whom apocalyptic literature seemed more accurately to describe reality as it actually was experienced than did the constructions of the philosophical idealists and the harmonious systems of the theological liberals. For Karl Barth in World War I and Hans Lilje in World War II, the Book of Revelation was far from absurd, being instead a profoundly truthful portrait of the forces contending for control of the world. And in this new, more severe world, those who dared to peer into the inner world of the psyche discerned a state of tension and conflict which reflected the realities of the outer world. A long career of such peering led Carl Jung to conclude:

JUNG

> The sad truth is that man's real life consists of a complex of opposites—day and night, birth and death, happiness and misery, good and evil. We are not even sure that one will prevail against the other, that good will overcome evil, or joy defeat pain. Life is a battleground. It always has been, and always will be; and if it were not so, existence would come to an end.[1]

As one adhering to a view of life as "a battleground," Carl Jung had a deep appreciation for the contribution which the myths of

2

antiquity could make to our understanding of life. For they were born of an age which perceived life as a tension-filled unity, thereby giving expression to the entire range of human experience, from spiritual to material, unconscious to conscious, inner to outer, subject to object, mind to matter, without dichotomization or the subsuming of one side in favor of the other. Ours is an age in which technological advances have seduced us into believing that the conscious world and the world of matter constitute the sum total of reality, and an age which suffers all of the psychoneurosis and world conflict generated by the neglect, abuse, and repression into the unconscious of the whole depth dimension of the human spirit. Such an age, according to Jung, needs to learn to reintegrate the whole from that earlier age, an age which expressed itself in the images and symbols of myth. What is more, that part of ourselves which is held in drugged stupor under the tyranny of technology can be awakened by the piercing intonations of mythology because of a collective memory ingrained by the Ages of our race.

The shocking images of that specific kind of mythology we call apocalyptic arrest the attention of increasing numbers of thoughtful moderns because they recognize that the apocalyptic themes of history's decline, imminent doom, and a new order beyond the cataclysm are far more descriptive of the world they live in – or should we say, of the world they are leaving and the world they yearn to enter – than the facile assurances of their civil leaders that the future is bright if efforts at technological development, materialistic production, and accumulation are merely redoubled.[2] There is in the *Zeitgeist* today a widespread "sense of an ending." Apocalypse is no further away than one error, human or electronic, in an underground nuclear command center. And apocalyptic literature, though to modern taste mythical and crude, portrays the conflict between life and death forces which once again seems to give accurate portrayal of life as it really is. This volume of essays therefore arises out of a concern I share with all those who include an appreciation of the writings of antiquity in their search for a more adequate way of being human. The ancient Jewish apocalyptic writings grew out of the courage to stare into the abyss on the edge of which an entire civilization tottered, and a willingness to describe what the fantasy of faith enabled the human eye to glimpse beyond tragedy. Our fantasy will not be identical with that of the ancient apocalypticist; what our eye beholds of the past decline, present crisis, and future hope will not reproduce the vision of the Jewish seer; but it is possible that the inspired fantasy and the daring vision encountered there may purge, enlarge, and enhance both our perspective and our

NB

concept of what is possible. For this reason we turn to examine a number of essays which contribute significant insights into the apocalyptic writings of the Bible.

The process of deciding which essays to include grew out of the classroom context, within which, over the years, I have sought to identify a handful of writings which prepare students to interpret, critically and appreciatively, the apocalyptic writings for themselves. Because I respect the ability of individuals to judge for themselves in matters where scholars disagree, I have included in this volume essays representing every significant point of view current today. In order to see how these points of view relate to each other as well as to earlier scholarship, we shall now give an overview of the scholarship on Jewish and early Christian apocalypticism.[3] As we see how others have understood the historical setting and meaning of apocalyptic writings, our own ability to comprehend this perplexing and often enigmatic literature should be strengthened.

The Interpretation of Apocalyptic Writings in Previous Scholarship

With the advent of the critical study of the Bible, the apocalyptic works found in Scripture were subjected to the questions of literary and historical inquiry. In 1832 Friedrich Lücke concluded that the apocalyptic writings developed out of prophecy, and were characterized especially by their unique view of history. He also sought to clarify the setting within which such writings arose, concluding that disillusionment with the course of history and infighting within the community were contributing factors.[4]

The historical-critical approach to the study of apocalyptic writings was placed on a firm foundation by Adolf Hilgenfeld, who in 1857 insisted that the essential qualities and the inner unity of apocalyptic could be understood only through the historical investigation of its origins. Though his own conclusions were heavily dependent on his Hegelian presuppositions, he treated these writings with a sympathy and respect which can serve as a model for today's scholar.[5]

Hilgenfeld's sympathetic attitude was soon replaced by a far more negative judgment in the monumental reconstruction of Israelite religion published by Julius Wellhausen in 1878. Since the apocalyptic writings fall on the post-exilic side of his division between the age of the spirit and the age of the law, they were regarded as the products of epigons borrowing alike from prophetic writings and Persian sources, signifying very little of theological value.[6]

4

Towering over all those applying Wellhausen's literary critical methods to the apocalyptic writings at the turn of the century was R. H. Charles, whose detailed attention to the texts themselves led him beyond blanket condemnation to a fascination with, and even an appreciation of, this often misunderstood material. Not only did he devote a lifetime to preparing critical editions and reliable translations of the many extrabiblical apocalyptic writings which were being discovered,[7] but he sought as well to describe the intrinsic qualities of apocalypticism.[8] He found its roots firmly in biblical prophecy rather than in Persian dualism, and demonstrated its parental relationship to Christianity. Whereas most of Wellhausen's students skipped over the apocalyptic writings in tracing the development of biblical religion from the great prophets ending with Second Isaiah to Christianity, Charles was sensitive to the contributions which apocalypticism added to prophecy and which prepared the way for Christianity, namely its universal scope, and its "great idea that all history, alike human, cosmological, and spiritual is a unity...."[9]

In the study of apocalyptic, as in many other areas of study related to the Bible, the contribution of Hermann Gunkel precipitated a methodological revolution. His traditio-historical method militated against a haphazard treatment of mythic fragments, seeking to relate them to the larger patterns of ancient Near Eastern mythology within which their true meaning and significance would be grasped. He sought as well to trace the development of apocalyptic out of prophecy with the aid of a careful study of the history of the literary genres found in this literature. Another aspect of his study involved the reconstruction of the social matrices within which the apocalyptic writings arose. The end result was a method of study with far greater promise than older approaches to aid in understanding the meaning of the apocalyptic writings within their original, concrete social settings.[10]

Here we can only make passing reference to Hugo Gressman's insightful probings of ancient mythical cycles as a source of biblical apocalyptic.[11] But we do need to give more direct attention to Sigmond Mowinckel's important thesis, based on his painstaking and creative investigation of the Psalms, that it was within the cult life of the Jerusalem temple that there were transmitted mythical traditions which were influential in the mutation of late prophetic eschatology into apocalyptic.[12] Mowinckel opened up an avenue of tracing the origins of important apocalyptic motifs which bore far more promise than hasty recourse to Persian dualism. While not denying ultimate roots in ancient Near Eastern – and especially

Canaanite – myth, he demonstrated that borrowing was usually not direct, but mediated through the royal cult, a phenomenon illustrated vividly by the cosmic imagery of Second Isaiah. Aage Bentzen pursued Mowinckel's cultic line of approach further, especially in examining Canaanite motifs which, through the mediation of the Jerusalem temple cult, reemerged in later Jewish apocalyptic writings (e.g., the El and Son of Man figures in Daniel 7).[13] A high degree of methodological precision has been added to the investigation of Canaanite sources and the Jewish adaptation of Northwest Semitic mythic motifs by F. M. Cross.[14]

Gunkel's methodological revolution, combined with the comparative dimension emphasized by Mowinckel, Bentzen, and Cross, set the stage for a new *Blütezeit* of apocalyptic scholarship. Thanks to an ongoing tradition of British scholarship, a theme earlier developed by Friedrich Lücke was not lost in this renewal, namely, the primary roots of apocalyptic in Old Testament prophecy. Noteworthy in this regard are the works of H. H. Rowley and D. S. Russell.[15] Less influential, though not lost, has been the opposing thesis argued by G. Hölscher early in the century that apocalyptic is primarily the offshoot of wisdom, a thesis revived by Gerhard von Rad,[16] and later refuted by Peter von der Osten-Sacken.[17] The fact that scholars concentrating on the earliest stages of apocalyptic tend to emphasize prophetic roots, whereas at least some of those centering their investigations on writings from the second century B.C.E. and beyond have drawn attention to wisdom connections, raises the question of whether Jewish apocalypticism, while having originally developed out of late prophecy, at a subsequent stage might not have been enriched by certain sapiential traditions. To this question we shall turn later.

New Impetus in Apocalyptic Research

The last twenty years have been characterized by intense new interest in the phenomenon of Jewish and early Christian apocalypticism. Writings within the Bible which fall into that category, extrabiblical apocalyptic writings which have long been known but neglected in scholarly study, and newly discovered writings have all become the objects of lively study. New textual editions have begun to appear, and various hypotheses seeking to explain the origin and development of ancient apocalypticism have evoked considerable discussion. What are the reasons for this renewed interest in a previously neglected subject?

One reason is the impact of recently discovered ancient texts.

Among these the ancient Canaanite mythic cycles discovered at Ras UGARITIC
Shamra have opened up to students a culture whose religious texts
incorporated many of the motifs which a millennium later resurfaced
in Jewish apocalyptic writings. Since this Ugaritic culture belongs
to the same Northwest Semitic cultural horizon as ancient Israel,
its bearing on Jewish religion is usually more direct than the
Mesopotamian texts utilized for comparative purposes by earlier
scholars.

The discovery of the Dead Sea Scrolls of Qumran brought to
light an actual apocalyptic community from the very period that
produced many of the most important ancient apocalyptic texts. In
fact, portions of 1 Enoch and the Testament of Levi were found
among these scrolls. And incorporated in the sectarian writings of
Qumran were teachings which were already familiar from previously
known apocalyptic writings. What is more, the scrolls of Qumran
pointed in the direction of the Essenes as the party within Judaism
which was particularly involved in the recrudescence of apocalyptic
notions in the second century B.C.E. On this basis scholars for the
first time were able to reconstruct the life context of a Jewish
apocalyptic movement of antiquity, for the texts in combination
with the mute archaeological finds revealed the general features of
the ritual practices, social structures, political views and religious
beliefs of the Essenes living at this desert site.

Another major find, the Nag Hammadi texts from Egypt, docu- NAG
ments the beliefs of a movement which in important respects can be HAMMADI
seen as the outgrowth of Jewish apocalypticism, namely, Gnosticism.
Motifs which were prominent in apocalyptic texts here were adapted
to a system of belief which moves beyond Jewish and Christian
apocalypticism in its pessimism vis-à-vis earthly structures and its
escape into other-worldly speculations.

Alongside these and other textual discoveries, new impetus came
from the side of theologians who asserted the importance of Jewish
apocalypticism for the understanding of early Christianity and for
Christian theology in general. When it is remembered that previous
generations of scholars had belittled the significance of apocalypticism by skipping over the entire Second Temple Period in tracing
the roots of Christianity back to the Old Testament prophets, this
change in attitude is especially noteworthy. A leading New Testament
theologian, Ernst Käsemann, in 1960 made the claim that apocalyptic was "the mother of Christian theology."[18] In the meantime,
systematic theologians were also turning their attention to this
literature. Wolfgang Pannenberg emphasized the importance of
apocalypticism for Christian theology, for in it the concept of

universal history was developed, a concept of central importance for Christian belief.[19] Further impetus has come from the writings of Jürgen Moltmann, who sees in the universal and cosmic perspective of apocalyptic an important safeguard against the snares of ethnocentricism and existentialistic narrowing of human history.[20]

Further abetting the renewed interest in apocalyptic is no doubt the precariousness of our times. Against the dark backdrop of the death clouds of Hiroshima and Nagasaki and the gas ovens of Dachau and Auschwitz there arises the dread awareness that nuclear proliferation has run out of control, making, in the minds of many sober scientists, nuclear war a statistical probability before the year 2000. A modern world slipping into a deeper and deeper pessimism regarding the future has turned to the literature of an ancient era similarly plagued by pessimism vis-à-vis human possibilities. Since the facile promises of the prophets of weal have run aground, there arises the hope that the hard look at reality found in apocalyptic may afford a glimpse beyond the tragedy which weighs so heavily upon the consciousness of thoughtful moderns.

An Overview of the Essays in this Volume

It seems appropriate that our first essay is taken from Klaus Koch's *The Rediscovery of Apocalyptic*. First published in German in 1970 under the title *Ratlos vor der Apokalyptik*, Koch's book documented the rise of interest in apocalypticism and offered a preliminary assessment of current trends in the research of this subject. In the chapter included here, Koch seeks to replace vague and impressionistic definitions with the attempt to analyze apocalypse as a genre by drawing on those works which are generally regarded as belonging to this type. He distinguishes from this formal analysis a second level of definition, namely, apocalyptic as "an intellectual movement." This distinction and the attempt at precise definitions are important contributions towards establishing a more reliable foundation under the study of apocalyptic than has been characteristic of the past.

In the article on "Apocalypticism" in the *Interpreter's Dictionary of the Bible, Supplementary Volume*, I distinguish between three levels of definition, apocalypse as genre, apocalyptic eschatology as a religious perspective, and apocalypticism as a religio-social movement.[21] These definitions are further refined in an appendix to the second edition of his book, *The Dawn of Apocalyptic*. An important contribution to the precise defining of the genre of apocalypse has been made by a seminar of the Society of Biblical Literature, as reported in *Semeia* 14.[22] Thus the desideratum expressed by Professor Koch has been at least partially fulfilled in recent literature.

The essential nature of Jewish apocalypticism and its source of origin are addressed in the second essay of this volume. Apocalyptic eschatology is seen primarily as a development out of prophecy abetted by the bitter experiences of the exilic and post-exilic period and the pessimistic attitude arising in visionary circles that Israel's sin was so deeply ingrained as to necessitate a radical break with the past and a new beginning initiated by Yahweh. This essay draws attention to the importance of social and political realities in understanding apocalyptic. Specifically in the case of the sixth and fifth century B.C., the early apocalyptic writings found in Isaiah 56–66 and Zechariah 9–14 are found to be the product of a visionary circle suffering oppression under the dominant, pragmatic Zadokite priestly party. Within this conflict the dialectical tension between vision and reality which was the hallmark of biblical prophecy begins to dissolve, leading to an unvisionary hierocracy and an unworldly apocalypticism, a pattern repeated in the second century B.C. amidst the conflict between *hasidim* and Hellenizers, and in many subsequent generations. In their attempts to keep faith alive in spite of earthly realities which seem to nullify their hopes, the visionaries draw deeply on mythic motifs mediated by the now defunct royal cult, for such motifs offer assurances of a realm of salvation unsullied by the harsh realities of this world.

In the third essay John Collins seeks to formulate the specific characteristic which distinguishes apocalyptic from prophecy. After expressing the inadequacies of "the idea of a definitive end," "the distinction of two periods," and "apocalyptic as mythology," he argues his thesis that the most characteristic feature of apocalyptic eschatology is its notion of the transcendence of death. As evidence Collins draws primarily on the Book of Daniel, though other works from the second and the first centuries B.C.E. are adduced in support of his argument. While one characteristic alone may be too narrow a base upon which to define a phenomenon as diverse as Jewish apocalypticism, Collins has described a theme which is of central importance to the understanding of the perspective of apocalyptic eschatology.

Michael Stone's contribution focuses on the wave of apocalyptic writings which appeared in the second century B.C.E. Drawing on the latest archaeological discoveries, he traces back to the third century B.C.E. the conflict between pietistic Judaism and Hellenism which exploded in the Maccabean revolt. Of particular importance to Stone are parts of the Book of Enoch (*1 Enoch*), which on the basis of manuscript evidence from the Dead Sea Scrolls can be dated to the third century B.C.E. Here, alongside archaeological themes, he notes the plethora of "pseudo-scientific" materials, dealing with astronomy, meteorology, and calendary lore. This speculative tradition, Stone feels, forces scholars into a reassessment of "the complexion of third century Judaism and of the origins of apocalyptic literature." And he goes on to suggest that such a reassessment will have to attribute a much larger role to speculative learning in the rise of apocalyptic literature, thus challenging the position which derives apocalypticism almost exclusively from prophetic eschatology. Stone thus raises one of the most important questions facing students of apocalyptic literature: What is the relation between eschatological and speculative (what some have called sapiential or wisdom) themes in apocalyptic writings? We shall return to this question below.

Jonathan Z. Smith pursues a line of inquiry related in certain ways to Stone's as he seeks to place the question of the interrelationship between wisdom and apocalyptic within a broad comparative framework. This leads him to recognize a common element underlying the "proto-apocalyptic" Babylonika of the third century B.C. Babylonian priest Berossus, Babylonian omen texts, and Egyptian compositions like the first century Potter's Oracle and the apocalypse preserved in the Hermetic *Asclepius*. That element is the scribal activity of ordering observed phenomena on the basis of paradigms which bridge past happenings and present experiences, leading to the science of compiling lists of patterns useful for the interpretation of new events. Once this activity was removed from the royal court with the cessation of native kingship, what was essentially a wisdom activity developed in the direction of apocalypticism. Smith thus not only contributes an intriguing thesis regarding the interrelationship between wisdom and apocalyptic, but invites scholars to see Jewish and Christian apocalypticism as a part of the broad development of Hellenistic religion.

The impact of recent discoveries on early Christian apocalypticism has been profound. What is affected is not only the material designated with the description "apocalypse" (e.g., the Apocalypse of John), but also diverse other materials related to an apocalyptic outlook, from traditions of the early church found in the Gospels to fragments embedded in letters and tracts found both in and outside of the New Testament. With conciseness and clarity, Norman Perrin covers this broad sweep of early Christian apocalyptic writings in Chapter 7 of our collection, which is taken from his *The New Testament – An Introduction: Proclamation and Parenesis, Myth and*

History; it has won wide critical acclaim in the field of biblical studies.

The last essay focuses on the most influential of all Christian apocalyptic writings, designated as the Apocalypse of John or the Book of Revelation. The importance of John Gager's essay lies in his emphasis on "the concrete situation (persecution and martyrdom) and purpose (consolation) of the book as a whole." Even as Stone and Smith breathed new life into Gunkel's concern to place the study of Jewish and Christian apocalyptic within a broad comparative religious context, Gager deepens Gunkel's definition of *Sitz im Leben* (i.e., the social situation and function of a composition) through the application of insights from structuralism and psychoanalysis. The Book of Revelation addresses a crisis in which the believing community is torn between hope and reality. Reality, intolerable in its present form, is transformed through the mythological enactment of an envisioned ideal future in the present, making the effect of the apocalyptic work a form of therapy.

The Future Shape of Apocalyptic Studies

In the future, as has been done in the past, progress will be made in the study of ancient apocalyptic writings from two sides. On the one hand we await the careful reexamination of the ancient texts themselves, including text-critical studies aimed at the clarification of the most ancient forms of these writings, literary studies which seek to determine the time and place of the writings and their authors, and form-critical studies which analyze the genres and motifs utilized by apocalyptic writers and place them in relation to similar forms found in other ancient cultures.[23] On the other hand we expect that efforts will continue to define the essential nature of apocalypticism, to reconstruct the broad social and political settings of apocalyptic movements, and to trace the development of apocalyptic traditions over long periods of time. Indeed, concrete textual studies and more hypothetical efforts at definition and reconstruction must go hand in hand if further insight is to be gained into the mysteries of apocalypticism. Only a superficial level of understanding can be expected from a study which analyzes a specific writing in isolation and gives scant attention to related writings both in the Jewish world and beyond. An interpretative framework incorporating definitions and reconstructions is an essential part of every creative exegesis. But such definitions and reconstructions function properly only if understood to be tentative and exploratory in nature, ever inviting revision on the basis of new insights derived from study of the individual texts themselves. It is no secret that writers easily become enamored with their own reconstructions, and those included in this volume are no exception. In the hope that each of them will continue to benefit from the criticism stemming from diverse perspectives, their programmatic statements have been placed side by side. We do not seek to "boil them down" into an inoffensive consensus, but rather seek only to encourage the most creative of proposals to remain vulnerable to the challenge of those who see matters differently. And while space did not allow inclusion of concrete textual studies, it is clear that the conversation we encourage always must be qualified and controlled by reference to the details of the ancient texts themselves.

As scholarship continues to develop within the dialectic of concrete textual studies and broader reconstructions, some conclusions which have emerged from recent writings seem to provide a solid basis for further research, whereas other questions seem poised to elicit spirited debate. Within the former category can be placed the distinction between discrete levels within the study of apocalyptic as essential to clarity and precision. In this connection the threefold division proposed by the present author in 1976 seems to have gained wide currency, namely, between apocalyptic as a genre, apocalyptic eschatology as a religious perspective, and apocalypticism as a socio-religious movement.

Another conclusion which has emerged as a major theme in recent scholarship is the primacy of prophetic eschatology in the origins of apocalypticism. Few would any longer argue that the taproot of apocalyptic eschatology is to be found in Persian dualism or in Egyptian wisdom. As the development of Jewish and then Christian apocalypticism is traced, however, a vexing question arises which belongs in the category of "questions poised to elicit spirited debate": Given the fact that wisdom elements constitute a very substantial part of several important apocalyptic writings in the second century B.C.E. and beyond, what is the relationship between the eschatological themes which can be traced back to prophetic origins and the wisdom themes which betray close affinities with a type of proto-scientific material which was being produced in diverse parts of the Hellenistic world? In relation to this question we can see the diversity of demands placed on the student of this literature. Contributions to clarifying this question will be made only as detailed studies of individual apocalyptic compositions containing wisdom elements are combined with a broad knowledge of related wisdom materials throughout the ancient Near Eastern and Aegean worlds and a thorough grasp of the history of the various traditions comprising apocalypticism. When one adds to these onerous requirements the weighty prerequisite of mastery of the many languages in which the relevant writings have been transmitted, it becomes clear that scholars working individually on specific texts and particular aspects of the overall problem must maintain close contact with each other, in order to benefit from the sharing of ideas and criticism. Such cooperation is imperative especially in attempts to sketch the broad picture of the development of apocalypticism over the centuries. This can be illustrated vividly when we recognize that apocalyptic writings of the period just before and after the turn to the common era incorporate mythical motifs and patterns which can be traced back to the second millennium B.C.E. and beyond. When an individual scholar evolves an overall theory of the origin and nature of apocalypticism from too narrow a base, say from the study of one particular writing or from research into one particular tradition or motif, the tendency is to distort the total picture through the overemphasis of some aspects and the neglect of others.

This leads to a further dimension in the study of apocalypticism, the importance of which lately has emerged with greater clarity and which is neglected at the cost of study becoming overly abstract and cut off from the ancient realities with which the origin and development of apocalypticism were so intimately related. This dimension involves the social, political, and economic realities which constituted the matrix within which apocalypticism unfolded. We are dealing with a phenomenon which developed not only on the level of the history of ideas, but also as an aspect of the total life of the ancient cultures in question. All that we know of ancient social customs, of political movements and economic structures is of vital concern to the student of apocalyptic. This in turn implies that as archaeological, epigraphical, and historical discoveries and studies add to our knowledge of these areas, they must be drawn immediately into the study of the apocalyptic writings.

We have noted that the mood of the times has contributed to the current interest in our subject. Now it is important to add that this apparent interest must not be answered by sensationalizing pseudo-scholarship which seeks only to exploit popular curiosity for personal attention or for the promulgation of some particular religious or ideological program. What is called for is scholarship which is sensitive both to the contemporary human issues on which the ancient Jewish and Christian writings may have some bearing and to the responsibility of the scholar to present the testimony of the past as faithfully and objectively as possible. The paperback bookshelves display many titles which violate both of these sensitivities. Scholars whose scholarly training evokes a loathing for such exploi-

Paul D. Hanson

tation must meet the challenge of taking common readers seriously enough to offer them responsible scholarship on this important and relevant material in an idiom they can understand. Cultures before our own have experienced the dread sense of ending which many persons are experiencing today, and out of those troubled times in the past there emerged those compositions we call apocalyptic, written by some of the wisest and most thoughtful savants of antiquity. It is not at all absurd to expect that from their insights we, too, may derive important perspectives on our own dilemma. From those trained in the study of ancient documents, interested readers also have a right to expect translations, interpretations, and reconstructions which can guide them as they seek to understand the present with an informed approach that includes knowledge of the past. As apocalyptic studies take shape in the future, we shall hope that they will include imaginative, readable interpretations from leading scholars dedicated to the enrichment not only of fellow scholars, but of a broad popular audience as well. The intrinsic value of the apocalyptic writings of antiquity is such as to merit no less a response.

NOTES

1 Carl G. Jung, "Approaching the Unconscious," in *Man and His Symbols* (New York: Dell, 1968) 75.

2 Those arrested by the themes of apocalyptic come from all fields of the natural and social sciences, the arts and the humanities. See, for example, the critique of the dominant economic theory in the Western world today: Robert S. Heilbroner, "The Demand for the Supply Side," *The New York Review* (June 11, 1981) 37–41; and Michael Mendelbaum, "The Bomb, Dread, and Eternity," *International Security* 5 (Fall, 1980) 3–23.

3 For further reading in the history of research, the following may be consulted: Johann M. Schmidt, *Die jüdische Apokalyptik: Die Geschichte ihrer Erforschung von den Anfangen bis zu den Textfunden von Qumran* (Neukirchen: Neukirchener, 1969); Paul D. Hanson, "Prolegomena to the Study of Jewish Apocalyptic," in *Magnalia Dei: The Mighty Acts of God*, ed. F. M. Cross (New York: Doubleday & Co., 1976) 389–413, and idem, "Apocalyptic Literature," forthcoming in *The Old Testament and its Modern Interpreters* (Fortress Press/Scholars Press).

4 F. Lücke, *Versuch einer vollständigen Einleitung in die Offenbarung Johannis und in die gesammte apokalyptische Literatur* (Bonn, 1832).

5 A. Hilgenfeld, *Die jüdische Apokalyptik in ihrer geschichtlichen Entwicklung* (Jena, 1857).

6 J. Wellhausen, *Prolegomena to the History of Ancient Israel* (Edinburgh, 1885).

7 See R. H. Charles' two-volume work, *The Apocrypha and Pseudepigrapha of the Old Testament* (Oxford: Clarendon Press, 1913), a classic in the field.

8   R. H. Charles, *Eschatology: The Doctrine of a Future Life in Israel, Judaism and Christianity* (New York: Schocken Books, 1963); first published in 1899.

9   Charles, *Eschatology*, 183.

10 Gunkel's contributions to the study of apocalyptic are scattered through a dozen or more books and articles, but of special importance was *Schöpfung und Chaos in Urzeit und Endzeit* (Göttingen: Vendenhoeck & Ruprecht, 1895).

11 Hugo Gressmann, *Der Ursprung der israelitisch-jüdischen Eschatologie* (Göttingen: Vandenhoeck & Ruprecht, 1905).

12 Sigmund Mowinckel, *He that Cometh* (Nashville: Abingdon Press, 1954). Another of Mowinckel's theses, however, has not found broad acceptance, namely his idea that eschatology developed as a part of Yahwistic faith only in the post-exilic period.

13 Aage Bentzen, *Daniel* (HAT 19; Tübingen: J. C. B. Mohr [Paul Siebeck], 1952). Similar themes are developed in S. B. Frost's *Old Testament Apocalyptic: Its Origins and Growth* (London: Epworth Press, 1952), and in "Eschatology and Myth," *VT* 2 (1952) 70–80.

14 F. M. Cross, *Canaanite Myth and Hebrew Epic* (Cambridge, Mass.: Harvard Univ. Press, 1975).

15 H. H. Rowley, *The Relevance of Apocalyptic* (London: Lutterworth Press, 1944). D. S. Russell, *The Method and Message of Jewish Apocalyptic* (OTL; Philadelphia: Westminster Press, 1964).

16 G. Hölscher, *Die Entstehung des Danielbuchs* (Giessen, 1919). Gerhard von Rad, *Old Testament Theology* (2 vols.; New York: Harper & Row, 1965).

17 Peter von der Osten-Sacken, *Die Apokalyptic in ihrem Verhältnis zu Prophetie und Weisheit* (Munich: Chr. Kaiser, 1969).

18 Ernst Käsemann, "On the Subject of Primitive Christian Apocalyptic," in *New Testament Questions of Today* (Philadelphia: Fortress Press; London: SCM Press, 1969) 108–37. (Cf. *JTC* 6 [1969] 17–46).

19 Wolfhart Pannenberg, *Revelation as History* (London: Sheed and Ward, 1969).

20 Jürgen Moltmann, *Theology of Hope* (New York: Harper & Row; SCM Press, 1967).

21 Paul D. Hanson, s.v. "Apocalypticism," IDBSup.

22 John J. Collins, ed., *Apocalypse: The Morphology of a Genre* (Semeia 14; Missoula, Mont.: Scholars Press, 1979).

23 In the area of basic resources, we await the volume of texts being edited by J. H. Charlesworth, for it will make available many of the early apocalyptic compositions in up-to-date translations which draw upon the latest manuscript discoveries. Important new commentaries on apocalyptic writings are also currently being written: *1 Enoch* by George W. E. Nickelsburg and *4 Ezra* by Michael E. Stone, both of which will appear in Hermeneia – A Critical and Historical Commentary on the Bible.

1

What is Apocalyptic? An Attempt at a Preliminary Definition*

KLAUS KOCH

---

1 *The Cloudiness of Current Definitions*

Apocalyptic is a Greek borrowing and smacks not only of the weird and menacing; it also suggests the abstruse and fantastic.[1] Since it is in its very origin a word derived from biblical scholarship, this meaning can only be explained by the fact that in the last century apocalyptic increasingly became for theologians "the quintessence of what is 'eschatologically' improper. Theological eschatology believed that it could best prove its legitimacy by abjuring apocalyptic as firmly and vocally as possible."[2] It is customary "to term 'apocalyptic' those descriptions of the future which serve as pure speculations merely to satisfy human curiosity, without any actual interest in salvation."[3]

Christians and Jews[4] are largely speaking at one in this rejection. It is astonishing, however, that the German translation of the original Greek noun *apokalypsis*, *Offenbarung*, or revelation, is high up on the list of "positive" theological terms. How can this discrepancy between the original word and its translation be explained?

The adjective apocalyptic is not directly derived from the general theological term *apokalypsis*, in the sense of revelation, at all; it comes from a second and narrower use of the word, also documented in the ancient church, as the title of literary compositions which resemble the Book of Revelation,[5] i.e., secret divine disclosures about the end of the world and the heavenly state. The word apocalypse has become the usual term for this

* First published in *The Rediscovery of Apocalyptic* by K. Koch (1972) 18–35, 132–38 (notes).

type of book. It is also applied to books and parts of books to which the ancient church did not as yet give this title – for example the synoptic apocalypse of Mark 13 (and its parallels). The ancient church already viewed the apocalyptic books with considerable reserve and hence excluded the *Apocalypses of Peter and Paul* from the canon, as well as Christian apocalypses which were attributed to OT figures (*5* and *6 Ezra*, for example).

Many early Christian apocalypses have as a result disappeared forever, or have only recently been rediscovered – the Greek version of the *Apocalypse of Peter*, for example, or the apocalyptic writings from the great Nag Hammadi discoveries.[6]

In the last two hundred years historical scholarship has gone over to the practice of classifying OT books and parts of books also as apocalypses, whenever (like the NT Book of Revelation) they contain visions of the events of the end-time and catechetical matter associated with these things. Many OT scholars would assign Isaiah 24—27 (the Isaiah Apocalypse), Trito-Zechariah (Zechariah 12—14) and the Book of Joel to this category; and all of them would include the Book of Daniel and the apocryphal 4 Ezra or Ezra Apocalypse. Nineteenth-century discoveries swelled the group of such writings in the OT field more than in the New. In 1800 Sayce published *1 Enoch* (Ethiopian Enoch), which had been brought back to England by the African traveller. In 1866 Ceriani brought out his edition of *2 Baruch* (or the Syriac Apocalypse of Baruch), which he had found in an Italian library. It was followed in 1897 by Bonwetsch's edition of the *Apocalypse of Abraham*, based on a Slavonic manuscript. The series continued, down to the discovery after the Second World War of the numerous Qumran texts in the caves of the Dead Sea area, among which there is considerable apocalyptic material,[7] much of it still awaiting publication.

Through the continual emergence of new writings, the centre of gravity of apocalyptic literature is increasingly shifting for the historical observer from the NT to the OT field. The number of late Israelite apocalypses is not only considerably greater today than the number of early Christian ones; the former are also, in the opinion of many scholars, much richer in content and show a greater depth of thought. That is why even "introductions to the New Testament," when talking about apocalypses other than Revelation, only think of the late Israelite ones and do not consider the other Christian apocalypses worth mentioning.[8]

According to the prevailing opinion, the great mass of apocalyptic literature came into being between 200 B.C. and A.D. 100 in the world of Semitic-speaking (or at least strongly Semitically influenced) Israel and Jewish Christianity. The church rejected the apocalyptic writings, viewing them as apocryphal to the degree in which it later found its centre of gravity in the Greek-speaking world. The same process of elimination took place in the early Judaism organized by the Rabbis after A.D. 70; perhaps this was due to disappointment over the breakdown of high-flown eschatological hopes in the two risings against Rome.

During the last century a collective term "apocalyptic" has come into general use, side by side with the generic name apocalypse. It is applied not only to the common mental and spiritual background of the relevant late Israelite and early Christian writings but is used to characterize a certain kind of religious speculation about the future of man and the world. The meaning of the adjective apocalyptic, which we mentioned above, is generally determined by this collective term.

Difficulties in defining the term apocalyptic more precisely, however, immediately arise once it ceases to be filled out merely speculatively, according to the subjective taste of the individual theologian or philosopher, but has also to be brought into accord with the historical texts.

The spiritual bond which unites the various writings classified as apocalypses is only difficult to establish because most of the OT apocalypses are not extant in their original form but only in second-hand or even third-hand translations – translations in whose reliability scholars have but little confidence, and in which, moreover, we have to reckon with additions, omissions, etc. In the case of the early Christian apocalypses, on the other hand, there is a problem of literary criticism, which is not unanimously settled: how far are these apocalypses revisions of late Israelite originals? This is already a matter of debate for the synoptic apocalypse, Mark 13, and for the Book of Revelation, and it is even more controversial for *5* and *6 Ezra* and the *Testaments of the Twelve Patriarchs*.

If there was really a community of ideas and spirit between the different books which we now call apocalypses, these books must go back to a common sociological starting point; they must have a comparable *Sitz im Leben*. The majority of scholars do in fact assume this to be the case with the OT apocalyptic. But as soon as it is a question of pinning down this assumption in precise terms, the secondary literature shows an unsurpassed jumble of opinions. During the period between 200 B.C. and A.D. 100 – that is to say the late Israelite period – in which the mass of the apocalyptic writings came into being, Israel had an appearance of anything but unity, whether in Palestine or in the Diaspora. Even in primitive Christianity there was a lack of that dogmatic and organizational unity which was later to be the mark of the catholic churches of East and West. Consequently the classification of a group of writings which contains no express information about its sociological setting forces the observer into conjecture. Every one of the groupings of the late Israelite period for which we have any evidence at all has been suggested as the *Sitz im Leben* of the apocalyptic writings. Were the authors of these writings obscure and simple people, far removed from the Jerusalem hierarchy and its theology (the view held by Bousset among others)? Or did they, on the contrary, belong to a small class of highly learned sages, who were also thoroughly familiar with the non-Israelite culture of their time?[9] Do the predominating East Aramaic element and the prevalence of Babylonian material in the Book of Daniel suggest that we must look for the beginnings in the Babylonian Diaspora or farther east in Persia?[10] Or was this a native Palestinian growth (the opinion held by most scholars)? Were the writers part of the Essene movement (Hilgenfeld's view),[11] like the Qumran sect from whom the Dead Sea manuscripts derive, or did they belong to the Essenes' forerunners, the Hasidim (Ploeger), the pietists of the Maccabean period? Was the Pharisaic lay movement, with its strict adherence to the Law – a movement both familiar and notorious from the pages of the NT – its matrix (Charles)? Or even the Zealots, the unremitting fomenters of rebellion against the foreign domination of Rome?[12]

But perhaps the attempts to find out to which of the religious parties the apocalyptists belonged is a fruitless one; perhaps they were to be found among all parties at the time (Russell)? Our survey indicates how completely obscure the sociological basis of the apocalyptic writings still is.

We are no better off as regards the *Sitz im Leben* of the NT apocalypses. Most commentators consider that the synoptic apocalypse had its origin in Palestine before A.D. 70. More can hardly be discovered. According to its opening chapter, the Book of Revelation was written on an Aegean island by a man called John, who merely describes himself as the servant of God or prophet and, on the evidence of his letters, had some kind of authority over the churches in Asia Minor. As for the noncanonical apocalypses, here scholars are completely in the dark.

Not only have scholars placed the *Sitz im Leben* of the apocalyptic writings as differently as it is possible to conceive; in addition it is a matter of doubt how far particular writings are to be classified as apocalypses at all. Does the so-called Isaiah Apocalypse (Isaiah

24–27) or the *Shepherd of Hermas* really deserve the name of apocalypse? Even where the ancient church assigned the title apocalypse to a particular writing, this classification is only useful for a literary and historical assessment up to a point. A title of this kind not only heads writings such as 2 *Baruch* and the *Apocalypse of Abraham*, which certainly derive from the Semitic linguistic area; it is also applied to originally Hellenistic works such as 2 *Enoch*, 4 *Baruch* and the *Apocalypse of Paul*, which certainly treat of heavenly journeys and cosmic geography, like the Semitic books, but which are lacking in an account of the end-time, as well as in paraenesis and historical surveys, which occupy large sections of the Hebrew and Aramaic apocalypses. The ancient church used the term from a different point of view from that of the modern literary historian. Since the Semitically determined apocalypses have come more and more to the fore during the last century, when scholars speak of apocalyptic today it is this group of writings of which they are primarily thinking.

2 *A Preliminary Demonstration of the Apocalypse as a Literary Type*

If we now enquire what can really be gathered from the writings generally classified as apocalypses about the actual apocalyptic content, the answers of different scholars vary just as much as their above-mentioned attempts to fix the *Sitz im Leben*. If, therefore, we are to have a standard of judgment for the following survey and for our criticism of present attempts, the only course open to us is to enumerate briefly a few facts about the writings which form the basis of the discussion, so that the reader may have a rough preliminary concept at his disposal. Consequently I may perhaps be permitted to formulate two dogmatic presuppositions, in the hope that unprejudiced fellow scholars will approve them as working hypotheses.

1   If we are to arrive at a historical perception of the background against which apocalyptic ideas grew up, as well as a serviceable and generally applicable concept of apocalyptic, we must start from the writings which were composed in Hebrew or Aramaic, or in which, at least, the Hebrew or Aramaic spirit is dominant. To this group belong first and foremost the Book of Daniel, *1 Enoch*, *2 Baruch*, 4 Ezra, the *Apocalypse of Abraham* and the Book of Revelation, with its Semitic tendencies.

2   We can only ascertain what is apocalyptic about these writings

if characteristics common to the type can be demonstrated.[13] If we are to succeed at all in the future in arriving at a binding definition of apocalyptic, a starting point in form criticism and literary and linguistic history is, in the nature of things, the only one possible.[14]

Given these assumptions, let me indicate in broad outline what can be discovered. I make no claim to an adequate description of apocalyptic as a historical phenomenon, much less to an answer to the question of what apocalyptic actually is. My aim is merely to furnish a number of aspects which at all events belong to the apocalyptic sphere – if, indeed, it is meaningful to use a word of this kind at all or to consider historical factors as contributing to the formation of the concept.

There are not a few scholars who declare that form-critical considerations are hopeless from the outset for apocalyptic material, which they find merely "a hotch-potch of the most varied literary forms."[15] This thesis cannot be refuted, strictly speaking, since there are as yet no form-critical investigations of the apocalyptic writings. But there are features of the texts which positively demand form-critical investigation and which, pending proof of the contrary, certainly convey the impression that there really was something like an apocalyptic type of writing. These features are as follows:

(*i*) As soon as one passes from the reading of the other OT writings, the great *discourse cycles* leap to the eye. As a rule they extend over several chapters and record a long dialogue between the apocalyptic seer and his heavenly counterpart. These discourse cycles are frequently called "visions,"[16] although the vision can be replaced by mere audition (as is already the case in Daniel 9). They reveal something about the destiny of mankind which has hitherto been a secret (*raz, mysterion*) guarded in heaven but which will soon come to pass on earth and which will be of absolutely decisive importance for everyone involved. The seer's partner is an exalted representative of the heavenly hierarchy. It is an obvious step to think of the OT prophetic books as being a preliminary stage to the apocalyptic discourse cycles; for there vision and audition were already coupled from the eighth century B.C. onwards (Amos 7) and a dialogue takes place between the prophet and his God, which is limited in the post-exilic period to a dialogue between the prophet and an *angelus interpres* (e.g., Zechariah's "night visions"). The apocalyptic cycle associates a whole series of formal characteristics with the account of the prophetic vision. To take only one of these: the first great vision cycle in Revelation begins like many other apocalyptic ones: "After this I looked, and lo, in heaven an open door" (4:1). Amos begins the account of his vision very similarly: "Thus the Lord God showed me: behold, he was forming locusts" (7:1). In both cases the word "see" is part of the introduction. Then follows the exclamation or imperative "lo" or "behold" accompanied by a participle (in both the Greek and the Hebrew) which points to a supernatural state of affairs,[17] which immediately changes into movement. If the discourse cycle does not begin with a divine visionary disclosure, then attention is first drawn to a tormenting problem which harasses the seer and even produces a bodily change in him. John, who was banished "on account of the word of God," found himself "in the Spirit on the Lord's day" (Rev. 1:10). Similarly, the introduction to 4 Ezra says that because of the destruction of Zion Ezra's "spirit was stirred profoundly."

(*ii*) These *spiritual turmoils* are, according to the unanimous assertion of the apocalyptists, also the result of the unexpected experience of vision and audition. In view of the prospects of the future which are opened up to him the seer is overcome by fear and dismay, which he reports in formalized phraseology. The recipient is beside himself; he falls to the ground, his trance sometimes being heightened to the point of unconsciousness.[18] This can even lead to the feeling of a violently produced change of place (*1 Enoch* 17:1; *Apocalypse of Abraham* 15).

It is hardly possible to ascertain how far descriptions of this kind are representations of an actual experience and how far they are a literary fashion – a mannered over-refinement of the prophet's account of his reception of the Word (Ezek. 2:1; 3:12–15; and frequently elsewhere). They are at least signs of a literary relationship.

(*iii*) The seer does not stop at the description of his own state or even at the secrets and revolutions of the future. He draws conclusions for his readers, offering them to his community, or his disciples or "sons," in the form of *paraenetic discourses*. These sections are invariably separate from the visionary or auditory discourse cycles. They unfold a kind of eschatological ethic, which calls still-faithful members of the people of God to endurance even under persecution, because the present age of darkness will soon be at an end (cf. the letters in Revelation; the final discourse and letter in *2 Baruch*; 4 Ezra 14:27–36; the paraenetic book in *1 Enoch*). The generic characteristics of the paraenetic sections, as well as the origins of the form, are still uninvestigated.[19] In Daniel and in the *Apocalypse of Abraham* the paraenetic sections are replaced by *introductory legends*, which are apparently intended to propound examples of proper behaviour. Here too the literary character is still obscure.[20]

But to unite visionary-auditory discourse cycles and paraenetic sections as component types evidently belongs to the true apocalypse.

(*iv*) It is a curious fact that later Israelite and early Christian apocalyptic writers do not reveal their names or the period in which they are writing, but positively hide behind a man of God belonging to the past: behind Enoch, for instance ("the seventh generation from Adam"): or Ezra and Daniel, men of the Exile; but also behind Peter or Paul, as the apostolic guarantors of the founding era of the church. The Book of Revelation seems to be a unique exception. This *pseudonymity* is a much discussed but not convincingly explained phenomenon.[21] It is only clear formally, as being the mark of a literary type. As such it differs from the contemporary Wisdom pseudonymous literature (Ecclesiastes, the Wisdom of Solomon) and its cultic counterpart (the *Psalms of Solomon*, the Prayer of Manasses) by its avoidance of royal names as literary cloak.

(*v*) The language takes on a concealed meaning by means of *mythical images rich in symbolism*. The forces of history and of the present, i.e., the forces of the world-time (*'olam, aion*), are reduced to their outstanding basic characteristics, appearing as dangerous, often unnaturally degenerate beasts or as huge trees or rushing waters.[22] The people of God and their leaders are also depicted correspondingly as land or lion or vine.[23] The beginnings of this codified language may already be found in the OT prophets. Isaiah describes Israel as a vineyard, for example (ch. 5); Jeremiah announces the coming of wild beasts from the north to tear Israel to pieces (5:6). But what is plain in the prophets – a transparently simple image – is heightened into the grotesque by the apocalyptic writers and is now incomprehensible without interpretation. The account of Alexander's empire and the rule of his successors, "Diadochi," given in Dan. 7:7f. belongs to the symbolic discourses which can be relatively easily understood:

> After this I saw in the night visions, and behold, a fourth beast, terrible and dreadful and exceedingly strong; and it had great iron teeth; it devoured and broke in pieces, and stamped the residue with its feet. It was different from all the beasts that were before it; and it had ten horns. I considered the horns, and behold, there came up among them another horn, a little one, before which three of the first horns were plucked up by the roots; and behold, in this horn were eyes like the eyes of a man, and a mouth speaking great things.

The apocalyptic descriptions suggest to many exegetes the suspicion that their authors were remythologizing the long-since demythologized religion – particularly since it is hard to discover how far such images are meant literally and how far they are intended to be pure metaphors.

The Semitic languages of the ancient world are invariably richer in symbols and more mythically charged than our rationalized modern European languages. To talk about an angel in heaven and the dead who sleep in the underworld, or about the devil who prowls around like a roaring lion, is nothing out of the way for a NT contemporary. There is not a single book in the Bible where mythical overtones are not to be heard or in which symbolic images are not used. None the less, the picture language of the apocalypses is so noticeable and so curious that it stands out clearly from the normal framework of the literature of the time and suggests a particular linguistic training, perhaps even a particular mentality.

(*vi*) All the apocalypses obviously have a long literary development behind them. The *composite character* is unmistakable – clearer than in other comparable literary works of the time (except, possibly, the late Mishna). Breaks in the train of thought and contradictions in detail crop up everywhere. The Book of Daniel even uses two languages, Hebrew in the opening chapter and chs. 8–12, Aramaic in chs. 2–7, thereby betraying its composite character in a particular way.

These outward characteristics would seem to be enough to allow us to view the apocalypse as a literary form current round about the turn of the era in the Hebrew-Aramaic linguistic area. If this is disputed it is because the linguistic structure is being ignored, i.e., it is a matter of different presuppositions, not of form-critical observations and methods based on linguistic history.

Yet from the outset apocalyptic presents a complex literary type which has absorbed into itself several component genres. Without a distinction between complex and component types[24] there can be no form-critical approach to these writings.

3 *A Preliminary Demonstration of Apocalyptic as a Historical Movement*

A literary type is not only a matter of formal characteristics; typical moods and ideas are equally important.[25] These are also amply present in the books in question – and so markedly that it would seem justifiable not only to talk about apocalypse as a form whose *Sitz im Leben* we do not yet know, but also to presuppose something like a movement of mind; and it is this which is indicated by the collective term apocalyptic. The pointers which can be cited for this are not so easy to pick out of the texts as the form-critical observations just mentioned; on the other hand these indications of an intellectual movement have played a part in secondary literature for a long time. I will try to confine myself to what is largely generally accepted opinion today.

(*i*) The writings are dominated by an *urgent expectation* of the impending overthrow of all earthly conditions *in the immediate future*. "Surely I am coming soon, Amen," proclaims the heavenly Christ at the close of Revelation. The same mood is noticeable in the other apocalypses. The hope of the speedy end of the world remains nebulous only where early figures such as Enoch or Abraham are the authorities for the vision. In all other cases it comes unmistakably to the fore. Daniel already expects only three and a half "times" till the end of the world – in another passage, more precisely, 1290 days or at most 1335 (12:11f). This keen expectation is especially striking in *2 Bar*. 85:10:

> The pitcher is near to the cistern,
> And the ship to the port,
> And the course of the journey to the city,
> And life to [its] consummation.

The same feeling is inherent in the image of the drops which continue to fall for a short time after rain, and the smoke which follows the fire (4 Ezra 4:50). Anyone who looks forward so longingly to the imminent end of the world makes a fantastic impression on the modern reader. This impression serves as justification for the commentators who treat the apocalyptic writers slightingly and do not give them credit for any logical train of thought.

(*ii*) The end appears as a vast *cosmic catastrophe*. There is no need to list expressly the horrors pictured in the Book of Revelation. In Daniel the reigning world power which is repressing mankind is found again at the end in an all-consuming stream of fire (7:11). The later apocalypses paint the age which preceeds the world judgment as a time of increasing horror.

> And it shall come to pass that whosoever gets safe out of the war shall die in the earthquake,
> And whosoever gets safe out of the earthquake shall be burned by the fire,
> And whosoever gets safe out of the fire shall be destroyed by famine (*2 Bar*. 70:8).

Then shall the sun suddenly shine forth by night and the moon by day:
And blood shall trickle forth from wood, and the stone utter its voice
4 Ezra 5:4f; cf. *Apocalypse of Abraham* 30

25

The series could be continued indefinitely. Descriptions of this kind have been a determining factor in forming the common notion of apocalyptic and cause it to be represented as *pessimism*.

(*iii*) The end-time is closely connected with the previous history of mankind and of the cosmos. The *time of this world* is divided into fixed segments; the content of these segments has been pre-determined from the days of creation and can be found alluded to in concealed form in certain sayings of the prophetic books.[26]

Numbers such as four, seven and twelve play a mysterious role. Talk about filled and bounded ages which tend towards salvation or disaster cause the apocalyptists to be reproached with *determinism*; but the behaviour of the individual is never accounted in these writings as being predestined towards good or evil – it is invariably only the behaviour of nations or epochs.

It remains a matter of dispute in this connection whether the apocalypses intend with their doctrine of time to depict world, or even cosmic, history as a meaningful process.

(*iv*) In order to explain the course of historical events and the happenings of the end-time, an army of *angels and demons* is mustered, divided into a hierarchy of orders; the leading powers even have their own names – Michael, Uriel or Belial, and Satan, for example. Earthly history, open to the sight of all men, is correlated to a supernatural and invisible history about which only chosen seers receive knowledge, through apocalyptic channels. Above all, the angels of the nations constantly intervene formatively in the events of the lower world[27] (whose decisive turning points cannot be explained by merely internal motivations), eager to promote the success of their own nations and to repulse the others.

In the future, with the beginning of the new epoch, the barriers between earthly and supernatural history will disappear and the faithful will join the good angels and shine like the stars in heaven.[28]

(*v*) Beyond the catastrophe a new *salvation* arises, paradisal in character. For this the remnant of the chosen people who have kept their faith in their God and remained true to their religion will be saved. Others will partake of it through resurrection.[29] The return of creation and the time of Moses or David (the heavenly Jerusalem) is comprehended in the scheme *primal period-end time*; i.e., the beginnings return in the Last Days.[30]

The members of the non-Israelite nations will also partake of the coming salvation. Every apocalypse expresses anxiety for the whole of mankind, although this is individually not easy to distinguish from the particular redemption of israel, which still remains a special one. A tendency to *universalism* is, however, unmistakable when compared, for example, with the future hope of the pre-exilic prophets or the views of the later Talmudic writings.

On the other hand, within Israel itself a distinction is made; it is no longer the people as a whole who are the heirs of eschatological salvation. Rather, the righteous in Israel are divided from the ungodly. The idea of the remnant of the chosen people which alone will be saved (a notion in evidence from Isaiah onwards) plays a great part. This differentiation has led to the apocalyptists' being today occasionally reproached with *individualism*.

(*vi*) The transition from disaster to final redemption is expected to take place by means of an act issuing from *the throne of God*. For this purpose God will solemnly ascend his throne or even permit that throne to be ascended by the Son of man.[31] From thence the final event will be initiated. Through this event the division between heavenly and earthly history will be abolished, the divine glory will appear and everything which is hidden will be revealed. This final ascent of the throne is a relatively old idea, which can already be demonstrated at the pre-apocalyptic stage in Isa. 24:23; it can be explained by the fact that the throne is viewed as the indispensable foundation of sovereignty.

The consequence of this ascent of the throne is that the *kingdom of God* becomes visible on earth (Dan. 7:14; *Enoch* 41; Rev. 11:15), replacing all earthly empires forever. In later apocalyptic the newly beginning age of the world, the age directly ruled by God, is designated as the age, or aeon, which is to come (4 Ezra; *2 Baruch*). Because of the "aeon" idea, it is customary to ascribe *dualism* to the apocalyptic writers, i.e., the conviction of a complete discontinuity between this evil world and that other good one. People then go on to conclude that the apocalyptic writers are not interested in the present world, let alone history, emphasizing them at most as a dark foil to the radiance of the future, which alone enthralls them. It is questionable, however, whether the "aeon" concept really has the purpose of emphasizing the "wholly other" character of the future age of the world. It is all too easily overlooked that the kingdom of God, or the future aeon, is undoubtedly thought of as being already present, though in concealed form (Dan. 3:33; Ezra 26ff; Rev. 1:9).[32] The kingdom's final realization and manifestation in the Last Days is, however, clearly distinguished from its present hidden power.

(*vii*) As has already been indicated in connection with the ascent of the throne in the end-time, *a mediator with royal functions* is frequently introduced to accomplish and guarantee final redemption. But at this point the apocalypses diverge widely in detail. The mediator has various names – for example, the Messiah, the Son of man, the Chosen One; and his function often differs as much as his title. Nor is it clear in many passages whether the mediator started out as an earthly person or as an angelic figure (e.g., Dan. 7:13f). He is angelic at least in *As. Mos.* 10:2 and in Dan. 12:1; and he is clearly human wherever he is called the Messiah. But in none of the apocalypses is God quite alone in what he does; it is never without some mediator or other that he brings about and eternally sustains eschatological redemption. The role of the eschatological mediator is particularly stressed by Christian theologians because of its christ-ological interest.[33] For the apocalyptic writers themselves it is doubt-less only a special example of the supreme role which supernatural beings as a whole play – not only angels and the just who have been taken up into heaven, but also efficacious forces such as glory, righteousness and wrath. This feature is often explained by the fact that for the late period God moved away into *remote transcendence* and that man's personal relationship to him thereby became so tenuous that religious feeling demanded intermediary courts of appeal. Where such an explanation is adopted it would seem only a short step to move apocalyptic into the vicinity of another spiritual movement, namely *Gnosticism.*[34]

(*viii*) The catchword *glory* is used wherever the final state of affairs is set apart from the present and whenever a final amalgamation of the earthly and heavenly spheres is prophesied. Glory is the portion of those who have been raised from the dead, who will thus become as the angels or the stars of heaven (Dan. 12:3, *1 Enoch* 50:1; 51:4). Glory is then the mark not only of man, however, but also of conditions, the "state" in which they live, the heavenly Jerusalem (Rev. 21:1ff; *2 Bar.* 32:4), or of the eschatological ruler (*2 Bar.* 30:1) who is above them. A bold man might conclude from this that the apocalyptic drama ends with a transformation of every social structure.[35] This is a remarkable difference from prophecy. Whereas the apocalyptic writers and pre-exilic prophets are at one in the conviction that the impending time of trial will bring with it the breakdown of all morals and order (e.g., Mark 13:12f; *2 Bar.* 70; 4 Ezra 6:21–24; 13:31; compare Isa. 1:21–23; Jer. 5:1–3), opinions differ about final conditions. An Isaiah expects the restoration of a sound, feudally organized Israelite state and for Jerusalem "judges as at the first, and your counselors as at the beginning" (1:26). Jeremiah's eschatology is tantamount to the view "that, in the land which at the moment is lying waste, conditions will return to normal and life will go on again."[36] For the apocalyptic writers, on the other hand, the normal state ties and the judicature will come to an end;

and work will become pleasure (*2 Baruch* 73f).[37] With these expectations in mind, every commentator who is ill-disposed towards the apocalypses reproaches them with longing for a Utopia.

The eight groups of motifs which I have picked out can be shown to be distributed more or less equally throughout the various apocalypses. Nearly every one of them can also be found outside the late Israelite and early Christian apocalyptic. But the way in which they are arranged is characteristic of apocalyptic, and probably of apocalyptic alone. It presupposes that the authors understand the eschatological events *as a sequence* and want to show a continuous scarlet thread running through the whole. They are concerned with a divine manifestation to the community present at the beginning of the end-time. In this way apocalypse means not only the revealing of details (revelation as the communication of doctrine) but the disclosure of possible participation in the final and unique, all-encompassing coming of God among men. An apocalypse is therefore designed to be "the revelation of the divine revelation"[38] as this takes place in the individual acts of a coherent historical pattern. But this never means a one-track systematic account, or a linear chronological one; rather, the *multiplicity of approaches* [39] always prevails as a matter of course in problems so important for the Semitic mind.

All this gives us the right to understand apocalyptic not only as a literary phenomenon but as the expression of a particular *attitude of mind*. The collective term apocalyptic, which came into use at the beginning of the nineteenth century,[40] can therefore still be retained today. We may define it with Ringgren as "speculation which – often in allegorical form ... – aims to interpret the course of history and to reveal the end of the world."[41]

4 *The Position of Apocalyptic in the Literature of Late Antiquity*

Which of the last Israelite parties known to us from other documents belonged to the apocalyptic movement must remain an open question, in view of what we have already said about the problem of its *Sitz im Leben*. But it seems likely that these speculations were not enjoyed by the whole of Israel in this late period. There are numerous books of similar date which pursue quite different interests. It is at least difficult to discover any close relationship to apocalyptic either in 1 and 2 Maccabees or in 3 and 4 Maccabees! And there are no apocalyptic traces at all in Philo's voluminous works.

In the case of many other writings the closeness to, or remoteness from, the apocalyptic movement is a matter of dispute. The *Testa-*

ments of the Twelve Patriarchs and the *Assumption of Moses* can be assigned to the apocalyptic writings straight away, on the basis of the characteristics of apocalyptic eschatology already mentioned, even though only some of the characteristics of the type previously noted can be found there.[42] The matter becomes more difficult with *Jubilees*.[43] A whole series of writings found in Qumran is clearly apocalyptic: for example the Book of Mysteries (1QMyst), the description of the New Jerusalem (1–2–5QJN), the Prayer of Nabonidus (4QPrNab), Pseudo-Daniel (4QPsDan)[44] and the Melchizedek scroll (11QMelch).[45] It is uncertain whether these writings derive from the sect itself or whether they were procured from outside. What has clearly been composed within the Qumran movement (e.g., the *Pesher* on OT texts or the *War Scroll*, 1QM), makes the reader doubt whether he should plead for apocalyptic or not.[46] What is bound to rouse ever-fresh astonishment is the fact that it is impossible to point to any genuine apocalypse in the huge field of rabbinic writings, in spite of the eschatological themes which the rabbis also assiduously cultivated.[47] Not a single apocalyptic book known to us, with the exception of the Book of Daniel, is quoted by a rabbinic writer.[48]

If apocalyptic is thus one trend among others within Israel and its literature, there are, on the other hand, indications that similar ideas were cultivated outside Israel as well, leading to a literature similar to the apocalypses. A connection with Hellenistic *oracle literature* can be shown at many points. The relationship is obvious, for example if one examines the Hellenistic-Egyptian tradition about the eight-footed and double-headed prophetic Lamb, adorned with the royal tokens of the Uraeus snake and the ostrich feathers, which is said to have appeared in the days of King Bocchoris,[49] and which prophesied:

Nine hundred years completed – I will smite Egypt.[50]

Since Hellenistic oracle literature is largely based on eastern prototypes, the beginnings of late Israelite apocalyptic may perhaps also derive from Iran or from the Chaldeans, who were active in Babylon and with whom the hero of the Book of Daniel is already brought into close contact. In view of the present state of research, however, it would be dangerous to draw fundamental conclusions from this relationship; for not only is the temporal and sociological emphasis of the OT apocalypses still obscure – above all we are still awaiting an adequate study of the relevant Hellenistic literature, to say nothing of the Iranian.[51]

It has not been my intention to review apocalyptic literature in detail or to bring to light new scholarly results, although that is urgently needed. My aim has merely been to convey a rough impression of apocalyptic round about the turn of the era, before going on to a survey and criticism of the present discussion. In view of the throng of contradictory theories, it would seem advisable to narrow down the criterion of what is apocalyptic, rather than to extend it, and to insist on starting from a strictly form-critical basis.

Even with so cautious and restricted a view of what apocalyptic is, the themes we have indicated are still explosive ones, theologically speaking; for the effect of such an apocalyptic on the place of the NT in the history of ideas could have been considerable. Consequently Cullmann's recent suggestion[52] that the word apocalyptic should only be used "in the neutral sense," as a mere term for literary types and themes, has little prospect of being generally adopted in the near future.

NOTES

1 The *Neue Brockhaus* (1964) 1:96, defines the German word "apokalyptisch" as "geheimnisvoll, dunkel," i.e., "mysterious, obscure," and so does the *Brockhaus Enzyklopädie* (1966) 1 612. The *Oxford English Dictionary*, on the other hand, with its definition "of the nature of revelation or disclosure," ignores these associations.

2 G. Sauter, *Zukunft und Verheissung* (1965) 95; cf. 229.

3 O. Cullmann, *Heil als Geschichte* (1965) 62; ET, *Salvation in History* (1967) 80.

4 For example the leading Jewish religious philosopher Martin Buber, cf. Freiherr von Hammerstein, "Das Messiasproblem bei M. Buber," *Studia Delitzschiana* 1 (1958) 23–5. A remarkable swing is taking place at present in American Judaism, however. In his foreword to the Dropsie College edition of Jewish Apocryphal Literature (in the first work to appear, S. Tedesche and S. Zeitlin, *The First Book of Maccabees* [1950] xf.), Abraham Neuman writes that *Enoch* and 4 Ezra reveal the spirit of the Jewish martyrs better than the writings of Josephus. The apocalyptic books are certainly nearer to the New Testament than to (late) Jewish literature. But nevertheless "we deem it an act of redemption to reclaim these works for the Jewish people and to restore them to their rightful place of honour in Jewish literature."

5 Hennecke-Schneemelcher, *Neutestamentliche Apocryphen* (1959) II:408 (ET, 582); E. Lohmeyer, *Die Offenbarung des Johannes* (2d ed. by H. Kraft; HNT 16 [1953] on Rev. 1:1).

6 Survey in J. E. Ménard, "Les manuscrits de Nag Hammadi," *Bibliotheca Orientalis* 13 (1956) 2–6, and in S. Schulz, *TR* 26 (1960) 237–50.

7 Survey in O. Eissfeldt, *Einleitung in das Alte Testament*, 1964³; ET, *The Old Testament: an Introduction*, 1965, section 110; C. Burchard, *Bibliographie zu den Handschriften vom Toten Meer* (BZAW 89 [1965]) II:333–6.

8 P. Feine and J. Behm, *Einleitung in das Neue Testament*, 14th ed. by W. G. Kümmel (1965); ET, *Introduction to the New Testament* (1966), section 33.

9 D. S. Russell, *The Method and Message of Jewish Apocalyptic* (1964) 28; G. von Rad, *Theologie des Alten Testaments* (1965⁴) II:327.

10 Eissfeldt, *Einleitung*, 711 (ET, 524); Kutscher, *Scripta Hierosolymitana* 4 (1958) 2. Russell contemplates people who reached Palestine from Mesopotamia during the Maccabean rebellion, *Method and Message*, 19.

11 At present vigorously supported by F. M. Cross: "That which places a gulf between the Essenes and the main stream of Judaism is their apocalypticism ... In no case can the Pharisees, much less the Sadducees, be called apocalyptists." *The Ancient Library of Qumran* (1958) 54, n. 33; cf. also B. Reicke *JBL* 79 (1960) 137–50.

12 "The Apocalyptic literature and the Zealot Movement went hand in hand, the one providing the dangerous food and the other feasting on it and calling for more." R. T. Herford, *The Pharisees* (1924) 188.

13 Cf. also von Rad in the first ed. of his *Theologie des Alten Testament* (1960) II:314; ET of first ed., *Old Testament Theology* (1965) II:301f.

14 My book *Was ist Formgeschichte?*, (1967²); ET, *The Growth of the Biblical Tradition* (1969) explains in detail why the approach offered by form criticism and literary history plays a decisive part for biblical and related writings (i.e., not only for the apocalypses). I can therefore confine myself here to a few key points.

15 The view taken by A. Nissen in "Tora und Geschichte in Spätjudentum," *NovT* 10 (1967) 246 (without detailed evidence); and by von Rad in *Theologie* (1965⁴) II:330, n. 28.

16 On *2 Baruch* and *4 Ezra* cf. B. Violet, *Die Apokalypsen des Esra und des Baruch in deutscher Gestalt* (GCS; 1924).

17 Cf. also Rev. 5:1; Dan. 7:2; *2 Bar.* 36:2f; 4 Ezra 13:2; *1 Enoch* 90:1f, cf. 1:2; *Apoc. Abr.* 21:2; and in the prophetic writings Ezek. 1:4; Zech. 1:8; and frequently elsewhere. If an actual vision has been described, the transition to the second, interpretative section is marked by the words: "This was the vision (word, dream) ... and its interpretation is ..." (Dan. 2:36; 4:18; 4 Ezra 10:40–3, cf. 12:10; *2 Bar.* 39:1f).

18 Rev. 1:17; 4:2; Daniel 10; *2 Bar.* 21:26; 4 Ezra 5:14; *1 Enoch* 65:4; *Apoc. Abr.* 10:2.

19 Whether the paraenetic (component) literary types have any close connection with the popularity of Wisdom discourses in the late Israelite period, or with the turning of post-exilic prophecy to hortatory discourses (Trito-Isaiah, Malachi) has not yet been clarified. The part played by ethics in the apocalypses cannot be too highly estimated. "Apocalyptic was essentially ethical" (R. H. Charles, *Apocrypha and Pseudepigraphia of the Old Testament* [1913] II:ix).

20 On the legends in the early parts of the Old Testament see *Was ist Formgeschichte?* (ET, *Growth*), section 16.

21 British and American scholars particularly have offered various explanations: (1) The absolute validity of the Law and the period staked out by the canon no longer allowed of contemporary prophecy (Charles, *Apocrypha* II:viii). (2) The author is falling back on a long oral tradition which circulated under the name in question (W. O. E. Oesterley, *The Jews and Judaism during the Greek Period* [1941] 74). (3) The dominating factor is the peculiar Hebrew

concept of an "extension of personality" (D. S. Russell, *Between the Testaments* [1959] 116; cf. also *The Method and Message*, 127–39). In Germany the old "deception" hypothesis is also still in vogue. According to this the apocalyptic writers, though knowing better, deliberately had recourse to a fiction in order to lend credibility to their writings (cf. von Rad, *Theologie des Alten Testaments* II⁴:320). English-speaking scholars dissociate themselves from this suspicion: "It is improbable that (the pseudonymity) deceived anyone, or was intended to" (H. H. Rowley, *The Relevance of Apocalyptic* [1944] 14). H. R. Balz's essay, "Anonymität und Pseudonymität in Urchristentum" (*ZTK* 66 [1969] 403–36), though full of useful material, is typical of the German attitude, with its remoteness from all the deeper problems. He finds Russell's thesis weighed down by "a whole series of prior judgments" (n. 39). He evidently imagines his own solution to be free of all such judgments. The answer he proposes for the book of Daniel is as follows: "If the author had written under his own name, however, he would no doubt have met with incredulity on the part of his contemporaries, for his visionary accounts are not descriptions of actual experiences; they are conscious literary inventions" (422). Balz unfortunately fails to reveal the source of his information.

22 Revelation 13; Daniel 7; *2 Bar*. 36f; 4 Ezra 11; *1 Enoch* 85ff; *Apocalypse of Abraham* 13. Von Rad (*Theologie* II:319) sees, however, in the "rational character of apocalyptic . . . the exact opposite of every kind of genuine mythological thinking."

23 Revelation 5; *2 Bar*. 35ff; 53ff; 4 Ezra 12. The symbols of redemption are generally taken from Old Testament prophecy.

24 For further explanation see my *Was ist Formgeschichte?* (ET, *Growth*), section 2D.

25 See *Was ist Formgeschichte?*, 5 (ET, 4f).

26 Rev. 20:6f; Daniel 9; *2 Baruch* 27; 4 Ezra 7:28; *1 Enoch* 85ff, 93; *Apocalypse of Abraham* 29.

27 Dan. 10:20f; *1 Enoch* 89:59ff, cf. Rev. 16:14; *Apoc. Abr*. 10:17.

28 Rev. 21:12; Dan. 12:3; *1 Enoch* 51:4; *2 Bar*. 51:5; 4 Ezra 7:97.

29 Rev. 20:4–6; Daniel 12; *2 Baruch* 50f; 4 Ezra 7:32; *1 Enoch* 22; 51.

30 Revelation 21; *2 Bar*. 6:8f; 4 Ezra 8:52–5; *1 Enoch* 48f; *Apoc. Abr*. 29:17.

31 Rev. 20:11; Dan. 7:19; *2 Bar*. 73:1; 4 Ezra 7:33; *Apocalypse of Abraham* 18.

32 Cf. my essay, "Der Schatz im Himmel," in *Leben jenseits des Todes, Festschrift für H. Thielicke* (1968) 47–60.

33 Scholars occasionally question whether a human or angelic mediator is an essential figure in apocalyptic eschatology, maintaining that the dominating feature is a *theocratic* view, according to which God alone brings about final redemption. Murdock (*Int*. 21 [1967] 175, n. 29) cites *1 Enoch* 16; 71f; 91; *2 Enoch* 33; 50:2 B; 65f; *As. Mos*. 9—10:6 as examples of "the expectation of the 'future aeon' without a messianic kingdom on earth." The discrepancy is most clearly emphasized by P. Vielhauer ("Gottesreich und Menschensohn in der Verkündigung Jesu" in *Festschrift G. Dehn* [1957] 51–79; reprinted in *Aufsätze zum Neuen Testament* [1965] 55–91; "Jesus und der Menschensohn," *ZTK* 60 (1963) 133–77, reprinted in *Aufsätze*, 92–140). Where the eschatological future is expected and designated as the rule of God, the Son of man is missing; "but in this case the Messiah, or any other judge-saviour figure, is missing as well" (*ZTK*, 135). Vielhauer cites the *Similitudes of Enoch* and 4 Ezra for the Son of

man as essential mediator, but he excludes Daniel 7 because there the Messiah is not an individual figure. For the sovereignty which relates to God alone he quotes Daniel 2; *Sibylline Oracles* II:767; *As. Mos.* 10:1ff.

Because this point is much discussed in connection with a noticeable relationship between apocalyptic and New Testament writings a few observations may perhaps not be out of place:

1 Of all the many interpretations of the well-worn passage in Daniel 7, the one suggested by Vielhauer is surely the most improbable; for according to 7:14 the Son of man of 7:13 (who, Vielhauer tells us, is a symbolic figure representing the eschatological kingdom) receives that very same eternal sovereignty and everlasting kingdom which are God's alone according to 3:33. According to Vielhauer, therefore, the symbol (Son of man = eschatological kingdom) has to "receive" the very thing (i.e., the kingdom) which it itself is initiating. What is this supposed to mean?

2 For *Enoch* a reference to 41:1, compared with 61:8; 69:26–29 and the throne concept in general, is enough to shake the theory of an unrelated parallelism between the rule of God and the figure of the mediator.

3 4 Ezra 13 certainly does not expressly mention the rule of God, but the (Son of) man cuts out for himself a great mountain (v. 6) and flies up upon it, which is undoubtedly a reference to Dan. 2:34, 44, where the stone which frees itself is expressly related to "the kingdom."

4 What is said in Dan. 2:34f, 44f, is interpreted by Vielhauer as referring to an absolutely established kingdom of God, without any human representatives. But Daniel talks about a new, fifth empire, which replaces the empires of the world which are ruled over by kings. What the structure of the new empire will be is not discussed. The question of "theocracy" or mediation in the Book of Daniel is not yet ready to be pronounced on in this passage.

5 It may be doubted whether the *Sibylline Oracles* (which derive from the Hellenistic world) are conclusive in the closest sense for the apocalyptic context. But if III:767 is drawn on at all, it should also be mentioned that the continuation in III:781f says that the prophets of the Mighty God are then "judges of mortal men and just kings."

6 Since the *Assumption of Moses* is not fully extant, only cautious conclusions can be drawn about its eschatology. But if arguments are based on the appearance of the kingdom of God throughout his creation (10:1), ought not the succeeding verse,

> Then the hands of the angel shall be filled
> Who has been appointed chief,

to be considered too? The connection of the chief angel (Michael) with the kingdom could actually be the key to the understanding of the statement about the Son of man in Daniel 7 (cf. J. Coppens and L. Dequeker, *Le fils de l'homme et les Saints du Très-Haut en Daniel VIII, dans les Apocryphes et dans le Nouveau Testament* = Analecta Lovaniensia Biblica et Orientalia [1961] III:23). Vielhauer's attempt at a proof grounded on the history of religion is therefore full of flaws in all the passages cited. We must ask, moreover, whether the idea of theocracy is not a typical notion of Hellenistic Israel. But this is not the place to pursue that question.

34 "Gnosis is of the very spirit of apocalyptic." R. Otto, *Reich Gottes und Menschensohn* (1934) 5; ET, *The Kingdom of God and the Son of Man* (1938) 15, quoting Gressmann.

35 A passage out of the Syriac *Apocalypse of Daniel*, col. III/IV, is significant: "The son shall speak to the father and say, 'Thou art not my father'. And the servant shall make himself equal to his lord. The maid shall be seated and the mistress shall serve. The youth shall lie down at table before him that is old." The unpublished manuscript is being prepared for publication by my pupil H. Schmoldt.

36 Von Rad, *Theologie* II:224; II⁴:220 (ET, 212).

37 B. Violet, *Die Apokalypsen des Esra und des Baruch in deutscher Gestalt* (1924) 312 (on Vision VI, 19:14 [= *2 Bar.* 74:1]).

38 The equivalents of the Hebrew root *glh* which are the basis of *apocalypsis/ apokalyptein* mean the disclosure of a historical background which becomes known for the first time through the apocalypse in question. This is generally interpreted psychologically by present-day scholars, as the experience of "divine" inspiration through the personality of the seer. But does that conform to the self-understanding of these men? What they write is hardly revelation literature after the style of medieval mysticism (cf. J. Lindblom, *Die literasiche Gattung der prophetischen Literatur* [1924]); it is rather a proclamation to a community, the writer merely acting as the messenger of a divine principal. What is laid bare is the eschatological drama, and that in such a fashion that the hearer or reader is in a position to make "faith" the direction of his life, thereby making possible personal salvation at the impending divine coming. It is in so far that the theme is "the revelation of the divine revelation." Modern theology's concept of revelation, for which the Old Testament offers no analogy (cf. R. Rendtorff in *Offenbarung als Geschichte*, ed. W. Pannenberg [1965³] 21–41; ET, "The Concept of Revelation in Ancient Israel," in *Revelation as History* [1969] 23–53) can in a sense be shown to be already present in apocalyptic.

39 See my article "Spätisraelitisches Geschichtsdenken am Beispiel des Buches Daniel," *HZ* 193 (1961) 7.

40 J. M. Schmidt, *Die jüdische Apokalyptik. Die Geschichte ihrer Erforschung von den Anfängen bis zu den Textfunden von Qumran* (1969).

41 *RGG³*, 1:col. 463.

42 Hennecke–Schneemelcher II:411 (ET, 586) therefore contemplates a further form, i.e., the farewell discourse – this, however, belonging to the same movement as the apocalypses themselves.

43 Nissen (cf. n. 15, above) marshals five reasons for assigning Jubilees to the apocalypses ("Tora und Geschichte," 246 n. 6), none of which is entirely conclusive:

    1 The secret revelation to a man of God – this already applies to Deuteronomy.

    2 History is divided into periods – which is already the case among the Deuteronomists.

    3 The Enoch tradition is taken over – but this is also true of the nonapocalyptic Ecclesiasticus.

    4 Heavenly tablets appear to the seer. The motif crops up in *1 Enoch*, where

past and present history is inscribed on the tablets (81:2; 93:2; 106:19; 107:1). According to *Jubilees*, on the other hand, what is written on the tablets is primarily ritual and criminal law.

5   In 1:6–18, 22–6; 23:1–31, proper apocalypses allegedly appear. But is every Ezekiel-like combination of historical survey and prophecy actually an apocalypse?

Russell (*Method and Message*, 54) is more cautious: "Jubilees is not, strictly speaking, an apocalyptic book; but it belongs to the same milieu."

44   Sources are cited in Burchard, *Bibliographie*, II:335f.

45   A.S.v.d. Woude, *OTS* 14 (1965) 354–73; J. A. Fitzmyer, *JBL* 86 (1967) 25–41.

46   A balanced consideration of the relationship between the Qumran community and apocalyptic can be found in Russell. Like Hanson, he holds Qumran to be "a cooled-down apocalyptic sect" (*Method and Message*, 24; see also his list of apocalyptic Qumran writings on 39).

47   "The apocalyptic literature of the Gaonic period is neither in form nor in matter a direct development of the pre-Talmudic Apocalypse," L. Ginsberg, *JBL* 41 (1922) 116 n.

48   The sole exception is to be found in *Sanh.* 9b, with a report of the discovery of a book in square script and in Hebrew – that is to say, a book with a canonical claim (Ginsberg, 119f).

49   E. Meyer, "Ein neues Bruchstück Manethos über das Lamm des Bokchoris," *Zeitschrift für Ägyptische Sprache und Altertumkunde* 45 (1908/09) 135f.

50   *Altorientalische Texte* (ed. by H. Gressmann [1926²]) 48f; K. Koch, "Das Lamm, das Ägypten vernichtet," *ZNW* 57 (1966) 79–93.

51   Extensive material on this theme-complex, combined with exemplary reserve in the evaluation of it, can now be found in M. Hengel, *Judentum und Hellenismus* (WUNT 10 [1969]) 319–94, esp. 335ff.

52   Cullmann *Heil als Geschichte*, 65 (ET, 83).

2

*Old Testament Apocalyptic Reexamined**

PAUL D. HANSON

Apocalypticism is in vogue. Whether one looks within the covers of a popular barometer of the *Zeitgeist*, such as the *Saturday Review*, glances through the program of a Society of Biblical Literature meeting, or ponders over the new releases from the publishing houses, there is ample evidence that apocalyptic has come out of a long eclipse into the full light of a wide audience.

This new popularity is not unrelated to a profound change which has swept over our country in the last decade. A young, headstrong nation suddenly came of age; the optimism of a long history of progress (only accentuated by glorious recovery from occasional setbacks) culminating in the prosperity of the Eisenhower Era (reserved to be sure for those smiled on by the system) began to falter and even to collapse. We are not speaking of a stock market crash, but of a collapse of a much more profound nature: a collapse of confidence in the *machine progress* to which our society had dedicated life and soul to perfect. For now that machine, like the Frankenstein monster infused with the breath of life, was making claims of his own: our rivers, forests, atmosphere, young members of our families (for various aspects of his operation – his war game, his narcotics game). Though many people deny these signs and continue to dedicate themselves to perpetuate the machine, a growing number have experienced the crisis sociologists find at the base of every apocalyptic movement: the collapse of a well-ordered world view which defines values and orders the universe for a people, thrusting them into the uncharted chaos of anomie and meaninglessness. For decades the well-defined legal structures found in the Torah and the pre-exilic prophets supplied a logical moral system for a well-ordered society, making the classical prophets popular to the exclusion of the later apocalyptic writings and causing scholars

* First published in *Int* 25 (1971) 454–79.

to trace the origins of normative Judaism and Christianity directly to the prophets, dismissing apocalyptic as a fall from pure religion into the dark realm of fantasy. But what happens when society falls into disorder; when an earlier generation's view of the irresistible progress of the machine is no longer tenable; when the machine to which we once sacrificed is seen as a demon out to sacrifice us; when the elemental spirits, Earth, Air, Water, and Fire, after having been silenced for two millennia by scientific man, again begin to cry out to heaven for vengeance upon mortals who have polluted their Earth? The answer is clear and written on the putrid air we breathe; those pondering over the signs begin to look upon the universe with a new respect, even as a place charged with ominous powers. A number, from among the ranks of such ponderers, experiencing complete alienation from these crumbling structures, withdraw into apocalyptic sects given to visions of the imminent collapse of this order and the dawn of a new era. These sects, such as Hari Krishna and the Process, are rediscovering the vitality of the apocalyptic literatures of the world; indeed, they are producing apocalyptic works before our eyes. The rest of us, disturbed by the signs but remaining within the system, account for the growing popularity of apocalypticism in the weekly magazines.

As students of a long-neglected field, it is gratifying to find our subject becoming popular. But popularity brings risks, especially the temptation to allow current interpretations of contemporary apocalyptic movements to become uncritically normative for our interpretation of ancient apocalyptic. Though certain features undeniably are shared by contemporary and ancient apocalyptists, it must never be forgotten that our world is vastly different from theirs, and symbols which are strikingly similar may have vastly divergent origins and significance in their ancient and modern contexts. For example, the current literature emphasizes the bizarre and the fantastic in contemporary apocalyptic, often connecting it with psychedelic experience and not infrequently with the use of hallucinogenic drugs. The source of apocalyptic imagery is thereby traced to the subjective consciousness of the individual, an evaluation commonly applied as well to ancient apocalyptic. But an important difference must be remembered: While the contemporary apocalyptist must go to his subjective fantasy to derive the appropriate images, ancient man, with a world view which we would designate mythopoeic, found his imagery in respectable religious systems. Many references to the bizarre, fantastic, disjointed, and eclectic nature of Jewish apocalyptic would be obviated were such contemporary analogies tested against historical investigation.

While thus welcoming the heightened interest in apocalyptic pre-cipitated by the contemporary *Zeitgeist*, our enthusiasm must be tempered with an appeal for a rigorous application of the historical-critical method as a corrective to the type of errors which modern analogies can deliver.

Johann M. Schmidt's recent book indicates that the study of apocalyptic most commonly has begun with Daniel.[1] Two negative results have stemmed from this practice: 1) The connections between prophecy and apocalyptic have either been neglected or misinter-preted: 2) The source of the "new" elements in apocalyptic have been sought in foreign religions contemporary with Daniel. Even in works where the study of apocalyptic has begun at an earlier period, the conclusions of the traditional approach have continued to influence the interpretation.

If, however – as study of the subject has led us to believe – the "taproot" of apocalyptic lies in prophecy, and if, further, the "new" influences giving rise to Jewish apocalyptic literature are to be traced *first* to the recrudescence of old mythic material long at home on Israelite soil, and *second* to the trying circumstances rending the Jewish community in the post-exilic period, then the beginning point will be in late prophecy. For it is there that one can detect prophetic eschatology being transformed into apocalyptic, thereby suggesting where the study of the nature and origins of Jewish apocalyptic must begin.

Before attention can be directed towards that crucial transition period, a word must be said about the phenomenon of prophecy in Israel, viewed against the background of the religious environment from which it emerged and within which it continued to struggle throughout its relatively brief life.[2] That preprophetic religious environment is especially important, inasmuch as apocalyptic in developing beyond classical prophecy harks back in many respects to that earlier environment.

Prophecy emerged from a mythopoeic religious environment, within which divine activity per se was regarded as occurring on a cosmic plane and within which the mundane sphere was regarded as a mere reflection of the drama of the gods. The task of the cult was to make the primeval activities of the gods efficacious for this world through reenactment of cosmic activities in the cult ritual. It was dedicated to safeguarding the order of things from change, thereby assuring the annual defeat of sterility and the attendant revivification of nature. Since the literature of this cult was concerned with the cosmic activities of the gods, historical events played no substantive part in the cultic drama, for history involved movement

39

and change, qualities which the ancient cult was dedicated to transcend. Before turning to prophecy, we note that the royal cult in Jerusalem, as indicated by the royal psalms, essentially retained this mythopoeic view and for obvious reasons: Emulating the dynasties of the great kingdoms, the House of Solomon was dedicated to a static order which safeguarded the monarch's rule from threat of change. The eternal cycle of myth suited well his dynastic aspirations.

Prophecy arose with kingship. The prophet established himself alongside the king as spokesman of a point of view which often opposed the royal theology, a view drawing heavily upon traditions of the League, tracing ultimately, it would seem, to the Amorite patron-deity type who guided his people in their wanderings and battles. Already present *in nuce* in the ancient promise to Abraham, this view recognized primary divine activity as involving a movement from promise to fulfilment, a movement stemming from a covenant relationship between tribe and deity.[3] The view of divine activity in this religion contrasts sharply with the mythopoeic view. While myth is dedicated to absolving the threat of change, this view embraces the flux and movement of history as the arena of divine activity. While myth recounts as its credo a cosmic drama, this view recites past historical events as the scenario of a drama, relating the cosmic deity to his earthly people. Myth therefore offers escape from the change of the historical process, while the prophetic view holds the cosmic and the historical in tension.

The prophetic view is seen emerging in Israel's earliest literature. It comes clearly into view in the Song of Miriam (Exodus 15), where the primordial conflict between Baal and Yamm is visible only in vestigial form; Yahweh is no longer battling Yamm, which has become completely passive, but Pharaoh, a historical figure.[4] Yet integration of the cosmic into the mundane is not complete, for the Divine Warrior effects his victory alone, and while he battles a historical foe, he utilizes no historical agent to aid him. The Song of Deborah (Judges 5) begins on the same level, with the Divine Warrior marching forth from his mountain accompanied by all of the natural disturbances appropriate to the theophany of the Storm God (vv. 4–5). But then the scene shifts from the cosmic realm to the historical plane where the tribes of Israel are going forth to battle the enemy. It is Yahweh's battle, but as the curse on Meroz indicates, the deity relies on historical agents: "Curse Meroz, ... because they came not to help of Yahweh" (v. 23). Only in verse 20 does one find a flashback to the cosmic level. In fact, the core of the poem, the description of Jael's single-handed defeat of Sisera, is rigorously humanistic in its attention to detail and its consistent realism. This part of the poem comes close to the humanism of the court history of David, where Yahweh does not intervene directly, but is left as an invisible mover behind the events of history.

The prophets were inheritors of this historical view of divine activity, which view they tempered with a continued attention to the cosmic perspective. If we may call the effort to integrate divine activity into the events and institutions of the historical realm a "realistic" impulse, and the orientation which views divine activity on a cosmic plane "visionary," we would suggest that one of the outstanding achievements of classical prophecy was its ability to maintain both elements in a dynamic tension. For example, it is obvious that Isaiah recognized actions of the divine assembly behind the events of his day. Yet if one aspect of his prophetic office stands out, it is his activity as a statesman, one fully involved in the politics of his nation, one constantly confronting the king with Yahweh's will. This determination to maintain the balance between reality and vision explains the significance of the prophet's self-consciousness as a messenger. He was called by Yahweh to straddle two worlds, to view the deliberations and events of the cosmic realm, but then immediately to integrate that vision into the events of the politico-historical order. This tension accounts for the contrast often noted between the language of the indictment and that of the sentence in the judgment oracle (e.g. Amos 1—2), the sentence cast in the cosmic imagery of the Divine Warrior, the indictment in the concrete realism of the historical realm, thereby manifesting the prophetic integration of cosmic and mundane. In Isaiah's call vision in chapter 6 we witness the tension experienced by a man straddling two worlds. He finds himself in the divine assembly, yet he does not belong there: "for I am a man of unclean lips, and I dwell in the midst of a people of unclean lips; for my eyes have seen the King, the LORD of hosts!" Once purified, he is enabled to pause in this holy sphere, but not to tarry. His access to the divine realm is not unqualified privilege, but is bound to the task of relating that experience to the normal realm of men. This tension between vision and reality in the prophets is of central importance in the question of the relation between prophecy and apocalyptic. Contrast Isaiah's vision to that of Daniel in chapter 12, which ends not with the words of Isaiah 6, "Go and say to this people": but with the instructions, "But you Daniel, shut up the words, and seal the book, until the time of the end."[5] The tremendous tension between the vision and the mundane realm in Isaiah is absent in Daniel; they are two separate spheres which Daniel is not required to integrate.

In keeping with the political nature of the prophetic office, the historical realm is taken very seriously in the classical prophets as a realm of primary divine activity. This activity is seen as a part of the covenant relationship which Yahweh has established with his human community. The relationship is a genuine one with both partners acting freely in response to each other. This genuine inter-action stems from the fact that in prophecy Yahweh's saving activity is recognized in the events of history. Events and persons of this world become charged with cosmic significance. Yahweh acts through "Assyria, the rod of my anger," through "the waters of the River, mighty and many," through the king of Assyria, the Babylonians, the Scythians, through Cyrus his servant. But the balance between vision and reality was a delicate one to maintain. In the tense centuries after Isaiah that balance was often lost. In the Deuteronomistic History Yahweh's cosmic activity was neglected in favor of his involvement in the events of Israel's history. The pendulum later swung far in the other direction with apocalyptic being preoccupied with the vision, to the neglect of mundane reality.

The abundant use that the Deuteronomistic historian made of old northern league traditions is well known, and the close affinities which his work has with the covenant theology of the classical prophets requires no further demonstration. Indeed, the structure of that history is based strictly on the prophetic theme of promise and fulfilment, making it the single most consistent application of the prophetic view of history. Nevertheless, a critical change in the application of that theme has occurred. While it was a theme within the context of a dynamic covenant relationship in the prophets, in the Deuteronomistic History it has become employed as the frame-work of a propaganda work for the imperial program of Josiah.[6] The prophetic theme of an open-ended, unpredictable bond between God and man has become an inflexible principle applied to demonstrate one fact: that the hope of Israel was bound to the central cult in Jerusalem. The movement of the entire history of Israel is towards the reign of Josiah, that ideal king whose faithfulness to the central cult would usher in a new era of glory.[7]

There is no denying the landmark achievement represented by the Deuteronomistic History. It represents the first genuine histori-ography of the ancient world,[8] and for the era of the Josianic reform it gave a very adequate interpretation of Israel's national history. Its theological insight into the nature of divine activity in human history is profound, as is its melding of old prophetic hopes and themes into a unified whole. But like all theologies, it was based on pre-suppositions too narrow to claim validity for all eras. By reducing the theme of promise-fulfillment to a dogmatic principle connected to the law of cultic centrality, and by placing this theme in the service of legitimatizing a particular institution, the Deuteronomistic theology became vulnerable in the crisis years which followed. In earlier prophecy the theme of promise-fulfilment maintained an aura of the ambivalent, for the authenticity claim of an oracle was never tied to specific results. The Deuteronomistic theology brings to a conclusion a purge of mythic elements from Yahwism which gained much impetus from the bitter struggle with Baalism during the Omride dynasty. However, the peculiar strength of myth was thereby lost, the aura of the mysterious, the opaque, the unpredictable, the cosmic encompassing the deity. Yahweh became predictable; history became transparent to his activity, allowing historical events to be fitted precisely and definitively into a schema of promise and fulfillment which culminated in the reign of Josiah.

Because the picture was drawn so precisely, it could ill tolerate events which contradicted it. One can imagine the crisis in the Deuteronomistic theology when a rapid succession of events did contradict the central theme of the entire history. The heart of that theology said that the Davidide who restored Yahweh's central sanctuary would be beneficiary of the covenant blessings. But Josiah, the *David redivivus*, no sooner completed his reform than he was cut down by Necco II; his successors fell prey to Egyptian and Assyrian intrigues; the land was ravaged, and then the culminating blow, Yahweh's central sanctuary itself was desecrated and destroyed. That which should have been the dawn of a second golden age, according to the Deuteronomistic theology, turned into national calamity. Attempts were made within the Deuteronomistic tradition to accommodate the old orthodoxy to the new crisis, as indicated especially by the additions of the post-exilic editor who blames the disaster on the sins of Manasseh (2 Kings 21:2–15). The Book of Lamentations is another example of this effort. More common in the literature, however, are echoes of despair which can be heard reverberating through the prophetic and wisdom literature of the period: "Yahweh will not do good, nor will he do ill" (Zeph. 1:12; cf. Ezek. 8:12; 18:25; Isa. 57:1). Perhaps the harshest indictment on the Josianic reform comes from the exiles in Egypt. So long as they had worshipped the queen of heaven, "we had plenty of food, and prospered, and saw no evil. But since we left off burning incense to the queen of heaven, and pouring out libations to her, we have lacked everything and have been consumed by the sword and by famine" (Jer. 44:17f). Though the question of the date of Job remains disputed, the original sections of that book are harshly critical of the retributive principle upon which the Deuteronomistic theology is

43

firmly based. It seems very possible that this book reflects the same crisis in the Deuteronomistic theology which we have been describing. Job's experience belies the doctrine that the godly shall inherit the earth (21:7). Rejecting the idea that the events of the historical order are transparent to the acts of the deity, Job embraces instead an El-type god of nature.[9] Much restudy of the Wisdom literature of the exilic and early post-exilic period is urgent, the cynicism of Qohelet already suggests, however, that the well-worn path of Wisdom, that of justifying the ways of God to men, was leading up a dead end from which there would be no easy exit.

Conceivably, Yahwism would have died with this crisis in the Deuteronomistic theology, or at least been radically altered – as it was among exiles to Egypt – had it not been for a bold new reformulation of the faith springing from prophetic circles during the exile. Prophecy remained very much alive during the years of crisis following the death of Josiah. As both Jeremiah and Ezekiel indicate, in certain prophetic circles the temptation of reducing divine activity to the mundane sphere was resisted. As in Isaiah, so too in these books, a dynamic tension between cosmic vision and mundane reality is maintained.

For Jeremiah, the true prophet is one who has stood in Yahweh's council (e.g., 23:16–22), and similar to Isaiah, he hears Yahweh say, "I appointed you a prophet to the nations." Jeremiah's entire career involves him deeply in the events of his nation (e.g., 38:17ff). Yahweh's activity is interpreted in the light of the events of his time (25:8f; also 27:6f; 32:26ff). Yahweh of Hosts is the Warrior who will destroy the land; yet he commands not the cosmic hosts, but agents of this world (e.g., 6:1–8). There is evidence also that the oracles are not intended merely to foretell future events, but are spoken within the context of Israel's covenant with Yahweh. Thus in chapter 3, harsh condemnation can prepare the way for an appeal for Israel to repent and return (3:11–14; cf. 18:11, 4:14). Besides recognizing these similarities with the earlier prophets, however, we also detect distinct developments in Jeremiah. First, there is a growing sense that such appeals to repentance are really futile; the two verses which follow the appeal to return in 18:11 indicate this. Chapter 11 indicates that the curse has fallen, because the people have broken the covenant. Indeed, Yahweh tells his prophet, "Therefore do not pray for this people or lift up a cry on their behalf, for I will not listen when they call me in the time of their trouble" (v. 14). The history of Israel's covenant relationship with Yahweh has become unmitigated *Unheilsgeschichte* (e.g., ch. 2). Therefore

You shall be put to shame by Egypt
as you were put to shame by Assyria. (v. 36).

This pessimistic view of the past will ultimately have profound effects upon the nature of prophecy, for as the impending judgment becomes more and more an inevitable catastrophe, prophecy will become less an aspect of a living covenant relationship aimed at returning the people to obedience and more the foretelling of cataclysmic future events. Jeremiah even pleads at times with Yahweh not to have mercy on the people, but to destroy them (18:19–23). Israel is nearly beyond the pale (19:11). The second development which follows from this pessimism is this: Hope is held out no longer for repentance within Israel's existing covenant with Yahweh. Rather a new and radically different covenant is deemed necessary. That is, Yahweh's initial relationship with Israel has failed. A new beginning initiated by a new covenant will be necessary (31:31–34). Taken together these two notions, the pessimistic view of Israel's past and the belief that only a radical new beginning will recreate the covenant, point in the direction of apocalyptic.

The Book of Ezekiel is important in the discussion of the origins of apocalyptic. Ezekiel, in good prophetic tradition, integrates his elaborate visions of the cosmic Yahweh into the events and institutions of the mundane sphere. For example, after his bizarre call vision Yahweh says, "Son of man, I send you to the people of Israel, to a nation of rebels, ..." Following the great vision of Yahweh's departure from Jerusalem, he is immediately transported back to the exiles in Chaldea: "And I told the exiles all the things that the Lord had showed me." After the vision of the dry bones in chapter 37, the prophet is commanded straightaway to preach to the people about the vision (cf. 40:4, 44:5f). The function of the vision in Ezekiel, as in the other classical prophets, is distinct from its function in apocalyptic, where the vision constitutes esoteric knowledge which the visionary is to keep secret.[10] A clear difference exists between the roles of the prophet and the apocalyptic seer; the prophet sees himself as a messenger of Yahweh and his divine council charged with relating his vision of the cosmic realm to the earthly realm, translating it into the categories and events of the mundane order. The apocalyptic seer is content to leave his vision on the cosmic level.

Whereas the increased use of the vision in general and certain details in the vision accounts in particular[11] indicate that Ezekiel brings us to the threshold of apocalyptic, yet his ties to the prophetic tradition remain firm: Vision and reality are held together. Though Yahweh is punishing Israel for her sin, his agent is the earthly monarch Nebuchadnezzar; though Yahweh will restore Israel by the return of his Glory, that restoration will occur in the historical city of Jerusalem.[12]

This balance between visionary and realistic elements accounts for the frequent attempts in the history of criticism to divide the book between two "Ezekiels." It also explains Ezekiel's unique position in post-exilic Judaism: On the one hand he is claimed as the father of the hierocratic temple community – a fact in keeping with his fidelity to the Priestly tradition and thorough familiarity with the temple cult – and on the other he exerts influence on apocalyptic circles, especially on the level of style and form.

While Ezekiel preserves the prophetic tradition into the exilic period, clear signs indicate that the demise of prophecy is at hand. Israel's past has become *Unheilsgeschichte*, pure and simple.[13] It seems that pessimism regarding the redemptive quality of Israel's past has reached a climax: No longer are instances of obedience cited alongside examples of backsliding; Israel's whole history has been one of unmitigated rebellion. The picture of the normal historical order as an arena of God's saving acts thus assumes a very dark hue. The faithful must look to a future act which would revivify the community of dry bones (37:12–14) and give the people a new heart and spirit (11:19; 36:26). When Ezekiel goes on in chapters 40–48 to explain how this renewal would occur, however, a difference in emphasis from Jeremiah becomes apparent, and his affinity with hierocratic elements in the post-exilic community becomes evident: Not an absolute break with the past, not further judgment followed by a new creation, but the return of the Glory of Yahweh and the rebuilding of the temple cult along the traditional patterns of the period immediately prior to the exile will inaugurate Israel's new era. While the prophetic dialectic of vision and reality does not dissolve in Ezekiel, it at least promises to find resolution in the very realistic program of restoration in chapters 40–48. Whereas the tension remains acute in Jeremiah, calling for a new eschatological act of Yahweh, Ezekiel's stress on continuity with the structures of the immediate past relieves the eschatological stress found in Jeremiah, making him in a genuine sense the founder of the post-exilic hierocratic community and limiting his influence on apocalyptic largely to the areas of genre and style.

Though Jeremiah and Ezekiel are important documents in the study of the rise of apocalyptic, even more crucial are the last 27 chapters of Isaiah, comprising the collections designated as Second and Third Isaiah. That Yahwism during the exilic period fell neither to the despair of Lamentations nor the cynicism of the Wisdom movement can largely be attributed to the message of Second Isaiah. The

twin doubts of Yahweh's sovereignty and his grace in Lamentations
were answered by Second Isaiah in the form of a brilliant new vision
of Israel's future: Far from calling into question the sovereignty of
Yahweh, the events of the early sixth century demonstrated that
Israel's God had purposes vastly surpassing those of the Josianic
reform. For Yahweh was no local deity whose purposes had been
frustrated by the Babylonians. Rather he is the one

> ... who sits above the circle of the earth,
>   and its inhabitants are like grasshoppers;
>   who stretches out the heavens like a curtain,
>   and spreads them like a tent to dwell in; ... (40:22).

Yahweh himself had given Israel to her spoilers (42:24f), and far
from being a proof of his impotence, he had done so only to prepare
for a far more glorious plan (43:18–21; 46:12f; 49:14–23; 52:7–10).
How was it that Second Isaiah was able to revivify a languishing
Yahwism in a way impossible to the Deuteronomistic tradition? It was
by reintroducing the cosmic vision into prophecy, by using mythical
motifs drawn from the by then defunct royal cult to place Yahweh's
historical acts in a context bursting the confining limits imposed by
the Deuteronomistic History, thereby demonstrating that the historical manifestations of Yahweh's acts were but ripples on a vast sea
of activity embracing the cosmos and affecting both the natural and
historical realms.[14] If Jeremiah and Ezekiel managed to maintain
the vision in balance with the realities of this world and made modest
use of myth, Second Isaiah greatly enhanced the vision and drew
profoundly on the cosmic dimension of myth. Indeed, Second Isaiah
would have been Israel's first apocalyptic seer if at the same time he
had not maintained the other side of the dialectic of prophecy, the
integration of the cosmic vision into the realities of this world. This
balance he was able to uphold, for in his work we see the brief
afterglow of the prophetic office. True, kingship had ceased in Israel,
but the sense of nationhood was still intact in Chaldea; and for
Second Isaiah, Cyrus, the anointed Servant of Yahweh, served as
surrogate for the Israelite king. This means that his message of
restoration, while based on a vision of proceedings in the divine
assembly (40:1–8), was yet thoroughly translated into the historical
realities of his time. A historical event made the restoration possible
– the fall of Babylon; a historical conqueror acted as Yahweh's
agent – Cyrus; a historical nation in a historical land would be
recipients of Yahweh's salvation – Israel. The prophetic function of
translating the cosmic vision of Yahweh's activity into the politico-
historical realm thus continues in an unbroken manner in the prophet

of the exile.[15] It is illustrated perhaps most dramatically by 51:9–11, a passage connecting the myth of Baal's defeat over Rahab/Yamm with Yahweh's victory over the Pharaoh at the sea, and then relating this primeval historical event to the imminent salvation event in which Yahweh would return his redeemed to Zion. This interlocking of primeval-past, historical-future has a profound effect on the total message of Second Isaiah: It lends cosmic significance to the future event, while yet keeping Yahweh's cosmic acts firmly moored in the historical experience of the people. Moreover, it affirms the continuity running through all of Yahweh's acts, from those in primordial times through those of Israel's past to those of the future.

Second Isaiah thus maintains the classical prophetic tradition; yet there are indications also in his ministry that prophecy is nearing its demise. The tension between vision and reality, between past and future act, between myth and history which was maintained so creatively in the classical prophets becomes strained in Second Isaiah nearly to the breaking point. The vision in chapter 40 tugs heavily at its historical moorings; the myth in chapter 51 seems ready to break loose from mundane realities, and the disjunction coming between past and future acts threatens to split those acts asunder:

> Remember not the former things,
> nor consider the things of old.
> Behold, I am doing a new thing; ... (43:18f).

Few added strains would be required to produce apocalyptic.

If apocalyptic was conceived in Ezekiel, manifested its first contractions in the destruction of the temple, and was carried to full term in exile by Second Isaiah, it was born shortly after the return of the *gola* in Third Isaiah. Though probably not stemming from one single author, the oracles of Isaiah 56–66 are closely bound by a common theme and setting. The exiles have returned, tensions have grown, Second Isaiah's glorious promises have failed to materialize. Two principal parties are discernible in the period between 538 and 500: a Zadokite-led group stemming from the *gola* and basing restoration hopes on the program of Ezekiel 40–48 and a mixed group comprising followers of Second Isaiah and dissident Levites, a good number of which probably had not shared the experience of the exile. A growing polarity begins to divide these parties: the Zadokite group accepting vassalship under the Persians and making a realistic attempt to reestablish the temple cult as it had existed just prior to the exile; the other espousing a more visionary hope for restoration based on the prophecy of Second Isaiah and awaiting Yahweh's intervention to defeat the enemies, both within the Jewish community and outside. In the eyes of the visionaries, Second Isaiah's promised restoration had been delayed because of the corruption of the normative party. Yet Yahweh would remain faithful to his promises, though the apostasy of the majority cried out for a further act of judgment before the restoration could occur. Here we find a deep difference between this group and the temple party; for the latter, feeling that no further judgment was imminent, dedicated its every energy to rebuilding the temple so as to restore the land as Yahweh's dwelling place. The ensuing conflict was bitter, as manifested by the acrimonious oracles in Isaiah 57, 59, 65, and 66; nowhere in Scripture is such vindictiveness spent on fellow Israelites. The result was a cleavage in the post-exilic community between a minority designating themselves as Yahweh's "servants" and a majority which they deemed defiled and liable to judgment (cf. 65:13ff). The vindictiveness of the minority was further hardened by oppression: "... Your brethren say, who hate you, and thrust you out for the sake of my name: 'Let Yahweh display his glory that we may see!' You I will gladden, but they shall be confounded."[16] This and evidence from the Book of Ezra suggests that a group which earlier played an important role in Israel's cult has been denied any part in the restoration.

How was it that the mode of eschatology which we call apocalyptic originated in this community situation? We have been describing prophetic eschatology as the prophet's vision of Yahweh's plans for this people which the prophet is commissioned to translate into the politico-historical events of his time. Prophetic eschatology is transformed into apocalyptic at the point where the task of translating the cosmic vision into the categories of mundane reality is abdicated. Why did the followers of Second Isaiah begin to abdicate this task? Because their view of this world grew so pessimistic that the mundane order assumed a guise unsuitable for their restoration hopes: "Therefore justice is far removed from us, and righteousness cannot overtake us; we look for light, but all is darkness, for brightness, but all is gloom" (59:9). In Third Isaiah the pessimism has deepened far beyond that of Amos or Isaiah; the latter could announce judgment in no uncertain terms, but behind the judgment was always the belief that once having been judged, Israel would yet be restored. Therefore judgment words and salvation words were directed at the nation as a whole. Different is the situation in Third Isaiah where a new oracle type, the salvation-judgment oracle, splits the pronouncement into two parts: To those elements in the community which are condemned, no prospect for later salvation is envisaged; for those promised salvation, this salvation is not construed within the context of the nation as a whole. The curse of a broken covenant rests heavily upon the land; because of the polluted cult of the normative party, exacerbated by their self-righteousness,[11] the nation is no longer one people which might be recipient of Yahweh's final saving act; as the antitheses in 65:13–15 indicate . . . a type of salvation must be envisaged which will draw out a righteous segment from the spoiled whole (see Isa. 65:8). What type of salvation can this be? One marked by an utter break with Israel's unholy past (65:16c–17a). The history of Israel's sin and the future of Yahweh's saving activity are split apart; indeed, one can begin to speak of two orders, an old order of corruption and the creation of a new holy order.

How could followers of Second Isaiah apply their vision to realities such as these? Remember, they no longer serve as spokesmen of their community, but as members of a disenfranchised minority. Their oracles indicate that the delicate balance maintained by Second Isaiah between vision and reality was being lost; moreover, Second Isaiah's lavish use of myth was becoming a tempting escape from the contradiction between glorious promises and a fallen order which contradicted those promises. For in its untranslated form, myth spoke of salvation which drew men above the flux of the mundane sphere, a salvation won on a timeless, cosmic level which offered an escape from this fallen order into a new creation which returned man to the security of the primeval state of nature before its fall to corruption and change. Increasingly, the post-exilic descendants of the prophets fell to this temptation and in so doing abdicated their political office of integrating their message into the politico-historical realm. As they made less and less effort to relate their visions of Yahweh's plans to historical realities, the dialectic between vision and reality began to break down. Their attitude towards the historical realm as the arena of Yahweh's saving acts first became one of indifference, finally of hostility. The move was very strong in the direction of two cardinal features of apocalyptic, a dualistic world view and belief in world epochs.

We shall now cite several passages from Third Isaiah to indicate how mythic patterns, mediated to the visionaries of the early post-exilic period by the now defunct royal cult, became the means for expressing a restoration hope uninhibited by the harsh realities of the mundane world. In Isa. 59:15b–20, after the fallen state of this order has been described, the future salvation is celebrated in the archaic League form of the Divine Warrior hymn. This adaptation of old forms to new situations is reminiscent of Second Isaiah, with the significant difference that no effort is made here to relate the myth to the historical realm. Salvation is a cosmic event effected by the Divine Warrior alone, who is visible from the west to the rising of the sun.

In 65:17–25, after a salvation-judgment oracle has described the cleavage between those blessed and those cursed by Yahweh, the *Endzeit wird Urzeit* pattern forms the basis of a song celebrating the new creation (vv. 16*b*–17*a*, 25).

In 66:15–16, also after a salvation-judgment oracle, Yahweh is portrayed as the storm god of ancient Near Eastern mythology, be he Baal, "rider of the clouds," or Marduk, mounting his storm chariot as he sets out to battle Tiamat. His weapon is the fire of the storm god's lightning bolt; the judgment is universal, "upon all flesh," and the cosmic drama is in no way related to the historical order. Neither the community of the faithful nor foreign human agents participate in the battle, which remains a pure cosmic happening. In passages like these the visionaries have gone far beyond Second Isaiah, who used myth in the restricted sense of adding a cosmic dimension to Yahweh's saving acts in the history of his people; myth is here used in its primary sense as a means by which oppressed and discouraged visionaries, for whom history has belied their most fervent hopes of salvation, can renew that hope by looking to a deliverance raised far above the harsh realities of this world. Salvation is described in the cosmic terms of myth, and the task of relating that vision to the realities of this world has been abandoned. Sociologically speaking, we are witnessing the emergence of apocalyptic sectarianism.

The Isaiah Apocalypse also fits the general period of Third Isaiah, that is, the late sixth or early fifth century. From this corpus, contrast Second Isaiah's use of myth in 51:7–11 with 27:1:

> In that day Yahweh will visit
> with his hard, great, strong sword
> Leviathan, the sliding serpent
> Leviathan, the twisting serpent
> And he will slay the dragon which is in the sea.

In 51:7–11 the primordial events of myth are bound to Yahweh's acts in the historical events of Israel, both past and future. In 27:1 raw myth is applied directly to the future hope of the people; a single change is made, the myth is eschatologized. Yet the return to a purely mythopoeic view has been completed in neither Third Isaiah nor the Isaiah Apocalypse. Though the effort to relate the vision to the events of the politico-historical realm has been abdicated, the hope of salvation has not broken all ties with mundane realities. In Third Isaiah, the servants will yet inherit Zion, they will yet inhabit the mountains of Judah, though to be sure, the Zion and mountains of Judah are much transfigured in the vision. Similarly, the historical Zion still forms the basis of the hope in the Isaiah Apocalypse (24:21, 23). Later apocalyptic, however, will go further in separating the vision from mundane reality. We thus designate Third Isaiah and the Isaiah Apocalypse as early apocalyptic.

Zechariah 9 is another example of early apocalyptic, comprising a Divine Warrior song which illustrates well an important aspect of the development of apocalyptic, its deep drawing on mythic patterns from the liturgical hymns of the royal cult and the Divine Warrior hymns of the League. Once again the contrast with Second Isaiah suggests that this song should be placed somewhat later than the exile for the ritual pattern of myth in this composition is not recapitulated to lend a cosmic dimension to divine acts in history, but is used in celebration of the Divine Warrior's single-handed victory, without Second Isaiah's firm mooring of mythic motifs in the realm of historical events: Yahweh acts not through human instruments like Cyrus, but leads his host alone. And his victory is universal, if not yet cosmic: "His dominion will stretch from sea to sea, from the River to the ends of the earth." This song thus furnishes another important link in our tracing the visionary stream as it develops from classical prophecy into late apocalyptic, especially since it preserves in a complete way the liturgical form of myth and the royal cult:

1–8	Combat (in terms of ritual conquest) – Victory
9	Victory shout – Procession to Zion
10	Manifestation of Yahweh's universal reign
11–13	Salvation: release of captives
14	Reenactment of Divine Warrior's victory
15	Banquet
16	Renewed fertility of the land.

This basic liturgical pattern can be traced all the way from ancient Near Eastern myth through the royal psalms and early apocalyptic down to fully developed apocalyptic, thus lending corroboration on the level of *Gattungsgeschichte* to our argument that apocalyptic develops in an unbroken fashion out of native roots.

This same liturgical pattern underlies Zechariah 14, a composition which brings us to the threshold of full-grown apocalyptic. Together with the closely related unit in Zechariah 12 it furnishes an important link in the study, for manifested in this fifth-century composition are the essential features of fully developed apocalyptic: (1) the dualism and division of history into eras; (2) the lavish description of cataclysmic disturbances in nature accompanying Yahweh's final theophany and judgment; (3) the *Endzeit wird Urzeit* motif; (4) the complete abdication of relating the cosmic drama of the Divine Warrior and his hosts to the events and agents of the historical realm. We thus come to the Book of Daniel via the prophetic tradition with all of the essential features of apocalyptic already present within Jewish literature by the beginning of the fourth century. For these essential features recourse to Persian dualism is not only unnecessary, it is unacceptable.

Having approached Daniel via this route through prophecy and early apocalyptic, we bring a vastly different perspective than that furnished by the traditional approach. The latter views the book purely as a second-century phenomenon with no essential connections with classical prophecy but with very intimate connections with Persian dualism. Our approach views Daniel as one station along a continuum reaching from pre-exilic prophecy to full-grown apocalyptic, very much at home on Jewish soil, and manifesting foreign borrowing only as peripheral embellishments.

The sociological setting of Daniel is analogous to that discernible behind Third Isaiah. Especially chapters 7—12 are intimately related to the faith of the *ḥasidim* during the Maccabean revolt. Like the communities behind Third Isaiah, the Isaiah Apocalypse, and Second Zechariah, they are a visionary minority living under oppression in a world seemingly fallen into the hands of enemies of Yahweh, convincing them that fulfillment of Yahweh's promises could no longer be anticipated within the existing order. Clinging to their vision, the community of Daniel passively awaits Yahweh's intervention. 1 Macc. 2:42 indicates that they joined in the revolt in its initial stages but soon withdrew, regarding it as but "little help," if this is the correct meaning of Dan. 11:34. If Tcherikover's interpretation of the *ḥasidim* as authoritative interpreters of the Torah is accurate, the sociological settings behind Third Isaiah and Daniel are drawn even closer: both involve the losing struggle of a group which, having once enjoyed an important role in the cult, has witnessed that role being undermined by a temple party which in both cases has established itself through collaboration with the foreign overlords. In each case the central dispute is the same, struggle over control of the cult. Rejecting alliances with foreign powers, both cling to a vision of Yahweh's final battle and judgment which will restore the faithful to their rightful place of glory.

When we speak of the continuity which binds the visionaries of the sixth through the second centuries, we are not suggesting the existence of a continuous visionary party, but rather of a visionary perspective which is embodied by different circles throughout the post-exilic period. The common affiliation shared by apocalyptic circles is therefore not membership in a particular party, but is more readily definable along sociological lines; whatever their party affiliation, the visionaries stem from the disenfranchised, especially those having fallen from positions of power. In times of community stress the visionary and realistic elements polarize, as in the time of Third Isaiah and Daniel. In times of community harmony the visionary and realistic elements are melded, as in the Chronicler's work.

The Book of Daniel focuses on the vision of Yahweh's plan for his faithful, by means of which he will bring to fulfilment the promises of the covenant. This vision represents the constant which binds together Isaiah, Second and Third Isaiah, Second Zechariah, and Daniel in an unbroken stream. The variable in the development is the way in which this vision is related to mundane reality. Second Isaiah, like the classical prophets before him, persistently related the vision to the reality. This dialectic began to dissolve in Third Isaiah. We now turn to consider how the vision is related to the politico-historical realm in Daniel.

In chapter 7 we have a vision and its interpretation from the time of Antiochus Epiphanes. It offers an excellent test case for our problem of the rise and development of apocalyptic, for it contains that central element of the visionary stream, the vision of the cosmic realm of Yahweh. Equally significant is the scenario developed in the vision, for it is the same as that found in Zechariah 9, which in turn was found to recapitulate the ancient liturgical pattern of the royal cult, of the League, and ultimately of ancient Near Eastern myth: (1) threat to the divine council, here by four beasts emerging from that inimical foe, sea; (2) the conflict, here taking the forensic form of the El-like Ancient of Days seated upon his fiery throne and consuming his enemies with a stream of fire; (3) the victory, with the Son of Man coming like Baal on the clouds of heaven and receiving dominion and glory and kingdom; (4) the salvation of the faithful, with the Saints of the Most High receiving the kingdom and possessing it forever. The fact that the scene recapitulates the royal liturgy of the Jerusalem cult can be demonstrated by comparison with at least a dozen royal psalms.[18] And the contact with ancient myth, especially the Baal cycle, is obvious both in the overall pattern and in detail. A feature of the visionary stream, all the way from Second Isaiah on, is thus found, the application of forms and motifs from myth to give expression to the vision of Yahweh's cosmic activity.

Next we ask how this vision is related to the politico-historical realm. This relation is effected in this chapter (as also in ch. 2 and chs. 10—12) through a borrowing of a concept widespread in the ancient Persian and Hellenistic worlds, that of the successive world empires. The foe threatening the divine council is not just Yamm, but four beasts emerging from Yamm. This notion itself probably stems from ancient conflict myths: Note for example the monsters created by Tiamat to aid her in her struggle, and the list of monsters associated with Yamm which Anat claims she has destroyed (Gordon V AB D 36ff). But whatever its ultimate source, by the second century it had developed into a common expression of world history. What function does this concept serve in Daniel? This question can better be answered in connection with chapters 10—12, and here we merely shall note that the narration of the rise and fall of these beasts (standing for Babylon, Persia, Media, and Greece) serves one function only in the vision, that of indicating the point when the cosmic event at the center of the vision would occur. This is made clear in the interpretation given Daniel by one of those standing before the throne of the Most High: "These four great beasts are four kings who shall arise out of the earth. But the Saints of the Most High shall receive the kingdom, and possess the kingdom forever, forever and ever" (Dan. 7:17–18). To answer our question concerning the relation between vision and reality, we can conclude that in Daniel 7 the dialectic has dissolved. The historical realm is seen as one given over to powers inimical to the Most High, which powers the Most High would vanquish and judge, so as to wrest from their control his people, to whom would be given an eternal kingdom. Connections with politico-historical realities have been lost: Neither the human community, nor any other human agent, takes part in the conflict which would be won "by no human hand" (8:25); nor does the kingdom given to the saints betray any connections with the mundane; they are saved by being lifted out of this order into the cosmic sphere of the vision.

Daniel 10—12 develops the same theme as Daniel 7, though with a greater attention to the concept of the world empires. The framework within which the succession of the empires is described is again cosmic and again comes to Daniel in the form of a vision. A heavenly being appears to Daniel, who explains that he has been battling with the prince of the kingdom of Persia. Indeed, the battle continues, though the heavenly being has been able to take leave long enough to appear to Daniel, because Michael, "your prince," carries forth the battle alone. He has come to Daniel "to make you understand what is to befall your people in the latter days. For the vision is for days yet to come" (10:14). But the heavenly being cannot linger, for the cosmic battle between the princes yet rages (10:20f). Whereas the cosmic conflict standing as prototype of the earthly struggles in chapter 7 was seen in terms of the conflict between beasts of the sea, in this account another ancient way of viewing cosmic drama is present which is equally indifferent to relating the cosmic to the mundane realm; in charge of each nation is a cosmic figure, a prince (cf. Deut. 32:8, LXX 4QDt.). Events on earth merely reflect phases in the cosmic drama, involving struggles between the patron princes. The world view is the mythopoeic one which forms the basis of a myth like the *Enuma elish*, further corroboration of our contention that apocalyptic involves a return to a mythopoeic view of reality.

After the cosmic drama which stands behind the world events has been revealed in the vision, the heavenly being goes on to explain how the earthly events are reflecting the cosmic drama, with the purpose of indicating to the seer how near history is to the final victory which will result in the salvation of the faithful. The timetable in this *vaticinium ex eventu* indicates two down, two to go; that is, the Babylonian and the Median kingdoms have fallen, the Persian and Greek remain. The events from the reigns of Antiochus III and Antiochus Epiphanes are narrated in considerable detail, culminating with the attack of the latter on the *Maskilim* and his blasphemy against the God of gods. Once the narrative comes to describe the fall of Antiochus Epiphanes, it suddenly reverts to the cosmic realm in 12:1f. It again is made clear to the reader that the real conflict is not between Antiochus and the *Maskilim*, but between Michael and the Prince of Yawan. The victory of Michael leads to the deliverance of a limited number to everlasting glory, of another to everlasting shame. The salvation of the *Maskilim* is then described in remarkable terms: "And those who are wise shall shine like the brightness of the firmament; and those who turn many to righteousness, like the stars forever and ever (12:3)." This description of salvation at the climax of the vision is very significant for our understanding of the relation between vision and reality in the stages of fully developed apocalyptic. Even as the battle was being fought by the heavenly princes alone (10:21), so too salvation takes the form of being lifted out of the historical realm into the cosmic. Present is a notion with ancient roots in the Old Testament which identified the astral bodies with Yahweh's host (cf. Judg. 5:20). Remember the scene in Daniel 7:10, where the Ancient of Days is seated on his throne, and "a thousand thousands served him, and ten thousand times ten thousand stood before him." Within this host the *Maskilim* would take their place, to shine like the stars forever, a notion recurring in later apocalyptic (e.g., *1 Enoch* 104:2.6; *As. Mos.* 10:9). With this conception of deliverance the tension between vision and mundane reality has nearly dissolved. The visionary tradition in Daniel, for the moment at least, has abdicated its responsibility to the politico-historical realm, a realm which has been given up as hopeless and fallen to the dark powers of the cosmos.[19] This view of salvation gives us the basis for interpreting the function of the detailed historical resume in chapter 11. No interest is evident for history as such: The *Maskilim* take no active part in historical events, since the historical plane is not the arena within which the decisive battles are being fought. In classical prophecy the realm of human history was the realm within which the covenant relationship between Yahweh and his people was being carried out; historical events were carriers of cosmic significance. They were not bound to an inevitable progression towards a predetermined end. The people could repent, Yahweh could change his mind, prophesied judgement could be transformed into salvation, all this because history was viewed as a realm within which the realization of the terms and promises of the covenant was possible. In Daniel the pessimism has grown much deeper than in proto-apocalyptic; the historical realm requires more than the return to sanctity envisaged by Ezekiel, for it is locked in the grip of dark powers. The ethical dualism of early apocalyptic even begins to assume ontological dimensions. No longer the context of a salvation history and a fulfilment of the promises of the covenant, the historical order assumes two new functions in Daniel, and in late apocalyptic in general: (1) *Vaticinium ex eventu* is used to establish the credibility of the seer; (2) History is used as a timetable indicating how close men are to the ultimate event which would break the power which the inimical powers hold on the elect. The dynamic of a history which is the living out of genuine covenant relationship yields to the inflexibility of a history which becomes a timetable of cosmic events: "for what is determined shall be done" (11:36). With this basically timeless view, one has entered not only the world view of myth, but has come close to the cosmic view of the Wisdom tradition which is based on the idea of a timeless order lifted above the flux and change of history. In all three, in apocalyptic, in myth, and in wisdom, the seer finds significant events and truths not within the historical order of change, but in the eternal order. Specifically in wisdom, God is no longer one engaged in the events of history, but rather is protector of a fixed, eternal order, a being aloof to the ebb and flow of historical events. While denying von Rad's theory of the origin of apocalyptic in wisdom, and while maintaining that one can trace the stage by stage development of apocalyptic out of Israelite prophecy, nevertheless I feel that once the visionary stream had dissolved the dialectic between the cosmic vision and the mundane reality, it had created a matrix congenial to the timeless material of the wisdom tradition.

We have set out to show in these pages how in apocalyptic the tension between vision and reality, between myth and history, which forms the restless heart of the classical prophets, nearly dissolved. The security and repose of a timeless realm of the vision of myth established itself as the hope of a people made weary by an overly harsh world.

This world-weariness has been the mark of every apocalyptic movement. It is shared today by men of vision who find a harshly brutal world denying them the opportunity to integrate their vision into the institutions of the historical realm. For them, too, myth often becomes a source of repose from a reality which they find too brutal to integrate into their apocalyptic vision.

NOTES

Editor's Note: Biblical translations are the author's when not the Revised Standard Version.

1 J. M. Schmidt, *Die jüdische Apokalyptik* (Neukirchen: Neukirchener, 1969). Especially in Germany the resurgence of interest in the subject of apocalypticism is evident. Of special significance in that country is the application which the study of apocalyptic is finding in theology, as evidenced by the writings of Wolfhart Pannenberg and Jürgen Moltmann. Unfortunately, this article must forgo both discussion of such contemporary treatments of the subject and the survey of past scholarship. Hopefully these two aspects can be treated in a subsequent article. For now, two excellent German studies may be consulted: for the contemporary scene, Klaus Koch, *Ratlos von der Apokalyptik* (Gütersloh: Gerd Mohn, 1970); ET *The Rediscovery of Apocalyptic* (tr. M. Kohl; London: SCM Press, 1972); for a survey of past scholarship, the above-cited work by Schmidt.

2 See P. D. Hanson, "Jewish Apocalyptic Against Its Near Eastern Environment," *RB* 78 (Jan., 1971) 31–58 for a fuller treatment of backgrounds.

3 The most archaic formulations of this promise-fulfillment pattern seem to be preserved in the Elohist and the Priestly writing. J on the other hand betrays influence from the royal theology; i.e., in Genesis 15 the covenant established with Abraham is based on a divine oath resembling a royal decree which is self-fulfilling. This stands in sharp contrast to the prophetic notion of covenant as a dynamic and open-ended relationship between God and nation.

4 See F. M. Cross, Jr., "The Song of the Sea and Canaanite Myth," in *God and Christ: Existence and Providence* (JTC 5: New York: Harper & Row, 1968) 1–25.

5 Similarly, Dan. 8:26, *Test. Levi* 8:19, and 4 Ezra 12:36–38.

6 F. M. Cross, Jr., "The Structure of the Deuteronomic History," *Perspectives in Jewish Learning* III: 9–24.

7 See, e.g., 2 Kings 23:25.

8 In defining a historiography as a consistent interpretation of the history of a people on the basis of an idea of history, the Assyrian annals represent beginnings in this direction, but nevertheless remain limited to episodes without connection (see J. J. Finkelstein, "Mesopotamian Historiography," *Proceedings of the American Philosophical Society* [1963] 107).

9 See F. M. Cross, Jr., "Will Ye Speak Falsely for God?" in *Contemporary Accents in Liberal Religion*, ed. Bradford E. Gale (Boston: Beacon Press, 1960) 92–105.

10 E.g., Dan. 8:26, 12:4.

11 E.g., the supernatural being which transports the prophet in Ezek. 8:3 and 40:3, foreshadowing the *angelus interpres* of apocalyptic.

12 The balance between vision and reality in Ezekiel is illustrated by chs. 40—48. The careful plan for rebuilding the temple, betraying the prophet's intimate acquaintance with the temple precincts, and furnishing the blueprint for the reconstruction of the post-exilic temple cult is realism in finest detail; yet it is cast in the form of the vision.

13 See for example chs. 16, 23.

14 Especially important in the study of the relationship between Second Isaiah and apocalyptic is Cross's article, "The Divine Warrior in Israel's Early Cult," in *Studies and Texts: Biblical Motifs: Origins and Transformations*, ed. A. Altman (Cambridge, Mass.: Harvard Univ. Press, 1966) III: 11–30.

15 This translation of vision into political terms can be seen throughout chs. 40—56; e.g., 41:2–4, 8–10, 25; 42:1–9; 44:26–28; 45:1–7, 13; 48:14–15; 49:1ff.

16 Isa. 66:5, reading *wsmḥtkm* instead of *bśmḥtkm*, since this conjecture of Torrey restores sense and metric structure.

17 See for example Isa. 65:5*a*: "Keep your distance, approach me not, or I'll communicate holiness to you."

18 See P. D. Hanson, "Studies in the Origins of Jewish Apocalyptic" (Diss.; Cambridge, Mass.: Harvard Univ., 1969) 280ff.

19 In dealing with Jewish apocalyptic we must speak of abdication of responsibility to the historical realm, and not the collapse of the notion of the historical. Whereas Daniel 7 and chs. 10—12 indicate that the apocalyptic circles tread far in the direction of Gnosticism, the historical experience of ancient Israel could not be entirely forgotten by these descendants of the prophets. Thus even the *ḥasidim* joined the Maccabees in the initial stages of the revolt, and the Essenes entered into the war against Rome. Both early and late apocalyptic writings envision the age when Israel would assume her rightful position among the nations. The polarity between the visionary and realistic stances always must be understood in sociological terms in Jewish apocalyptic; abdication of responsibility to the mundane realm and flight into the realm of myth, thereby dissolving the tension between vision and reality, is never a theological position adopted by Jewish apocalyptic circles; it is always an expedient stance prompted by the exigencies of a hostile world. For this reason we have chosen to deal with the phenomenon of Jewish apocalyptic within a conceptual framework which is largely sociologically conditioned. Visionary and realistic elements within the

community are not parties with fixed visionary and realistic doctrines; they are rather elements within one religious tradition which are restlessly caught within a tension which lies at the heart of Yahwism and which at times of political and social stress polarize into the extremes of the continuum for reasons which can be discerned partially within the political and sociological circumstances of the given period.

3

Apocalyptic Eschatology as the Transcendence of Death[*]

JOHN J. COLLINS

Ever since the work of Albert Schweitzer,[1] the terms "apocalyptic" and "eschatology" have occasioned lively debate in NT studies.[2] More recently they have again come to the forefront in the assertion by Ernst Käsemann that "Apocalyptic is the mother of Christian theology,"[3] and in the theological writings of Jürgen Moltmann and Wolfhart Pannenberg.[4] Despite the theological weight often placed on these terms, their connotation is far from clear. Not only is the relation between the two terms disputed but neither term individually carries a clear meaning.[5] In the case of eschatology, some scholars distinguish between a stricter and a looser understanding of the term.[6] Others refuse to describe as "eschatological" anything which does not involve the end of the world.[7] The term "apocalyptic" has been used with nuances ranging from a particular literary form of revelation literature to a philosophy of life prevalent in the intertestamental period.[8] The juxtaposition of the words "eschatology" and "apocalyptic" in our title potentially evokes the shades of several different scholarly debates. Did the pre-exilic prophets have an eschatology? What is the relation between eschatology and history? Is apocalyptic the child of prophecy? Should apocalyptic be defined by its form or its content? What is the theological value of apocalyptic? and so forth. It is important therefore that we begin by sorting out those questions and making clear which ones we will address and which we will pass.

Let us start from the minimum which is universally agreed – both "eschatology" and "apocalyptic" have some assocation with future expectation. Further, every scholar agrees that the future expectation of the pre-exilic prophets was significantly different from the type of future expectation found in the Book of Daniel and certain works of intertestamental Judaism which are usually referred to as "apocalyptic." The existence of these two types of future expectation

[*] First published in *CBQ* 36 (1974) 21–43.

is admitted by all, even though there is much disputation as to the names by which we may refer to them. Much of this disputation is purely terminological and makes no real contribution to our understanding of their phenomenon. Accordingly, I do not wish to enter into the purely terminological discussion which has recently been maintained by Carmignac and van der Ploeg.[9] Rather I wish to consider the phenomenon of future expectation in the Jewish tradition, in particular the later type, found in Daniel and the intertestamental works. By the term "apocalyptic eschatology" I merely wish to refer to this type of future expectation.[10]

I am aware that not all the material in the so-called "apocalyptic books" is explicitly relevant to future expectations. Apocalypses, as their name suggests, are largely revelations of heavenly secrets. As examples of this fact we might mention the heavenly journeys of Enoch in *1 Enoch* 1–36 or the description of the movements of the stars in the so-called "book of the heavenly luminaries" in *1 Enoch* 72–82.[11] I will argue later in this paper that the revelation of these heavenly secrets is not in fact irrelevant to the future expectations of their writer. However, in deliminating my subject I am guided primarily by the passages which deal explicitly with future expectations. I do not propose to discuss all aspects of the phenomenon of apocalyptic but only the aspect of future expectation.

Two further points I take as given.

First, the distinction between the manner in which the future expectation of the prophets is presented and the manner of presentation in apocalyptic has been adequately described.[12] Apocalyptic is marked by pseudonymity and its revelations are mediated by visions and dreams to a far greater extent than is the case in the prophetic writings. These literary devices lessen the immediacy of the apocalypticist's visions. As a result the visions appear to impart information about a predetermined future rather than an existential call to repentance.[13] This difference in immediacy I take to be generally accepted. My concern is different. I ask rather about the content of the future expectation. Irrespective of whether the future was predetermined or not, was the apocalyptic view of what was going to happen in any way different from what the prophets expected? It will become evident that the literary form of the apocalypses is in fact significant for their future expectation.

Secondly, I take it that all scholars agree that the expectation of the prophets focused on the life of the nation. Whether they prophesied doom or salvation, the issue was the peace and prosperity of Israel in the promised land. As we shall see, there is no such unanimity on the central issue of apocalyptic.

Many attempts to distingish the central issue of the later type of future expectation from the prophetic type have been blurred by the confusing data of post-exilic prophecy. For that reason I wish to omit post-exilic prophecy from my discussion, and concentrate on the fully developed apocalyptic eschatology of which the earliest example is Daniel.[14]

My objective, then, is to clarify the distinctive character of the later type of Jewish future expectation as found in the Book of Daniel and the intertestamental apocalypses, over against the expectation of the prophets. My paper will have three parts. (1) First, I will examine some attempts which have been made to formulate the distinctive character of apocalyptic eschatology and which I consider unsuccessful. (2) Secondly, I will present my own formulation and support it by an examination of apocalyptic texts. (3) Thirdly, I will comment on the historical and theological significance of this particular type of future expectation.

Unsuccessful Formulations

Although the existence of two types of future expectation in the OT is generally admitted, and although several scholars of note have attempted to formulate the distinction, no clear and consistent formulation has yet, to my knowledge, been made.

We may begin by discussing some of the formulations which have been proposed.

(a) The Idea of a Definitive End

Julius Wellhausen and his followers felt that only the future expectation of the post-exilic period could rightly be called eschatology. This term they then reserved for a belief in the end of the world.[15] This formulation emphasizes a dualism which is both temporal and cosmological. With some slight variations, it is still the formulation most widely found. So Th. C. Vriezen, in distinguishing the looser and stricter senses of eschatology, writes:

"In a narrower sense the only thing we can understand by it is the apocalyptic form of *'olam hazze'* as against the *'olam habba'*, or life in heaven as against life on earth," while he also argued for the validity of applying the term eschatology to the earlier form of prophetic expectation "even if there is no question of the destruction of the kosmos."[16] Here, as in Wellhausen, the essential difference between the two types is that in the later type the world is destroyed.

Similarly Sigmund Mowinckel, while less clear-cut in his definition, also seems to share this view. He writes:

Eschatology is a doctrine or a complex of ideas about "the last things," which is more or less organically coherent and developed. Every eschatology includes in some form or other a dualistic conception of the course of history, and implies that the present state of things and the present world order will suddenly come to an end and be superseded by another of an essentially different kind.... The universe itself is thrown into the melting pot...."[17]

Mowinckel goes on to say that eschatology in this sense was not found in the pre-exilic prophets.

Further:

Any sober historical consideration which avoids the confusion of different ideas will recognize that Deutero-Isaiah himself does not yet present a true eschatology. We miss the idea of a definite end to the present order, and of a new world of an essentially different character from this one.[18]

Such expressions as "the present order of things" are extremely vague. All future hope can be described as the hope for "a new order of things." This in itself gives us no basis for distinguishing one type of future hope from another. Mowinckel would certainly admit that Deutero-Isaiah hoped for a new order of things. What is essential in his definition is the idea of *a definite end*. There are two facets to this idea. One is the cosmological destruction of the world and the other is the temporal end of history. We may discuss those two facets separately since they do not necessarily coincide. Human history can come to an end without the destruction of the world. Neither facet, however, provides an adequate formulation of the distinctive character of apocalyptic eschatology. First, the cosmological end of the world is certainly a very important motif in some apocalyptic texts. Perhaps its classical expression is that found in 4 Ezra 7:30–31: "Then shall the world be returned to primeval silence seven days, like as the first beginnings, so that no man is left. And it shall be, after seven days, that the Age which is not yet awake shall be aroused, and that which is corruptible shall perish." We might also mention the gospel passage, "Heaven and earth shall pass away but my word will not pass away."[19] However, there are important apocalyptic texts which do not refer to an end of the world. Notable among these is our prime example of pre-Christian apocalyptic – the Book of Daniel. There we read of a resurrection, and we are told that the just will shine like stars, but nothing is said of a transition to a new world. The term *qēṣ*, which is usually translated "end," occurs in Daniel but never as the "end" of anything in particular and seems to refer to "a time of crisis" rather than to a definitive end.[20] Again in the Qumran Scrolls, there is only one passage, in the third column of 1QH, which possibly speaks of the destruction of the world.[21] Yet the Scrolls are generally recognized as the literature of an "apocalyptic community."[22] The idea of the definitive destruction of the world is also missing in certain sections of *1 Enoch* (chs. 1–36 and 91–the end, apart from the Apocalypse of Weeks). Yet no one will deny that these texts exemplify the later, fuller, type of future hope, which is described as apocalyptic eschatology. It is clear then that the distinctive character of this type of future expectation does not consist of the belief in the end of the world.

The second aspect of the formulation of Wellhausen and Mowinckel, which sees *a definitive end* as the essential character of the later expectation, is the idea of a temporal end, an end of history. Now the only sense in which we could unambiguously speak of an "end of history" is with reference to the final destruction of all human life. This of course is never the case, in any of the Jewish or Christian texts. In any looser sense, we can only speak of the end of one period of history, which really means the transition from one period to another. If history means the account of human actions, then we can obviously find a new period of history even in a new creation, as can be seen in Isa. 65:17ff:

> Lo I am about to create new heavens and a new earth; ... No longer shall there be in it an infant who lives but a few days, or an old man who does not round out his full life-time; he dies a mere youth who reaches but a hundred years, and he who fails of a hundred shall be thought accursed. They shall live in the houses they build, and eat the fruit of the vineyards they plant...

Most of all a formulation based on the idea of the "end of history" cannot provide us with an adequate conceptual framework to contain a notion like Dodd's "realized eschatology" or the belief of the Qumran community that it had already made the transition to a new form of life, while still in this life, in history.[23]

In short, despite the fact that the term *eschatology* is normally used to describe it, the future hope of late post-exilic and intertestamental Judaism cannot be defined with reference to "the end" of something.

By this conclusion I repudiate the recent attempt of J. van der Ploeg to reduce the term "eschatology" to a narrow etymological connotation.[24] Even apart from the questionable appropriateness of trying to equate the meaning of a word with its etymology, the attempt manifestly fails to work. For van der Ploeg, "It is abundantly clear what Old or New Testament eschatology should mean in theology, the knowledge of the end of this period, this time, and of the rather short space of time which precedes the end. It is more specified by what precedes than by what follows." So, even though van der Ploeg admits that Second Isaiah pronounces the end of an era, he cannot be said to have an eschatology because he "is interested above all in what comes after." Van der Ploeg does not want to deny that there is any concern in "eschatology" passages for what comes after the end, but he insists that it is secondary and not essential. Yet he admits that "in the New Testament the accent lies rather on the birth of salvation" (p. 91). While it is true that most of the passages containing the word "eschaton" deal with the end of something (naturally enough), it is surely wrong to consider these passages decisive for the main interest of the books in which they occur. If the apocalyptic books were written, as is widely believed, to give hope to the faithful in times of oppression, it would be indeed extraordinary if they were primarily concerned with "the end" and not with what lies beyond it. This is in fact borne out by several passages in such recognized apocalyptic books as the Apocalypse of John (Revelation), 4 Ezra, and *2 Apocalypse of Baruch* which speak at length of what lies beyond the destruction.[25]

In fairness to van der Ploeg it must be stated that his objective was merely to clarify the use of a term, not to outline a particular type of future expectation. Nevertheless, when he states that "true and explicit eschatology belongs to the apocalyptic literature," and proceeds to define eschatology in a narrow etymological sense, he is suggesting a false understanding of the apocalyptic books.

(b) The Distinction of Two Periods

There is another type of formulation which has frequently been used to express the distinctive element of apocalyptic eschatology. This type of formulation focuses not on the definitive end, but on the transition from one period or age to another. So Johannes Lindblom has written that "our starting point must be the idea of two ages rather than the end of all things."[26] Similarly, van der Ploeg does not speak of the end of the world, but of the end of "this period." However, the crucial point about this type of formulation is what one considers to be the end of a period. We have already seen that Mowinckel did not find the expectation of a new world order adequately expressed in Second Isaiah because that prophet did not speak of a definitive end to the old order. If the distinction between two ages requires the destruction of the world in between, then the doctrine of the two ages becomes a variant of the idea of the end of the world.[27]

If on the other hand, the distinction is made between two historical periods, we cannot deny that such a distinction was made already by the pre-exilic prophets. Georg Fohrer has argued that the point of transition between the two types of expectation came when the "either-or" of the great prophets was transformed into a temporal doctrine of two ages.[28] As examples of the latter he points to the emergence, in Second and Third Isaiah of an "eternal covenant" (Isa. 55:3, 61:8) with "eternal signs" (Isa. 55:13), "eternal prosperity" (Isa. 45:17; 51:6, 8) and "eternal peace" (Isa. 51:11). But these expectations were not a purely post-exilic phenomenon as Fohrer claims. Even apart from more controversial passages such as Isaiah 2 and 11 and Micah 4, the new covenant promised in Jeremiah 31 and the return to the desert followed by a new covenant in Hosea 2 already mark the transition from an age of change to an age of lasting good relations between Israel and God.[29]

Similarly Gerhard von Rad has said "the message of the prophets has to be termed eschatological wherever it regards the old historical bases of salvation as null and void."[30] He draws attention here to a highly significant point of transition in Israel's future hope, but one which was made already at the beginning of the period of the classical prophets. The hope for new institutions modeled on the old ones remained an important aspect of the future hope of the Jews right through the NT period.[31] However, this feature can already be found in the pre-exilic prophets, notably in Hosea 2 and Jeremiah 31. It became more frequent and more emphatic in later literature, but this shows how a continuous theme runs through prophetic and apocalyptic eschatology and is gradually developed. It illustrates the continuity between the two types of future hope. It does not show us the difference.

(c) Apocalyptic as Mythology

A further type of formulation which has been applied to apocalyptic eschatology, is, if not entirely successful, distinctly more fruitful. This approach considers apocalyptic as a form of mythology. We may consider the recent formulation by Paul D. Hanson. Hanson defines *prophetic eschatology* as

> the announcement to the nation of the divine plans for Israel and the world which the prophet, with his insight into Yahweh's divine council, has witnessed unfolding within the covenant relationship between Israel and Yahweh, which plans the prophet proceeds to translate into the terms of plain history, real politics and human instrumentality,

whereas apocalyptic (more accurately apocalyptic eschatology) is the disclosure (usually esoteric in nature) to the elect of the prophetic vision of Yahweh's sovereignty (including his future dealings with his people, the inner secrets of the cosmos, etc.) which vision the visionaries have ceased to translate into terms of plain history, real politics and human instrumentality because of a pessimistic view of reality growing out of the bleak postexilic conditions in which the visionary group found itself.[32]

These definitions, in a sense, deal with the form of presentation rather than the content. Even as formal descriptions they are not entirely satisfactory. The suggestion that the OT prophets "translated" a mythical message into "plain history" smacks too much of twentieth-century demythologizing. Surely both prophets and apocalypticists presented their message as they themselves saw it. If, however, we insist that both types of visionaries are reporting what they saw, then Hanson's definitions provide a good illustration of the intrinsic relation of the form to the message. For the prophets the most significant action takes place on earth. Even if a decision is taken in the divine council, it is acted out on earth, in "plain history." For the apocalypticists however, the most significant action takes place between heavenly mythological beings, in the conflict of God and Belial, Christ and Anti-Christ, angels and demons, sons of light and sons of darkness. In this respect apocalyptic shares the world-view of the ancient cosmic mythologies.[33] This shift of focus from earthly to heavenly events first emerges clearly in the Book of Daniel, although it is partially visible in some of the post-exilic prophets, notably Isaiah 24–27 and Zechariah. It carries with it a radical change in the nature of future hope. We the most significant action is situated among the heavenly beings then the main hope of human beings is to be elevated to this higher sphere of life. If human beings are elevated to the heavenly form of life, whether this happens by a resurrection after death or already before death, the restrictions of the human condition are cast off and in particular death is transcended.

In classical biblical prophecy the issue had always been the life of the nation. Apocalyptic still deals with a communal context, whether it be the nation or, more often, the just. However, its concern has extended to the life of the individual. By its focus on heavenly, supernatural realities it provides a possibility that the human life can transcend death, not merely by the future generations of the nation but by passing to the higher, heavenly sphere. It is this hope for the transcendence of death which is the distinctive character of apocalyptic over against prophecy.

Apocalyptic Eschatology as the Transcendence of Death

In support of this thesis I shall now adduce some texts from the second century B.C. which are usually classified as "apocalyptic." My selection is determined by a number of factors. First, I adduce nothing earlier than the second century because the material in the late prophetic books, which is sometimes described as "apocalyptic" or "proto-apocalyptic" – such as Isaianic apocalypse or the book of Zechariah – represents the transition from prophetic to apocalyptic eschatology, but is not regarded as a full development of the later type of future hope. Secondly, I adduce nothing later than the first century B.C.–i.e., I do not include the Apocalypse of John, 4 Ezra or *2 Apocalypse of Baruch*, because they represent a further, later stage in the development of Jewish and Christian future expectation. In so limiting my texts I confine myself to one phase of Jewish apocalyptic. Later apocalyptic expressed the transcendence of death in different terms. Almost 300 years separate the Book of Daniel from 4 Ezra and we cannot speak of both in one breath as "Jewish Apocalyptic." Thirdly, I avoid as far as possible works of uncertain origin such as the *Testaments of the Twelve Patriarchs* and the *Apocalypse of Abraham*. Much needs to be clarified about the provenance of these works before we can purposefully integrate them into the thought of any given period.

My main text is the Book of Daniel, and I will supplement this with reference to the Qumran Scrolls, the book of *Enoch*, *Jubilees* and the *Assumption of Moses*, all of which appear to have been written in Palestine in the second, or at latest, first century B.C.[34]

First, let us consider the second half of the book of Daniel.[35] Chapters 7 and 8 both consist of visions of heavenly events. These are followed by a prayer in chapter 9. This in turn is followed by two visions of the angel Gabriel, the first of which contains the famous prophecy of seventy weeks; the second of which contains a figurative description of the Hellenistic wars, culminating in the judgment scene in Daniel 12.

The first point we may notice is that chapters 7 and 8 deal with heavenly events and are not merely figurative descriptions of earthly battles. I base this assertion chiefly on the use of the word $q^e d\bar{o}sh\bar{i}m$ (Aramaic $qadd\bar{i}sh\bar{i}n$) "the saints of the Most High." In chapter 7 we read that the "little horn" was waging war with the saints and overcoming them, until the Ancient of Days came (7:21). In chapter 8 (10–11) "the little horn pitted its strength against the host of heaven and some of the stars of heaven he cast to the ground."

69

From the parallelism of these two verses, we can see that the $q^e d\bar{o}sh\bar{\imath}m$, the saints of the Most High, in Daniel refers to the angelic host.[36]

This is in fact the usual meaning of the term $q^e d\bar{o}sh\bar{\imath}m$ in the OT and at Qumran.[37] In the Book of Daniel this interpretation is borne out by the use of the term $q\bar{a}d\bar{o}sh$ to designate an angelic figure in Dan. 8:13, and the fact that in chapters 10 and 11 the heavenly battle is fought between Michael and Gabriel on the one hand and the princes of Greece and Persia on the other.

The "people of the saints" (7:27 and 8:24), however, surely refers to Israel.[38] The possessive form is used to express the relationship between heavenly patrons and human people. In Dan. 10:21 – Michael is "your prince." In Daniel 7 the expression is inverted – Israel is the people of Michael and his fellow angels. The kingdom attributed to the people is all *under* heaven and might be considered as a subdivision of the entire angelic kingdom.

From the references in Daniel 10 to the angels of Greece and Persia it is apparent that the author of Daniel is working here with the old idea that each nation has a corresponding angelic "prince" who rules over it. This idea is old in biblical literature. Perhaps the *locus classicus* is Deuteronomy 32, where God set up the boundaries of the peoples according to the number of the sons of God.[39] Here the nations and their angels are not identical but stand in direct correspondence. A similar correspondence between humans on earth and the angelic host in heaven can be seen in Judg. 5:19–20. "The kings came and fought; then they fought, those kings of Canaan, at Taanach by the waters of Megiddo.... From the heavens the stars too fought; from their courses they fought against Sisera."[40] Again in Isa. 24:21 we read that Yahweh will punish "the host of heaven in the heavens and the kings of the earth on the earth." In all these passages we are dealing with a two-story universe, where events happen on one level on earth but also on another level in the heavens.

There are some glimpses in the OT of a tradition of a battle between angelic beings in heaven. The most noted of these is perhaps Isaiah 14 which tells of the revolt of Helal ben Shachar.[41] This however is only a glimpse of a tradition which seldom comes to direct expression before Daniel and the rise of apocalyptic. Usually in the OT, though Yahweh and his host fight from heaven, they fight against human, earthly enemies.[42] For a complete portrayal of battles between divine beings we must go all the way back to the cosmic myths of ancient Canaan and Mesopotamia.[43] In the ancient mythologies the cosmic battle in the heavens was *the* significant action, while the earthly counterpart was only a byproduct. The return of emphasis to the heavens as the locus of action is a very significant departure in Daniel and shows the acceptance of a world structure closely akin to the ancient mythologies.[44]

Daniel, however, takes a significant step beyond what we find in either the ancient mythologies or in the earlier books of the Bible. It suggests that the just can be elevated to the heavenly sphere of life to join the angelic host. The text reads: "Many of those who sleep in the dust of the earth shall awake; some shall live forever, others shall be an everlasting disgrace. But the wise shall shine brightly like the splendour of the firmament, and those who lead the many to justice shall be like the stars forever" (Dan. 12:2–3).

Some scholars have considered the reference to the stars here as a simple comparison.[45] This, however, is unlikely. The stars had long been identified with the angelic host in biblical tradition. In Judg. 5:20 the stars were said to fight against Sisera.[46] The identification is explicit in Dan. 8:10: "its power extended to the host of heaven, so that it cast down to earth some of the host and some of the stars and trampled on them."

The entire second half of Daniel deals with the heavenly counterpart of the battle of the Jews with Antiochus Epiphanes on earth. There is nothing to suggest that the author was interested in the revival of earthly life. Rather, Dan. 12:1–3 describes the final coming together of the two spheres of life by the elevation of the just to join the angelic host.

This interpretation is confirmed by several passages in the contemporary literature. In particular we may cite *1 Enoch* 104:2 which promises the just that "you will shine as the stars of heaven" and 104:6, "you will become companions to the hosts of heaven." Again in the *Similitudes of Enoch* (39:5) the dwelling places of the righteous are with the holy angels.[47]

In Daniel this elevation is the result at once of a final judgment and a final battle.[48] It is, therefore, a vindication of the righteous. At the time at which Daniel was written this vindication was necessary especially for the martyred righteous who had lost their lives for their faith. The promise of elevation showed that this loss was not as absolute as might appear since the just were raised to a higher, lasting form of life.

In Daniel the promise of elevation comes in temporal sequence at a future time. It involves the raising of the dead, although the elevation of the living is not excluded.[49] The impression is given that it only takes place at the end of a period, after a time of great tribulation. This is also the case in certain other works of the second century B.C. In *Jub.* 23:27–31 the just are promised that "their bodies

71

will rest in the earth and their spirits will have much joy." Here no resurrection is promised, but the just are assured that they will transcend death *at a future time*. Again, in the final section of *1 Enoch* the elevation of the just to the stars comes at the conclusion of the judgment of a period and is definitely future.[50] This is also true of the corporate elevation of Israel in the *As. Mos.* 10:9.

However, the transcendence of death was not necessarily to be awaited as strictly future. It could also be experienced as present reality. This seems to have been the case at least in the Qumran community. Although the Qumran sect is generally recognized as an apocalyptic community, there is no clear reference to the resurrection of the dead. Various interpretations of the community's attitude to death and afterlife have been put forward. Chaim Rabin, amazingly, finds ample evidence of a belief in resurrection to confirm his thesis that the scrolls are Pharisaic.[51] At the other extreme R. B. Laurin finds no evidence of either immortality of the soul or resurrection of the body.[52] In between, most scholars find some form of spiritual immortality other than physical resurrection.[53] Most penetrating, perhaps, is the analysis of H. W. Kuhn, who finds in the Scrolls and particularly in 1QH the conviction of present participation in angelic life, coupled with the expectation of further fulfillment in the future.[54]

In fact death does not arise as a theological problem in 1QH, because the community believed that it had already transcended death by passing over into the community of the angels. This is well illustrated by a passage in 1QH iii:19–23:

I give thanks to you, O Lord,
For you have redeemed me from the pit
And from Sheol Abaddon you have lifted me up to the *eternal height* (*rwm 'wlam*)
And I will walk to and fro on an unsearchable plain
And I know that there is hope for him whom you have created from the dust of the *eternal assembly*;
And the perverse spirit you have cleansed from great transgression to be stationed with *the host of the holy ones*,
And to enter into fellowship with the congregation of the children of heaven,
And you have apportioned to man an eternal destiny with the spirits of knowledge.

In this text it is apparent that the author is convinced that he already possesses eternal life. This conviction is repeated in 1QH xi:3–14: "You have cleansed man from sin ... that he might be joined with the sons of your truth, and in a lot with your holy ones ... with the everlasting host."[55] The conviction of the presence of the angelic host in the community is reflected in the rules of 1QS: "Nor shall anyone who is afflicted by any form of human uncleanness whatsoever be admitted into the assembly of God ... for holy angels are present in their congregation."[56]

In more general terms 1QS iv:6–8 promises "abundance of bliss, with length of days and fruitfulness and all blessings without end and eternal joy in perpetual life and the glorious crown and garment of honor in everlasting light." Here again we find the promise of eternal life, with no mention of the fact of death. We cannot suppose that the authors of these documents believed that members of the community would not in fact die.[57] In any case the literature was produced over more than one generation, some of it surely after the Teacher of Righteousness had passed away.[58] Yet no need was apparently felt for any statement of belief in the resurrection of the dead. The reason for this can only be that the community believed that death was already transcended by its fellowship with the angelic host.

The fact that such a conception was possible for the Qumran community shows that the most significant aspect of the future hope of second century Judaism was not the physical resurrection of the body, which was hardly envisaged at the time, nor a transformation of the earth, nor the ushering in of a new age, but the transition from one sphere of life to another. Such a transition is vertical rather than horizontal, spatial rather than temporal. I do not mean that it must be conceived in crudely spatial terms, that life with the heavenly host must be lived in a heaven distinct from earth. Evidently the Qumran community enjoyed this higher level of life right here on earth. Rather I mean that there is another sphere of life parallel to this. In the words of 4 Ezra, "the Most High made not one world, but two."[59] These two, however, are not only in temporal succession, as envisaged by 4 Ezra, and often thought to be typical of all Jewish apocalyptic. They are also contemporaneous, as envisaged by Daniel, *1 Enoch*, and Qumran. The religious ideal of a life of heightened intensity and perfection was not entirely relegated to a future utopia. It was also something eternally present in the heavenly court. This belief inevitably opened the way for some form of mystic participation in the higher form of life, even if only on a communal basis, as was the case at Qumran.[60]

We may note that if we regard the world view of apocalyptic as a two-story universe rather than as a theory of two world ages, we can see that revelations of heavenly secrets, such as we get in the heavenly journeys of Enoch and again in *Enoch* 72—82, are not irrelevant to the eschatology of these works.[61] If the future hope of the apocalypticist was to be elevated to a heavenly life, then any information about the heavenly regions where such life is most fully lived is relevant to that hope. In this way it is possible to find a unified world view in the apocalyptic writings.[62]

Theological Conclusions

There are two conclusions relevant to biblical theology which I wish to draw from the foregoing. One concerns the contrast of Greek and Hebrew thought which has been fashionable for some time in biblical theology. The other regards the logic of eschatological expectations, or the function filled by future expectation in the living out of present experience.

(a) Similarity to Greek Thought

The hope for the transcendence of death in late post-exilic Judaism inevitably reminds us of the Platonic idea of the immortality of the soul.[63] Plato also believed in the existence of a higher world, the world of ideas, to which the good soul could be elevated upon death. As in most of the Jewish texts this transition in its complete form was basically something to be hoped for in the future, after the death of the individual, although he could participate in it proleptically by a good life and contemplation of the ideas here on earth. Both traditions believed that the righteous would experience an ultimate vindication which would not be cut off by death.

Inevitably there were important differences between the Platonic tradition and Jewish apocalyptic eschatology. One was the far greater emphasis on personal mysticism in the Platonic tradition while the Jewish tradition remained predominantly interested in the community. In this, Jewish apocalyptic showed its roots in biblical prophecy. However the common ground remains highly significant. The essential point in both traditions is that earthly biological life is not the highest form of experience for which human beings can hope. There is a whole higher realm of life, expressed in the Jewish tradition by reference to the divine council and in the Platonic tradition by the world of ideas. Both traditions allow for some possibility of experiencing this higher life proleptically before death by living a just life.[64]

The similarity between the two traditions can be well illustrated from the ambiguities of the Wisdom of Solomon. Some scholars have interpreted this book fairly successfully, from an almost exclusively Greek background.[65] Others have gone so far as to argue that it was written in Hebrew.[66] On the one hand we find such characteristically Greek statements as that "the corruptible body weighs down the soul" (9:15), and we may suspect Greek influence of a Platonizing kind in the statement that "God created man for incorruption" (2:23). On the other hand, we find the vindication of the just man expressed not merely as immortality of the soul but also as being "numbered among the sons of God" and having "a portion among the saints" (5:5), precisely the hope of Jewish apocalyptic in Daniel, *Enoch* and Qumran.[67] The Greek hope of immortality of the soul and the eschatology of the Jewish apocalypses was not precisely the same, but Wisdom shows how far the two could be successfully combined.[68]

The similarity between certain patterns of Greek thought and apocalyptic eschatology might be explained in part by Hellenistic influence on Jewish thought in the intertestamental period.[69] The fact of Hellenistic influence or at least the influence of Hellenistic-oriental syncretism can hardly be doubted.[70] The spread of the belief in astral immortality in the Hellenistic world undoubtedly helped prepare the way for the idea of elevation to the heavenly host.[71] There is no reason however to regard apocalyptic eschatology as a foreign growth in the Jewish tradition. The idea of a two-story universe which made apocalyptic eschatology possible was always present to some degree in the biblical tradition and indeed in the ancient Near East as a whole. Recent studies have shown the importance of the divine council in the OT.[72] The prophets had access to this higher sphere as a source of information.[73] A few chosen individuals such as Enoch and Elijah seem to have gained permanent access to it. Furthermore the psalms and wisdom literature both speak of "life" in absolute terms which suggest a higher sphere of life, even though it is not specifically associated with the divine council.[74] The great emphasis on "history" in modern biblical theology has often led to the impression that Israel had a one-dimensional, or nearly one-dimensional view of the world.[75] This view must be modified. While Israel certainly had a distinctive world view, and one in which emphasis on human history played an important part, there remain important analogies with Greek tradition in the concept of a higher realm of life.[76] The affinities of late Jewish hope for the transcendence of death expressed in categories drawn from OT tradition, with the Platonic hope of the immortality of the soul expressed in terms drawn from Greek philosophy, go a long way to disprove the strong contrast between Greek and Hebrew thought advocated by some biblical theologians.[77]

(b) The Logic of Apocalyptic Escahtology

The apocalyptic writings had no one literally intended portrayal of the manner in which the elevation to the higher form of life will take place. Daniel speaks of a resurrection. *Jubilees* 23 says that the bodies of the just will remain in the earth but their spirits will rejoice. The Qumran community experienced the transition as a present reality, but also expected a future vindication which was variously described in 1QM, 11Q Melchizedek, etc. This variety of expression can hardly surprise us. Hope is by nature of things unseen, which can only be figuratively or symbolically expressed, and no one symbol can exhaust the potentialities of the hope.

It is clear from the example of Qumran that the transition to the higher form of life was essentially a depth experience in the present. Death was transcended by an intensity in this life, which was not destroyed by physical decease, rather than by future revivification. In recent years certain theologians have pointed out that eschatological formulations are essentially projections of hopes experienced in the present. In that respect they indicate a present depth experience, rather than an objective future expectation. So Rudolf Bultmann wrote: "The meaning in history lies in the present and when the present is conceived as the eschatological present by Christian faith, the meaning in history is realized."[78]

Also Karl Rahner: "Man's knowledge of the future still to come, even his revealed knowledge, is confined to such prospects as can be derived from a reading of his present eschatological experience."[79]

These assertions are in some degree supported by the evidence of Qumran or by the assertion in the Wisdom of Solomon that "Righteousness is eternal" (1:15). However, they can hardly be said to do justice to the logic of eschatology as found in the apocalyptic texts. In those texts, while the present experience of righteousness gives rise to the hope of final vindication, it is also true that the hope of final vindication confirms and even makes possible the present experience of righteousness and divine approval. Neither present experience nor future hope can be ignored. They are mutually interdependent.

This interdependence is evident again and again in the apocalyptic texts. When in Dan. 12:12 the angel sums up the message of the preceding visions in the words "blessed are they who stand firm" he is encouraging the just to stand firm by the promise of resurrection which has been given at the beginning of the chapter, but also assuring them that even while they are standing firm they are blessed. Again in *1 Enoch* 104:14 the righteous are told to "be hopeful and cast not away hope, for ye shall have great joy as the angels of heaven," "for the paths of righteousness are worthy of acceptation but the paths of unrighteousness will suddenly be destroyed and vanish" (94:1). Here again the point of the writer is that the paths of righteousness should be accepted here and now, but he realizes that this requires a degree of hopefulness and confidence in the future which is made possible by the promise of future joy. Even at Qumran, where the emphasis is very heavily on present experience there remains a promise of future consummation for "God through the mysteries of His understanding and through His glorious wisdom has appointed a period for the existence of wrong-doing; but at the season of visitation He will destroy it forever; and then the truth of the world will appear forever."[80]

The logic of these texts might be described as follows. The objective is that people should live justly, responding in a free and uninhibited manner to the demands of righteousness, and so attain the experience of the approval of God. Now one of the main factors which inhibits such a free response to righteousness is the fear of personal loss, of pursuing an unprofitable course of action, and especially of the ultimate loss of death. So the impious in the Wisdom of Solomon reason:

> Our life is a passing shadow
> And ther is no retreat from our end . . .
> Come therefore let us enjoy the good things that are . . .
> Let us crown ourselves with rosebuds ere they wither . . .
> Let our strength be the rule of our righteousness,
> For weakness is proved to be unprofitable.[81]

These fears are countered by the hope of a form of life which transcends death. This hope gives the freedom necessary to respond freely to the demands of righteousness and so attain the present depth experience in life.

This logic of Jewish apocalyptic carries over into the NT. It is well expressed in a passage of Paul:

> We know that Christ, once raised from the dead, is never to die again: he is no longer under the dominion of death. For in dying as he died he died to sin, once for all, and in living as he lives, he lives to God. In the same way you must regard yourselves as dead to sin and alive to God . . . Put yourselves at the disposal of God as dead men raised to life, yield your bodies to him as implements for doing right (Rom. 6:9ff).

In this passage it is the assurance of resurrection which enables the Christian to give up his body to doing right with no interest other than living to God. The same point is made by the gospel saying: "Lay up for yourselves treasure in heaven" – not so that you may eventually enjoy them, but so that they may mediate a present depth experience of eternal life – "for where your treasure is, there is your heart also" (Matt. 6:19–21).

The important thing in this logic of eschatology is surely the attainment of the present depth experience, of liberation in response to the demands of righteousness. If this is attained the manner in which it is mediated is of lesser importance. It is undoubtedly true that this depth experience can be attained by some without a belief in the heavenly host, immortality of the soul or resurrection of the body. It is also true that belief in an after life does not necessarily involve liberation, or the attainment of a depth experience. However, if we are to understand the thought pattern of apocalyptic eschatology we must realize that, for the apocalypticists, present experience and future hope were intrinsically connected and mutually interdependent.[82]

Conclusion

This paper has been an attempt to clarify the distinctive nature of the future hope of late post-exilic Judaism. This hope cannot be understood as the expectation of a purely future event, and, despite the etymology of the word eschatology, it is not primarily concerned with the end of anything. Rather it is concerned with the transcendence of death by the attainment of a higher, angelic form of life. This hope shows considerable affinities with the Greek doctrines of the immortality of the soul. It cannot be adequately understood as either a future expectation or a present depth experience. It is essentially an interpenetration of both.

Editor's note: Translations of biblical passages are from the New English Bible.

NOTES

1 Albert Schweitzer, *The Quest of the Historical Jesus* with a new introduction by James M. Robinson (New York: Macmillan, 1969).

2 This article is the text of the Boylan lecture to the Irish Biblical Association, Dec. 6, 1972, at Earlsfort Terrace, Dublin. Translations of biblical passages are taken from the New American Bible.

3 Käsemann's thesis has been presented in two essays in *JTC* 6 (New York: Herder, 1969): "The Beginnings of Christian Theology" (17–46) and "On the Topic of Primitive Christian Apocalyptic" (99–133). The volume also contains reactions to Käsemann's views by Gerhard Ebeling and Ernst Fuchs.

4 Jürgen Moltmann, *Theology of Hope* (New York: Harper & Row; London: SCM Press, 1967): Wolfhart Pannenberg, *Revelation as History* (London: Sheed and Ward, 1969). The views of Pannenberg and his circle on apocalyptic depend

heavily on the work of Dietrich Rossler, *Gesetz und Geschichte* (Neukirchen: Neukirchener, 1960) and are most fully expressed by Ulrich Wilckens, "The Understanding of Revelation Within the History of Primitive Christianity," also in *Revelation as History*, 55–122.

5   On the history of the discussion of "apocalyptic" see especially two recent books, Johann M. Schmidt, *Die jüdische Apokalyptik* (Neukirchen: Neukirchener, 1969) and Klaus Koch, *The Rediscovery of Apocalyptic* (London: SCM Press, 1972). The debate on the term "eschatology" is summarized by Hans-Peter Mueller, *Ursprünge und Strukturen alttestamentlicher Eschatologie* (BZAW 109; Berlin: Töpelmann, 1969) 1–11. See also H. D. Preuss *Jahweglaube und Zukunft-serwartung* (BWANT 87; Stuttgart: Kohlhammer, 1968).

6   So, for example, Th. C. Vriezen, "Prophecy and Eschatology," VTSup I (Leiden: Brill, 1953) 199–229; G. von Rad *Old Testament Theology* (New York: Harper & Row; Edinburgh: Oliver and Boyd, 1965) II:114–115.

7   So G. Holscher, *Die Ursprünge der jüdischen Eschatologie* (Giessen, 1925) 3. S. Mowinckel, *He That Cometh* (Oxford: Blackwells, 1959) 126, and most recently, J. van der Ploeg, "Eschatology in the Old Testament," *OTS* 17 (1972) 89–99.

8   In addition to the literature listed in notes 3 and 4 above see the collection of essays in *Int* 25 (1971), and the discussions by Gerhard von Rad, *Theologie des Alten Testaments* (4th ed.; München: Kaiser, 1965) II:315–30 and Martin Hengel, *Judentum und Hellenismus* (WUNT 10; Tübingen: Mohr, 1969) 319–80.

9   Jean Carmignac, "La Notion d'Eschatologie dans la Bible et à Qumrân," *RQ* (1969) 17–31; van der Ploeg, "Eschatology in the Old Testament."

10   I borrow the phrase "apocalyptic eschatology" from Paul D. Hanson, "Jewish Apocalyptic Against its Environment," *RB* 68 (1971) 35.

11   This fact was stressed by von Rad, *Theology of the Old Testament* II:307 and, in greater detail, by Dr M. E. Stone of the Hebrew University in a forthcoming article.

12   Cf. the description by Robert North, "Prophecy to Apocalyptic via Zechariah," VTSup XXII (1972) 47–71. Von Rad, *Old Testament Theology* II:304–5.

13   On the question of determinism in apocalyptic see especially P. von der Osten-Sacken, "Die Apokalyptik in ihrem Verhältnis zu Prophetie und Weisheit," in *Theologische Existenz Heute* (München, 1969) 157.

14   This is not to dispute the crucial importance of post-exilic prophecy as the time of transition from the future expectation of the prophets to apocalyptic escha-tology. See Paul D. Hanson's Harvard Thesis (1970) "Studies in the Origin of Jewish Apocalyptic" and his articles "Jewish Apocalyptic Against its Near Eastern Environment," *RB* 68 (1971) 31–58 and "Old Testament Apocalyptic Re-examined," *Int* 25 (1971) 454–79 and herein, pp. 37–60. Also Otto Plöger, *Theo-cracy and Eschatology* (Oxford: Blackwell, 1968); R. North, "From Prophecy to Apocalyptic via Zechariah," VTSup XXII (1972) 47–71 and Samuel Amsler, "Zacharie et l'origine de l'apocalyptique," VTSup XXII (1972) 227–31.

15   See the review by H. P. Mueller, *Ursprünge und Strukturen*, 2ff. Hugo Gressmann shared this definition of eschatology but claimed to find it already in the pre-exilic prophets.

16   Th. C. Vriezen, "Prophecy and Eschatology," 199.

17 Mowinckel, *He That Cometh*, 125–6.

18 Mowinckel, *He That Cometh*, 266.

19 Luke 21:23; cf. also Apoc. 21:1.

20 It is used in parallelism to the word *mō'ēd* in 11:21, *kî 'ôd qēṣ lammō'ēd* and again in 11:35 *'ad 'ēth qēṣ kî 'ôd lammō'ēd*, and the word *mō'ēd* occurs in 11:29 in a noneschatological sense as "appointed time."

21 1QH 3:29–33: "Then the floods of Belial go over all steep banks like a fire that devoureth all their ... in order to destroy every green and dry tree by their channels, and it sweepeth with burning flames until all that drink of them are no more; it devoureth the foundations of clay and the extension of the dry land; and the foundations of the mountains become a burning, and the roots of flint become streams of pitch and it devoureth right down to the great deep." (Tr. Svend Holm-Nielsen, *Hodayot*; Aarhus: Universitetsforlaget [1960] 65.)

22 In the phrase of F. M. Cross, Jr., *The Ancient Library of Qumran and Modern Biblical Studies* (New York: Doubleday, 1958) 56.

23 On the "realized eschatology" of the Qumran community see especially H. W. Kuhn, *Enderwartung un Gegenwärtiges Heil* (SUNT 4; Göttingen: Vandenhoeck & Ruprecht, 1966). Similarity in the Apocalypse of Weeks (*Enoch* 93; 91:12–17) the crucial transition seems to take place within history, in the seventh of ten weeks.

24 J. van der Ploeg, "Eschatology in the Old Testament."

25 Apoc. 21–2; 4 Ezra 7:89–101; 10:25–8; *2 Apocalypse of Baruch* 49—52; 72—74.

26 Johannes Lindblom, *Prophecy in Ancient Israel* (Philadelphia: Fortress Press; Oxford: Blackwell, 1962) 360.

27 These two doctrines coincide in late apocalyptic texts such as Apocalypse of John and 4 Ezra.

28 G. Fohrer, "Die Struktur der alttestamentlichen Eschatologie" in *Studien zur Alttestamentlichen Prophetie* (BZAW 99; Berlin: Töpelmann, 1967) 32–58.

29 Note in this regard Hos. 2:19, "And I will espouse thee forever."

30 Von Rad, *Old Testament Theology* II:118.

31 Cf. the dictum "Urzeit gleicht Endzeit." Cf. F. M. Cross, "New Directions in the Study of Apocalyptic" in *JTC* 6 (1969) 157–74; Mowinckel, *He That Cometh*, 155ff.

32 P. D. Hanson, "Jewish Apocalyptic Against its Environment," 34–5.

33 The affinities of apocalyptic to the ancient myths had of course often been noted before, notably by Hermann Gunkel, *Schöpfung und Chaos* (Göttingen: Vandenhoeck & Ruprecht, 1895) and Hugo Gressmann, *Der Ursprung der israelitisch-jüdischen Eschatologie*. Cf. also S. B. Frost "Eschatology and Myth," *VT* 2 (1952) 70ff; F. M. Cross, "New Directions in the Study of Apocalyptic"; Amos Wilder, "Eschatological Imagery and Earthly Circumstance," *NTS* 5 (1959) 229–45 and on a more popular level, B. W. Anderson, *Creation versus Chaos* (New York: Association Press, 1967).

34 The Qumran community originated in the second century B.C. but many of the texts may not have originated until later. On the dating of individual documents see F. M. Cross, *The Ancient Library of Qumran* 34ff. On the dating of the various sections of *1 Enoch* I essentially follow R. H. Charles, *The Book of*

Enoch (Oxford: Clarendon Press, 1893). Cf. most recently J. T. Milik, "Problèmes de la littérature Hénochique à la Lumière des Fragments Araméens de Qumrân," *HTR* 64 (1971) 333–79. Milik's arguments for a late date for the *Similitudes of Enoch* are not convincing. See J. Collins, "Studies in the *Sibylline Oracles*," Harvard Thesis, 1972, 231 n. 78. On the date of the *Assumption of Moses*, and of *Jubilees* 23 see most recently G. W. Nickelsburg *Resurrection, Immortality and Eternal Life in Intertestamental Judaism* (HTS 26; Cambridge, Mass.: Harvard Univ. Press, 1972) 43–7.

35 The main commentaries on Daniel are those of Montgomery (ICC; New York, 1927), Charles (New York, 1917), Bentzen (Tübingen, 1937), Plöger (KAT; Gutersloh, 1965) Porteous (OTL, 1965) Nötscher (Echter-Bibel, 1948) and most recently Delcor (EBib, 1972).

36 There are three possible interpretations of the saints of the Most High in Daniel: (a) The term refers to Israel. This is the traditional interpretation, recently defended by C. W. Brekelmann, "The Saints of the Most High and their Kingdom," *OTS* 14 (1965) 305–29, and M. McNamara, *Daniel*, in *The New Catholic Commentary on Holy Scripture* (London: Nelson, 1969) 664. (b) It refers to the angelic host. So Noth, "The Understanding of History in Old Testament Apocalyptic" in *The Laws of the Pentateuch and other Essays* (Philadelphia: Fortress Press, 1967), 194–214. (c) It refers simultaneously to both Israel and the angelic host. So Annie Jaubert, *La Notion d'Alliance dans le Judaisme* (Paris: Editions du Seuil, 1963) and most recently, Lamberigts, "L'Idée de Qedōshīm dans les textes de Qumran," *Ephemerides theologicae lovanienses* 46 (1970) 24–40. I believe that the term *qedōshīm* refers to the angelic host, but that the "people of the saints" refers to Israel.

37 Ps. 34:10 is the only clear exception.

38 Contra Noth, who regards this phrase as synonymous with "the saints of the Most High," see "The Understanding of History," 223.

39 So LXX, confirmed now by evidence from Qumran. The MT has "sons of Israel." See P. W. Skehan, "A fragment of the 'Song of Moses' (Deuteronomy 32) from Qumran," *BASOR* 136 (1954) 12–15. Also D. Barthelemy, "Les Tiqqunē Sōpherīm et la Critique Textuelle de l'ancien Testament," VTSup IX (1962) 295.

40 The importance of the human part of this synergism is emphasized in the Song of Deborah by the curse against Meroz, in v. 23, because its inhabitants did not turn out to help Yahweh.

41 Cf. also the passage from Isaiah 24 quoted above.

42 Cf. the text from Judges 5 quoted above. Also Hab. 3:12: "In wrath you bestride the earth, in fury you trample the nations."

43 The alternative would be to posit influence from Persian dualism. In Plutarch, *De Iside et Osiride*, c.47ff, we read an account of the heavenly battle between the forces of Ormazd and Ahrimann, which may very possibly have influenced the formulation of the war between the sons of light and the sons of darkness at Qumran. See David Winston, "The Iranian Component in the Bible, Apocrypha and Qumran," *HR* 5 (1966) 183–216. However, the few passages in the Bible to which we have referred are sufficient to indicate that there was a Canaanite-Palestinian tradition of a battle in the heavens. On cosmic war in Ugarit and Mesopotamia see especially Patrick D. Miller, *The Divine Warrior in Early Israel* (HSM 5; Cambridge, Mass.: Harvard Univ. Press, 1973).

44 Daniel was not entirely original in this. Traces of this mythical pattern can already be found in the Isaiah Apocalypse (Isaiah 24—7) and Zechariah, but only in Daniel does it become fully evident.

45 So Aage Bentzen, *Daniel*, 52.

46 Cf. also Isaiah 14, where Lucifer tried to set his throne above the stars of heaven. Further *Enoch* 80:6; Job 38:7; Sir. 43:8f; *2 Apoc. Bar.* 51:10.

47 Cf. also *As. Mos.* 10:7, where Israel is elevated to the stars. Matt. 22:30: "At the resurrection men and women do not marry but are like angels in heaven."

48 See the discussion by Nickelsburg, *Resurrection*, 11–28.

49 Cf. 1 Thess. 4:13–18.

50 On the eschatology of this section of *1 Enoch* see Pierre Grelot, "L'Eschatologie des Esséniens et le Livre d'Hénoch," *RQ* 1 (1958/9) 113–31, and Nickelsburg. *Resurrection*, 112–30. In the first section of *1 Enoch* (chapters 1—36) ch. 22 describes the abode of the souls while they await the day of judgment. The *Similitudes of Enoch* do not give a consistent picture. In 38:5 the righteous already dwell with the angels, but in ch. 51 a future resurrection is expected. The fourth section of *1 Enoch* (chs. 83—90) apparently expects a future resurrection in 90:33.

51 C. Rabin, *Qumran Studies* (Oxford, 1957). For two possible references to resurrection in 1QH vi:29, 34 cf. Nickelsburg, *Resurrection*, 150–51, who, like most scholars, rejects Rabin's interpretation.

52 R. B. Laurin, "The Question of Immortality in the Qumran Hodayot," *Journal of Semitic Studies* 3 (1958) 344–55.

53 For a summary of the debate, with references, see Nickelsburg, *Resurrection*, 144–45.

54 H. W. Kuhn, *Enderwartung und Gegenwärtiges Heil*. A very similar position is held by Helmer Ringgren, *The Faith of Qumran Theology of the Dead Sea Scrolls* (Philadelphia: Fortress Press, 1963).

55 For a summary of the discussion of these passages with full references see Nickelsburg, *Resurrection*, 152–6. I follow Nickelsburg's translations here.

56 1QSa 2:3–11. Cf. also 1QM 7:4–6. On the parallel to 1 Cor. 11:10 see Joseph A. Fitzmyer, "A Feature of Qumran Angelology and the Angels of 1 Cor. 11:10," *NTS* 4 (1957–8) 48–58 (= *Paul and Qumran*, ed. J. Murphy-O'Connor; London: Chapman, 1968) 31–47.

57 On the evidence of burials at Qumran see Roland de Vaux. *L'Archéologie et les Mss de la Mer Morte* (London: Oxford Univ. Press, 1961) 46–7.

58 This contradicts the view of Ringgren that the community ignored the belief in resurrection because earlier generations were of no relevance.

59 4 Ezra 7:40.

60 On an individual basis we should note the heightened interest in such figures as Enoch and Elijah in the intertestamental period.

61 If the apocalyptic is a form of mythology (above nn. 32 and 33) it presupposes a mythical geography, and therefore a two-story universe.

62 This observation may cast some light on the debate whether apocalyptic derives more directly from prophecy or from wisdom (cf. above n. 11).

63 For Plato's teaching on immortality see especially the Phaedo and the myth of Er at the end of the Republic.

64 We may describe this higher form of life as the life of the spirit if we are careful to note that spirituality does not necessarily mean immateriality. Cf. R. North "Separated Spiritual Substances," *CBQ* 29 (1967) 419–49. In the Jewish texts the angelic form of life seems to be a state intermediate between God and man but the question of immateriality is simply not an issue.

65 So most recently J. M. Reese, *Hellenistic Influence on the Book of Wisdom* (Rome: Biblical Institute Press, 1970).

66 See Joseph Reider, *The Book of Wisdom* (Dropsie College Series; New York: Harper & Bros., 1957) 22–9. The main champion of the Hebrew original of Wisdom was Margoliouth, "Was the Book of Wisdom written in Hebrew?" *Journal of the Royal Asiatic Society* (1890) 263ff. More recently others have maintained a Hebrew original for the first 10 chapters – so E. A. Speiser, *JQR* XIV (1923–4) 455ff, and C. E. Purinton, *JBL* 47 (1928) 276ff.

67 On the affinities between the Greek doctrine of immortality of the soul and the Jewish doctrine of elevation to the heavenly host see G. W. Nickelsburg, *Resurrection*, 177–80. On the eschatology of the Book of Wisdom see P. Grelot, "L'Eschatologie de la Sagesse et les Apocalypses juives," *A La Rencontre de Dieu*, in *Mem. Gelin* (Le Puy: Xavier Mappus, 1961) 165–78; Paul Beauchamp, "Le salut corporel des justes et la conclusion du livre de la Sagesse," *Bib* 45 (1964) 491–526; C. Larcher, *Etudes sur le Livre de la Sagesse*, 103–32, 301–28; M. Delcor, "L'immortalité de l'âme dans le livre de la Sagesse et dans les documents de Qumrân," *NRT* 77 (1955) 627–30. For a possible reference to astral immortality in Wis. 3:7f see Nickelsburg, *Resurrection*, 60.

68 A distinctly physical idea of the resurrection of the body, which contrasts sharply with Greek ideas, is found already in 2 Maccabees 7 and in some later Jewish apocalypses.

69 For alleged Greek influence on Jewish eschatology see T. F. Glasson, *Greek Influence on Jewish Eschatology* (SPCK Biblical Monograph; London, 1961); Martin Hengel, *Judentum und Hellenismus* (WUNT 10; Tübingen: Mohr, 1969); and H. D. Betz, "On the Problem of the Religio-historical understanding of Apocalypticism" *JTC* 6 (1969) 134–56, argue for a more general Greek influence on Jewish apocalyptic.

70 Cf. the work of Saul Liebermann, especially his *Hellenism in Jewish Palestine* (New York: Jewish Theological Seminary, 1962).

71 On astral immortality in the Hellenistic world see especially Franz Cumont, *Lux Perpetua* (Paris: Librairie Orientaliste, Paul Geuthner, 1949) Ch. 3, 142–88.

72 F. M. Cross, "The Council of Yahweh in Second Isaiah," *JNES* 12 (1953) 274–8; R. N. Whybray, *The Heavenly Counsellor in Is. 40:13–14.* (Cambridge: Cambridge Univ. Press, 1971); R. E. Brown, "The Pre-Christian Semitic Concept of Mystery," *CBQ* 20 (1958) 417–20; H. W. Robinson, "The Council of Yahweh," *JTS* 45 (1944) 151–7.

73 Cf. Jer. 23:18, 22 where the false prophets are denounced because they had not stood in Yahweh's council.

74 For "life" used absolutely in the Wisdom literature, cf. Prov. 2:19; 5:6; 6:23; 10:17; 15:24, etc. On the eschatology of the Psalms see L. Sabourin, *The Psalms*, (Staten

Island N.Y.: Society of St Paul, 1969) I:145–51 and the literature there cited. The future hope of the apocalyptic writings may in a sense be considered as an insertion of the hope of "life" in the psalms and wisdom literature into the communal and political framework of the prophetic tradition. Much more work must be done on the relation between the Psalms and apocalyptic especially in view of recent emphasis on the cult as the carrier of old mythical traditions which re-emerge in apocalyptic.

75 Cf. the use made of biblical theology by Harvey Cox in *The Secular City* (New York: Macmillan, 1965) 15–32.

76 Cf. in this respect the article of N. P. Bratsiotis, "Nephesch-Psyche, Ein Beitrag zur Erforschung der Sprache und der Theologie der Septuaginta," VTSup (1966) 58–89, especially his conclusion on p. 87. "Der hebräische Terminus 'nephesch' und der sehr alte griechische Begriff 'psyche' weisen im grossen und ganzen dieselbe Breite der Bedeutung und dieselbe Mannigfältigkeit in der Abwandlung ihrer Bedeutung auf." Bratsiotis is concerned here primarily with pre-Platonic Greek thought.

77 See especially Thorlief Boman, *Hebrew Thought Compared with Greek* (London: SCM Press, 1960). Contrast James Barr, *The Semantics of Biblical Language* (London: Oxford Univ. Press, 1961). See the comments of Brevard S. Childs on the debate, *Biblical Theology in Crisis* (Philadelphia: Westminster Press, 1970) 44–7.

78 R. Bultmann, *History and Eschatology*, Gifford Lectures, 1955 (New York: Harper & Row, 1957) 155.

79 K. Rahner, "The Hermeneutics of Eschatological Assertions" in *Theological Investigations*, 4 (London: Darton, Longman & Todd, 1966) 334.

80 1QS iv:18–19 tr. W. H. Brownlee; *BASOR*, Supplementary Studies 10–12 (1951) 16. Cf. also 1QM.

81 2:5ff. Trans. Reider.

82 Cf. Carl E. Braaten, *History and Hermeneutics* (New Directions in Theology Today 2; London: Lutterworth Press, 1968) 179: "The present without its past and future is fleeting and meaningless. Eschatology must point out the realm of future hope beyond death." Also Karl Rahner, "The Hermeneutics of Eschatological Assertions," in *Theological Investigations* 4:326: "The self-understanding of Scripture itself, no matter how existentially interpreted, undoubtedly excludes an elimination of eschatology."

4

*New Light on the Third Century**

MICHAEL E. STONE

The situation created by the character of the sources results in a lacuna in our knowledge not only of the religious and intellectual history of Judah in the fourth and third centuries B.C.E., but also of its social, political and economic history. These latter areas of knowledge have been somewhat illuminated by two finds of papyri. One lot, in Greek, comes from Egypt and contains the reports sent by Zenon, the steward of Apollonius, the "finance minister" of Ptolemy II Philadelphus, about his dealings with Palestine and the trips he made to that country on his master's behalf, including an extensive journey in the year 259 B.C.E. This body of texts sheds some light on economic and social matters, but is of little or no help to the historian of ideas or religion.

The second group of texts is the so-called Dāliyeh papyri, named after the area of the Jordan rift where they were found, some miles north of Jericho. These were copied in the fourth century B.C.E., and are predominantly legal documents written in the Aramaic language. They were taken by refugees who fled from Samaria before Alexander in the year 331 B.C.E., and whose bones, together with the papyri, were found in a cave. They have not yet been published in full, but according to the preliminary reports they seem unlikely to contribute much to our knowledge of matters other than chronological or legal affairs. In these latter realms, however, their importance is considerable. What is evident already, from the Wadi Dāliyeh texts and even more from the Zenon papyri, is that the process of Hellenization was well under way at the end of the fourth and early in the third centuries B.C.E., and started to some extent, even before Alexander the Great. It is difficult to learn more than this, however, about matters of religious or intellectual interest.

In addition to these two papyrus discoveries, in recent years there have been a number of attempts by scholars to penetrate into the social and religious history of the fourth and third centuries. One

* First published in *Scriptures, Sects, and Visions* by M. E. Stone (1980) 27–35.

such attempt works back from the first period at which the historical sources become relatively abundant again, after 200 B.C.E. When the situation in Maccabean Judea is examined, what first strikes even the most superficial student is the bitter conflict between Judaism and Hellenism that characterized the early part of the second century B.C.E. This conflict became so intense as to lead to open warfare in the Maccabean revolt.

The Maccabean revolt, these historians point out, cannot have been the result of a sudden development. Their view is that the conflict was basically one between Hellenizing and anti-Hellenizing parties in Jerusalem itself, although other factors (notably Seleucid policy) may have played a role. There is a good deal to be said for this view. The forces that eventually exploded in revolt in 175 B.C.E. must have been building up tension in Jewish society for a considerable period of time. The process of the Hellenization discerned in the Dāliyeh, and particularly in the Zenon papyri, must have been fostered by groups or circles in Judean society, just as groups which opposed Hellenism must have arisen in reaction to it. Thus, the pietistic trends and groups represented at the start of the Maccabean revolt by the Hasideans must have had a "pre-history."

At the start of the Maccabean uprising, these groups observed the Sabbath with such rigour that they allowed themselves to be killed rather than desecrate it by taking up arms to oppose their enemies. Groups which developed the sort of approach that made this action seem necessary cannot have arisen spontaneously. Some scholars have maintained that they must have originated in the third century B.C.E. This is an important insight which contributes notably to our understanding of the social and religious situation in the third century B.C.E. Unfortunately, some of those espousing this view have made it into the general principle by which they analyse and describe all aspects of the period preceding the Maccabean revolt. At the point at which this happens doubts begin to arise.

One matter that has been intimately tied to the Maccabean revolt and particularly to the Hasideans is the origin of apocalyptic literature. This is a type of writing which was widespread in Jewish circles in the last pre-Christian centuries. It had considerable vogue, furthermore, in Jewish and Christian circles alike through most of the first millennium C.E. The remarks made here will bear on the oldest part of this continuous literary tradition. The apocalypses are typically presented as a literature of visions written in the name of an ancient sage, that is to say that they are pseudepigraphic in form. These books revealed the secrets of the heavens and the earth, including information about the end of days. Studies continue in the attempt to reach a clear formulation of the characteristics of the literary *genre* of the apocalypse. Among its most typical features are a mysteriousness of form, esotericism (often assumed) and symbolic visions, most often interpreted by an angelic mediator, and sometimes very complicated indeed. Moreover, the authors of this literature frequently wrote under the deep impression that the end of days was imminent. This attitude is not found in all the apocalypses, but is prevalent in many of them. The apocalypses were a major vehicle of theological and conceptual innovation in the Second Temple period.

The view that asserts the dominance of conflict concerning Hellenism in third-century Judaism and the antiquity of the Hasidean type of pietism also attributes the first group of apocalypses to these pietists. Generally the apocalypses are regarded as a new phenomenon, emerging from the crisis engendered by the persecutions by Antiochus IV Epiphanes, King of Syria, and the revolt that followed. These persecutions and the martyrdoms which came in their train produced an intolerable situation: the righteous were suffering and dying for their very righteousness. Out of this the apocalypses were born; it is the eschatological message of vindication that lies at the heart of the apocalypses.

Almost all the sources from which Judaism of the period of the First Temple and the age of the Restoration is known are biblical. Moreover, when the Judaism of the period after 200 B.C.E. is compared with that of the age of the Restoration before 400 B.C.E., it exhibits very striking innovations, not the least among which is the apocalyptic literature. Now, in contrast with the sources for the earlier period, which are all biblical, the sources for the "surprising" Judaism after 200 B.C.E. are all preserved outside the Hebrew Bible. With scarcely an exception, they are not cherished by the Jewish tradition, but have been transmitted by the various Christian churches. Some have come to light through archaeological chance. This means, of course, that when the extrabiblical literature of the period after 200 B.C.E. shows us dimensions of religious thought which are new in comparison with that of an earlier age, various explanations may be sought. They could be new developments in Judaism, either indigenous or under the influence of foreign cultures —Greek, Persian or even Phoenician. They could well also be the first literary expression of points of view and attitudes which may have existed from earlier days, but which are not reflected by the biblical sources, due to the selectivity with which these latter were transmitted.

Against this series of problems, the recent publication of the manuscripts of the *Book of Enoch*, from among the Dead Sea Scrolls, must be assessed. The original Semitic text of this writing was lost in antiquity, along with all but fragments of the Greek translation of it. Some quotations of the Greek have survived. The first is in the New Testament (Jude v. 14), while the most extensive are passages quoted by the Byzantine chronographers, particularly the ninth-century writer, George the Syncellus. We do not know why the Greek text disappeared, but George the Syncellus does not seem to have had direct access to it. Instead, like many Byzantine authors, he drew his quotations from those incorporated in the writings of the chronographers who preceded him, in a tradition going back to Eusebius. Two papyri of the middle of the first millennium C.E. also contain some parts of this Greek text.

The text of the *Book of Enoch* first became widely and completely known with the recovery, publication and translation of its Ethiopic text in the late eighteenth and early nineteenth centuries by the English scholar, Richard Laurence. The book is replete with material for the understanding of Judaism. Among the Dead Sea Scrolls, fragments of ten or so manuscripts of the *Book of Enoch* were discovered and were recently published by their appointed editor, J. T. Milik. Much of interest is to be learned from these manuscripts. Of immediate significance here are their dates. The *Book of Enoch*, as it is preserved in Ethiopic, is a compendium of five separate writings. The first and third parts of it survive at Qumrân in manuscripts clearly dated in the late third or early second century B.C.E. on palaeographic grounds. They are not the authors' original autographs, but copies of them or copies of copies of them. Consequently, these two parts of the *Book of Enoch* must have been composed by the third century at the latest. Moreover, the first part of the *Book of Enoch*, the so-called *Book of the Watchers* (i.e. the fallen angels, Gen. 6:1–2) is a composite literary work whose author has taken advantage of sources he had before him. This can readily be discerned in the text of the book. It follows, of course, that these sources which are already combined in our oldest manuscript must be even earlier.

From this it also follows that these parts of the *Book of Enoch* are the oldest surviving Jewish documents of religious character outside the Bible. They are the chief evidence we now possess for Judaism in the third century B.C.E., and they were written well before the Maccabean revolt. Their importance is manifold, and some aspects of it will be explored.

What do these documents, then, contain? The *Book of the Watchers* contains various sorts of information. At its heart is the story of the fallen angels, the "sons of God" of Gen. 6:1–2, who sinned with the daughters of men; the secret information which they revealed to women; and the corruption which their bastard offspring of giants brought about. This story had wide circulation in connection with Enoch and Noah, and it recurs elsewhere in the literature associated with Enoch. It is also found in the *Book of Jubilees* (an early second-century B.C.E. composition) and other later sources. This body of legend served various purposes. One was etiological—it dealt with the origins of evil, of various forbidden teachings, of demons (the spirits of the giants who drowned in the Flood), of illness (*Jub.* 10:1–15), and more. It most probably also preserved ancient mythological traditions of a "Prometheus" or culture-hero type, and also of a heavenly revolt.

The *Book of the Watchers* reports the ascent of Enoch to the heavenly realm and his experiences there. He reaches the presence of God and witnesses the steps taken by him against the Watchers and their offspring. This section of the book is important since it is the oldest Jewish ascent vision. The Hebrew Bible records various types of religious experience such as visions, dreams, bodily transportations, auditions and others. It does not contain any visions relating in detail the ascent of the recipient of the vision to the heavens, a type of experience which was widespread in a number of surrounding cultures. This absence of the ascent vision has been attributed to the fact that the view of man in the Hebrew Bible does not distinguish between body and soul in such a way as to set them in opposition or contrast, or even to regard the soul as the essential part of man. This distinction was known to the Greeks from the sixth or fifth centuries B.C.E. on, and was particularly current in the Hellenistic age. Admittedly, we have ascent visions recorded (in later texts) in which it is not clear whether the ascent was in the body or not in the body (compare Paul's words in 2 Cor. 12:2–3). Nonetheless, it seems notable that this type of religious experience should start to appear in Jewish texts in an age when the idea of the separable soul had considerable currency. Thus, the ascent vision of Enoch represents the first occurrence of a type of religious experience which became very prevalent in later times. It also seems to mark a change in the view of man which was to have very considerable repercussions.

In this vision there is a description of the divine palace, the heavenly environs of God, through which the visionary ascends. The experience peaks in the vision of the Throne of God and in the revelation which Enoch receives there. The oldest Jewish mystical texts are called the *Merkabah* or "Chariot" texts. The term "Chariot" was the name given to the winged throne of God, described by the prophet Ezekiel (Ezekiel 1). Indeed, as was pointed out some decades ago, the "Chariot" texts employ a very distinctive technical terminology to describe the environs of God. This terminology derives from the first chapter of the Book of Ezekiel, and the speculation based on that chapter was a constitutive element of this oldest type of Jewish mystical writing.

The "Chariot" mystical books have been dated to the middle of the first millennium C.E., the later Talmudic period. G. G. Scholem demonstrated that this terminological tradition could be traced back into early rabbinic sources, and into still earlier works dated in the late pre-Christian period. Fragments of a writing entitled the *Angelic Liturgy* from among the Dead Sea Scrolls showed that this same terminological tradition was known in the circles which produced the Scrolls. It is also found to exist in a developed form in chapter 14 of the *Book of Enoch*, part of the *Book of the Watchers*. This means that it was not just the idea of a heavenly ascent which was well developed by the time that this part of the *Book of Enoch* was written, in the third century B.C.E. at the latest. It also demonstrates the antiquity of the tradition of speculation upon the Chariot vision of Ezekiel as the mode by which the heavenly realm is to be described and which was already well formulated by the third century B.C.E., many years before anyone thought that it could have happened.

It is quite important to be clear that this does not mean that mysticism was practised in Jewish circles in the third century B.C.E. The ascent vision and the terminology for the description of the heavenly realm are shared by the *Book of Enoch*, chapter 14, and by the "Chariot" mystical texts. The end or purpose of the ascent differs. One great authority has described the purpose of ascent in the "Chariot" books as the "perception of (God's) appearance on the Throne, as described by Ezekiel, and the cognition of the mysteries of the celestial throne world" (Scholem, *Major Trends*, 44). In Enoch's case, however, the purpose of the ascent is the revelation of certain matters having to do first and foremost with the Watchers and their fate.

The biblical writings do not exhibit any interest in the technical description of the environs of the Godhead as seen by a visionary. This sort of interest was already well developed, however, by the third century, a fact which casts a rather unexpected light into the gloom of those dark centuries. The Bible does show some interest, however, in the associated matter of angelology, and peripherally in demonology. In the *Book of Enoch* these spirit realms are well represented. The archangels are known by name, and are very active, while the origins and functions of demons are much discussed.

Following the vision of the divine Throne and the punishment of the Watchers, Enoch is taken on two "guided tours." First, he sees visions of the underworld, the secrets of meteorology, the place of the fallen angels and their punishment and, finally, the names of the archangels and their tasks (chapters 17—20). On his second journey, he sees again the places where the angels are punished, Sheol and sundry distant places, parts of the mythological geography of earth, with special emphasis on their meteorological and astronomical features (chapters 26—36). From this material, the range of interests of the *Book of the Watchers* is evident. There is also some eschatological interest, particularly in chapters 1—6 and 10:14–16; this latter section, however, is not truly eschatological, for it describes events which will take place before the flood. Furthermore, these chapters contain the oldest known fragments of Jewish biblical exegesis. But it is the range of scientific (or, better, "pseudo-scientific") material in them that is astounding, and the impression made by it is reinforced by the contents of the other Enochic writing which stems from the third century, the *Astronomical Book*. In this writing, which was about twice as long in its Aramaic form (unfortunately mostly lost) as in its Ethiopic version, the sort of "learned" information referred to above abounds. It is full of astronomy and meteorology and calendary lore. The whole of the *Astronomical Book* is in the form of a heavenly journey upon which Enoch embarks under the tutelage of the archangel Uriel.

From these two writings, it is clear that there existed in the third century B.C.E. broad areas of speculation of a pseudoscientific kind in Judah and in Jewish circles. That they originate in Judah, in Jewish circles, is the most likely view; a Samaritan origin seems unlikely. Considered thus, these documents are quite surprising. The picture of a rather sophisticated and rich realm of speculation and "sacred science" within Judaism, the highly developed ascent vision and the broad interest in "scientific" matters are totally unexpected. Moreover, the documents in which these interests are presented are apocalypses. The new publications of the manuscripts of the *Book of Enoch*, then, force us to a reassessment of the complexion of third century Judaism and of the origins of apocalyptic literature. The origins of apocalyptic literature have been to the fore of scholarly debate in recent years. These parts of the *Book of Enoch* are the oldest surviving apocalypses. They antedate the apocalyptic parts of the Book of Daniel by half a century at least, and their evidence must be brought into account in any assessment of the development of apocalyptic literature.

5

*Enoch and Apocalyptic Origins**

MICHAEL E. STONE

In the last chapter we looked at the nature and character of Judaism in the third century B.C.E. as illuminated by the recently published manuscripts from among the Dead Sea Scrolls. The range of interests thus uncovered will probably be broadened and deepened as further manuscripts from Qumran are published. It seems very likely that the Aramaic *Testament of Levi* also stems from the third century, and perhaps other works will be added to this corpus as scholarship advances. The *Testament of Levi*, purporting to be the last will and testament of Jacob's son, is known in Aramaic from fragmentary manuscripts found in the famous Cairo Geniza. The Geniza was a repository for old books, papers and letters which was found in a synagogue in Cairo at the end of the last century. It contained an incomparable collection of thousands of fragments of Jewish writings from the Middle Ages.

A number of manuscripts from the Geniza have been identified as containing writings from a sectarian library like that of Qumran. It seems most likely that a mediaeval discovery of some Dead Sea Scrolls was made and that copies of writings from this find eventually made their way into the Geniza. These include the *Damascus Document* (a clearly sectarian work) and most probably the Hebrew fragments of Ben Sira (Ecclesiasticus) and the Aramaic *Testament of Levi*. A Greek translation of some parts of this last writing is known, and a number of fragmentary Aramaic manuscripts of it have turned up at Qumran. It, or a closely affiliated writing, must have been one of the sources of the *Book of Jubilees*, and also of the Greek *Testament of Levi* (a different work), which is included in the Greek writing called the *Testaments of the Twelve Patriarchs*.

The Aramaic *Testament of Levi*, then, only exists in fragments. It is instructive for the character of very ancient Jewish biblical exegesis. It also contains long and detailed instructions, supposedly given by Abraham to Isaac and transmitted to Levi. These instruc-

* First published in *Scriptures, Sects, and Visions* by M. E. Stone (1980) 37–47.

92

tions deal with a sacrificial cult which these patriarchs supposedly conducted. In a great many of their details these instructions differ from everything else known of Jewish sacrificial law. They also show some otherwise unknown material of botanical character, here related to the types of wood which are to be used for the fire upon the altar. This document also presents some Messianic expectations, all concentrated on a descendant of Levi who is expected at the end. It is written, like the manuscripts of the *Book of Enoch*, in the literary Aramaic of the age and, incidentally, contains what is probably the most ancient Aramaic poetry known.

The Aramaic *Testament of Levi* is not as firmly dated to the third century B.C.E., however, as are the manuscripts of the *Book of Enoch*. These are clearly third century, a dating established first and foremost by the palaeographic dating of their script; it may be that once the Aramaic *Testament of Levi* manuscripts are published in full, we will be able to date it with greater precision. But, even basing observations only on the manuscripts of the *Book of Enoch*, one must raise certain issues relating to the character of Judaism in earlier ages. For these, only the biblical sources survive, and their purpose or intent is certainly not to give a sampling of all types of Jewish culture and learning, but rather to promote or preserve certain very specific types of tradition and teaching. An example of a case where it may be possible to penetrate beyond the biblical text is in the Bible's representation of the figure of Enoch.

Enoch is first introduced by a few verses in the Book of Genesis (Gen. 5:21–24). He then reappears in a series of sources, mostly written from the second century B.C.E. onwards. It had been an open question whether the figure of Enoch as found in the sources from the early second century on was to be seen as a development of that age. Some scholars, pointing to the fact that Enoch is seventh from Adam, and that in Mesopotamian tradition the seventh antediluvian king was a wisdom figure, sought the origins of the traditions about Enoch in Mesopotamia. Indeed, there is an accumulation of new and older evidence which makes it appear quite probable that the scientific and learned traditions, with which we know that Enoch was associated at least from the third century, have strong Mesopotamian connections.

Two independent studies of the Mesopotamian sources suggest that an extensive tradition of learning was attached to Enoch because he was patterned after certain mythological Mesopotamian wisdom figures. Other scholars have commented that the scientific theories of the *Astronomical Book* were of Mesopotamian character and show no influence of the much more advanced Greek science of the

Hellenistic age. These observations, incidentally, were based solely on the Ethiopic text of the *Astronomical Book*. Now that the more ancient, longer Aramaic form of the book is partly available, a renewed examination of this matter seems called for. The *Book of the Watchers* assumes a particular mythological map of the world, over which Enoch travels, particularly in the second of his two journeys. This map of the world is most closely related to Mesopotamian geographic conceptions. At a different level of discussion, the *Book of the Giants*, another of the Enochic writings from Qumran, mentions Mesopotamian mythological personalities, including Gilgamesh.

All of this indicates that the learned tradition nurtured in certain Jewish circles by the third century B.C.E., if not rather earlier, was largely Mesopotamian in character, although expressed in our sources in Aramaic. It was associated with Enoch, who was already mentioned in the Bible, yet it seems abundantly clear that the figure of Enoch as he appears in the later sources is not just an exegetical development of Gen. 5:21–24. The growth of the figure of Enoch must be tied to the learned tradition of the age. It remains an open question whether this presentation of Enoch was itself a development of that tradition about him hinted at by the author of Genesis 5, some centuries earlier, rather than of Genesis itself. If due weight is given to the Mesopotamian evidence, this is not unlikely.

Another interesting parallel to the development of the Enoch figure is that of Daniel. The Book of Daniel is composed of two parts. The stories (chapters 1—6) were written by the third century at the latest, while the visions (chapters 7—12) come from the time of the Maccabean revolt (after 168 B.C.E.). Daniel is the purported author of the book, which is set in the time of the Babylonian and Persian monarchies. Yet the selection of this particular pseudepigraphic author is strange, for the Daniel figure of the Book of Daniel has no obvious antecedent in other biblical literature. The identity of the Moses of a Moses pseudepigraphon, or of an Elijah, or an Ezra, in the books attached to them, was clear, but who was Daniel?

Among the Dead Sea Scrolls tiny fragments of one work (and perhaps more) attributed to Daniel have turned up. They seem to be similar in character to the biblical book, but not identical with it. Again, the Greek translations of Daniel contain some stories not to be found in the form of the book which is preserved in the Hebrew Bible. These compositions were not necessarily (and not even probably) written under the inspiration of the canonical Book of Daniel. Instead, they show that the Book of Daniel was part of a wider literature whose hero or pseudepigraphic author was Daniel. So the question of his identity becomes even more intriguing. There was a mythological Canaanite wise man called Dan'il, mentioned in second-millennium Ugaritic epics and by the Book of Ezekiel, but his relationship to the Daniel of the biblical and apocryphal sources is tenuous. The *Book of Jubilees*, interestingly enough, knows Dan'il as Enoch's father-in-law.

Here, then, are two figures, Enoch and Daniel, who may have roots going back into mythological antiquity, and both of whom seem to reach special development in the late Persian or early Hellenistic periods. Both have wisdom dimensions, both reveal divine secrets and witness to the truth of the God of Israel. The parallel between them is quite striking. These developments of the pre-Maccabean age must come into account in re-exploring "dark ages" of post-exilic Judaism.

As a conclusion to this part of the discussion, it may be noticed that the development of a learned literature associated with a figure out of the ancient or mythological past is not limited to the Jewish sphere during the Hellenistic period. The Egyptian god of wisdom, Thoth, was identified with the Greek god Hermes, and a large literature of secret and revealed teaching was attributed to him. Similar, it appears, was the Phoenician god Taautos (see Eusebius, *Praeparatio evangelium* 1:9) who derived from Egyptian Thoth.

The publication of the new fragments of the *Book of Enoch*, then, serves to illustrate dramatically how dependent we are on the sources which have survived for our historical reconstructions, and how the character of these sources affects our reconstructions. The origins of the apocalyptic literature are not merely thrown back half a century or more as a result of these new data; the very character and context of its development must now be reassessed. Scholarly work in recent years has concentrated on the questions of the origins of apocalyptic eschatology, and on tracing its development from the future hope of the prophets. This particular issue has been at the centre of scholarly interest because of its importance for the study of Christianity and particularly of the New Testament, not for the study of the apocalypses.

The change from older forms of future hope into apocalyptic eschatology has been seen to result from the conflict between the groups in society which bore and nurtured the future hope of the prophets, and their environment. The new manuscripts of the *Book of Enoch* do not contradict this view; they are, however, the oldest existing Jewish apocalypses and the weight of their central interests lies elsewhere, not in the eschatological at all.

Some years ago, study of certain texts led me to maintain that the speculative interests are one of the core elements of the apocalypses. By the term "speculative interests" are intended such matters as cosmology, astronomy, calendar and so forth. Some scholars have suggested that a particular connection exists between the apocalyptic literature and that type of biblical and apocryphal literature called "wisdom literature." The wisdom literature comprises such books as Proverbs and Ecclesiastes, Ben Sira and the Wisdom of Solomon. In spite of the suggestive character of the term "wisdom literature," however, if in fact the preserved wisdom books are representative of the interests and concerns of the circles that produced them, then they were not particularly interested in these speculative matters. Now, the antiquity of the first and third parts of the *Book of Enoch* means that by the third century B.C.E. at the latest this speculative learning existed in Jewish circles; yet it seems amply clear that such interests as these were beyond the pale for the transmitters of biblical literature. The Book of Daniel, unique among the apocalypses for its lack of interest in such matters, is ample evidence of this; it is the only apocalypse that was accepted into the Bible. From this it seems to follow that to trace the eschatological axis as the chief one along which apocalyptic literature developed is to lay upon the evidence the same censorial rules as did the biblical editors themselves.

Instead, from consideration of the simple fact of the palaeographic dating of the Qumrân manuscripts of the *Book of Enoch* to the late third and early second centuries B.C.E., it can be inferred that this realm of speculative interest was much cultivated in pre-Maccabean Judea. Moreover, such speculations had reached a level of development such as to be embodied in the complex written form of the two oldest parts of the *Book of Enoch*. Furthermore, in the century after Alexander, this type of knowledge was still permeated by the learned tradition of Mesopotamia as its astronomical and geographical views indicate. Suddenly, a quite unexpected dimension of the intellectual world of Judaism in the third (and perhaps the fourth) century B.C.E. is unveiled. How does this fit into the pictures that have been drawn in recent years of the social and religious organization of the Jewish people at that time? How does it affect our understanding of the development of Judaism and Jewish religious literature?

None of the recent attempts to reconstruct a picture of third-century Judaism has taken this element into account. Generally, these attempts have tried to discern polemical tones in the literary remains or else have focussed on conflicts which were known to exist from the surviving historical sources. Attempts to write social and

political history have been made by assuming that polemics or conflicts imply the existence of groups that carried them on. The conflicts
that have been isolated as the basis for projecting the existence of
such differing groups within the Jewish people have focussed on two
issues – the nature of eschatological hope and assimilation or syncretism. The latter interest is clearly determined and, to a large extent
justifiably, by the events of the early second century which climaxed
in the Maccabean revolt (see above, chapter 4). The former, like
the attempt to describe apocalyptic literature in terms of eschatology
alone, is determined in part by the interests of the authors of the
biblical books and those who transmitted them. These gave the
biblical text its particular emphases and content. Since the Bible very
often plays a central role in the thinking of scholars of Judaism and
early Christianity, the complexion laid upon it by those who transmitted it led to the interest in certain matters and lack of interest
in others. The speculative and pseudoscientific matters are not
present in the Bible. They are new in the post-biblical sources. They
are almost completely absent from the New Testament. For these
reasons in the history of scholarship scarcely any serious attempt
has been made to understand this material and to study its role in
the Judaism of its day.

It is quite evident, then, that groupings like pietistic and Hellenizing Jews could scarcely have exhausted the types of groups and
trends in third-century Judaism. The conservative piety of a Ben
Sira must have had a place in it, just as did the speculations embodied
in the *Book of Enoch*. The circles which cultivated the latter must
have been well learned; they may also have had connections with
the traditional intellectual groups – the wise and the priests. Enoch
is patterned, after all, in the type of a wise man; indeed, he is the
founder of wisdom. A priestly connection may be suggested by the
interest in calendar, and astronomy. In the later Dead Sea sect, for
example, the interest in these matters was related to the calculation
of the sacred calendar and the service of the priestly courses in the
Temple. Such observations as these, however, remain purely speculative; there is no firm evidence for identifying the groups and circles
which nurtured these speculations.

As mentioned, their character as visions is central to the apocalypses. This feature, more than any other, appeared to speak for
the origins of apocalyptic literature lying within the prophetic
tradition. Certainly by the time of Zechariah, if not substantially
by that of Ezekiel, most of the elements distinctive of the literary
form of the apocalypse are to be found in prophetic writing. In many
ways the travels of Enoch described in the *Book of the Watchers*

are close to Ezekiel chapters 40—48, being this prophet's view of the ideal Jerusalem. This brings to mind another priestly connection – speculation about heavenly things is ancient when these things are related to the idea of the heavenly pattern of the Temple and its furnishings. This is clearly indicated already in Exodus and 2 Chronicles and the idea that the earthly Temple is patterned after the heavenly one has ancient, mythological roots. Now, however, in light of the new manuscripts and their date, the view that either the form or content of the apocalypses originated exclusively or predominantly from prophecy may well be strained.

In general, there seems no reason to think that the collection of literature transmitted in the Hebrew Bible represents all the types of Jewish literary creativity down to the third century B.C.E. Instead, it is a selection of texts, and that selection primarily reflects the judgement of certain groups in Jerusalem before and after the Babylonian exile. It seems specious, therefore, to seek the full explanation of a third- or second-century phenomenon from roots to be discerned in the Bible and, if such cannot be located, immediately to attribute it to foreign influence. Other circles than those responsible for the winnowing of biblical literature must have existed; the oldest extra-biblical books teach us that some of these were deeply involved in ascent vision activity and speculative sacred sciences. Such speculations had already taken on a sophisticated written form by the third century at the latest.

It had been observed in the past that those sections of the Bible which have closest relationship in form to the apocalypses show little contact with them in their eschatological type of content (e.g. Ezekiel 40—48; Zechariah 1—4; Ezekiel 16, 17, 19): on the other hand, those texts in which the development of apocalyptic eschatology can be traced seem to lack the formal elements of the apocalypses (e.g. Isaiah 24—27; Ezekiel 38—39; Isaiah 40—66; Zechariah 9—14). Could it be that formal elements of the apocalypses, which occur in full development in the *Book of the Watchers* and the *Astronomical Book*, were endowed with a heightened or almost exclusively eschatological content in response to the crisis brought about by the Antiochean persecution? The older parts of the *Book of Enoch* show some eschatological interest, but also exhibit a broad range of other concerns. It is the eschatological content that comes to play a central role in such writings as Daniel, the *Testament of Moses* and the *Dream Visions of Enoch*, which arose on exactly this background. We know of profound changes in eschatological views which came about at the same time.

The origins of the speculative material which plays such a large part in the oldest apocalypses is itself the subject of some speculation. It is certainly complex. A number of lines of development led into it, but at present it is difficult to make any final determination as to their exact interrelationship. The Mesopotamian affinities of some of this material, including the astronomical and geographical, seem indubitable. Most recently the possibility has been raised that the apocalypses drew, in this respect, particularly on the widespread mantic or oracular wisdom of ancient Mesopotamia. This was a tradition of learning associated with a particular class of wise men. Its chief subject was the interpretation of dreams and omens, and some associated matters. This sort of context seems particularly helpful when we come to study a figure like Daniel. Astronomy was subordinated to astrology, too, in Mesopotamia, and the Mesopotamian character of the astronomical lore of the *Book of Enoch* has been remarked upon.

Another possible tributary feeding into this stream is the priestly interest in the sacred calendar and the heavenly Temple. Yet a third point of view, less soundly based, points to the Israelite schools of didactic wisdom. The difficulty with this is that there is no evidence that these were concerned with the sort of speculative material being discussed here. Whatever the sources be, one thing is clear; no tradition, literary type or specific group can be identified in the biblical sources, which fostered this type of speculative wisdom. It does not necessarily follow that this sort of interest was imported from abroad into third-century Judaism. If there were foreign elements in it, it is still difficult to tell how long they had been there before this material finally surfaced in the preserved sources.

In any case, an additional stage in the development of the apocalyptic literature can now be traced. The biblical material which is analogous to the apocalypses may now be termed (with the exception of Daniel) "proto-apocalyptic." A new type of speculative apocalyptic writing is around in the third century, and it does not seem to be directly dependent on the biblical "proto-apocalyptic" texts. This body of material contained some eschatological teachings, but much other material as well. Those apocalypses which stem from the time of the Antiochean persecution and the Maccabean revolt show the schematizations of history and the shift of eschatological belief to that which will henceforth typify this literature. Certain apocalypses which are difficult to date, but which probably stem from the time before the destruction of the Second Temple in the year 70 C.E., are now more easily understood, since they have much more of the speculative material in them than do the works of the time of the Maccabean uprising. In them an old interest of the apocalypses is again to the fore. A final body of writings stemming from the period after the destruction of the Second Temple form a separate, distinct type, distinguished by their preoccupation with the problem of theodicy, formulated in highly theological terms. Their central concern is to understand how God's justice evinces itself in the world, particularly in view of the destruction of Jerusalem and of the Temple.

6

*Wisdom and Apocalyptic**

JONATHAN Z. SMITH

One of the more vexing problems in contemporary biblical scholarship is that of determining the relationship between Wisdom and
Apocalypticism. It is my hope that in this essay, writing as a historian
of religions, I shall raise a set of questions which stem from presuppositions different from those frequently employed by specialists
in biblical research, and shall utilize as evidence a wider range of
materials than those usually considered and thus achieve some
modest progress towards a resolution of this problem. Therefore I
shall not confine myself to questions such as the mythology of the
figure of Wisdom in apocalyptic literature or the relationship of
wisdom in apocalyptic literature or the relationship of wisdom and
apocalyptic literature to prophecy; rather, I shall take a more
oblique approach and focus on materials removed from a Jewish
or Christian provenance. I do so partly because I believe that such
an examination may raise new questions and categories for further
research and partly because of my own presuppositions as to the
international character of many religious phenomena (including
wisdom and apocalypticism) in the period of late Antiquity.[1] I
should like to join with Hans Dieter Betz in arguing that "Jewish and,
subsequently, Christian apocalypticism as well, cannot be understood from themselves or from the OT alone, but must be seen and
presented as peculiar expressions within the entire development of
Hellenistic syncretism;"[2] although I differ from Betz in largely
rejecting the explanatory utility of the concept of syncretism and by
emphasizing the continuity of Hellenistic religious forms with the
archaic.[3]

  I agree with Betz and von Rad that apocalypticism cannot be
reduced to a mere catalogue of elements such as secret or heavenly
books, journeys to heaven by a sage, etc., as these motifs can be
found within the archaic religions of the Near East and are typical
of all modes of Hellenistic religiosity.[4] What I should like to explore

* First published in *Religious Syncretism in Antiquity*, ed. B. A. Pearson (1975) 131–56.

101

in this paper is the pattern of these elements in combination and their underlying social structure in the apocalyptic literature of late Antiquity.

I BABYLONIA

A valuable starting point for our inquiry may be gained by a consideration of the fragments from the *Babyloniaka* of Berossus.[5] A priest of Marduk in Babylon, he wrote his book c. 290–280 B.C. and dedicated it to Antiochus I, Sotēr.

The *testimonia* concerning Berossus divide into two categories. From Greco-Roman authors we learn that he was an astronomer, astrologer (Vitruvius, *De arch.* 9.6.2; Pliny, *N.H.* 7.123) and an apocalyptist related to the Babylonian Sibyl (Pausanias, 10.12.9; the *Suda*, s.v. *Sibulla Delphis*; cf. Moses Chorene, *Hist. armen* 1.6). From Jewish and Christian sources, we learn that he was a mythographer and historian (Josephus and Eusebius, both apparently dependent upon the excerpts from Berossus by Alexander Polyhistor). While these two types of *testimonia* clearly value different aspects of Berossus and put him to different uses, *taken as a whole* they reveal an overall pattern familiar to us from apocalypticism: a history of the cosmos and a people from creation to final catastrophe which is dominated by astrological determinism.

It is tempting to begin our consideration of Berossus by exploring the relationship between him and the Babylonian Sibyl, and the Babylonian Sibyl's relationship to the Jewish *Sibyllines*, especially with respect to the redaction of *Oracula Sibyllina* III:97–154, 809–29. But the tradition is extremely obscure, as witnessed by its oldest testimony in Pausanias: "The Hebrews who lived beyond Palestine had a prophetess called Sabbē (more recently corrected to Sambēthē or Sambathis) whose father they say was Berossus and mother Erymanthē; but some say she was a Babylonian Sibyl and others an Egyptian" (10.12.9; cf. pseudo-Justin, *Cohor. ad Graecos*, 37.3).[6] Barring further clarification on this point, I propose instead merely to refer to some elements in Berossus, setting aside the more usual questions as to the historical accuracy of the traditions he transmits.[7]

The *Babyloniaka* describes the history of the world from its creation to its final destruction and offers a periodization of the history of Babylonia which stretches in between.[8] In the former, Berossos draws upon a learned mythic tradition; in the latter, upon an equally learned chronicle tradition. A number of details are of interest as paralleling motifs in apocalyptic literature: the tradition of the antediluvian books of Oannes (F1) (Jacoby) and the hidden

102

books of Xisuthrus (F4) which contain cosmogonical and flood traditions clearly related to those represented by the *Atrahasis* epic, *Enuma elish* and *Gilgamesh*;[9] the correlation of the rule of foreign kings with the rise of idolatry and religious desecration (F11), etc. In the key apocalyptic fragment which has survived (F21), the beginning and the end are clearly correlated. All things will be consumed by fire and the world will be flooded and return to the watery chaos that existed in the beginning.[10]

What is of importance for us with respect to this book, which might be described as "proto-apocalyptic," is not an argument as to the nature of the work and the erection of some pan-Babylonian theory of the origins of apocalypticism[11] but an argument as to the nature of its author. Berossus was a learned Babylonian priest during the Seleucid period at a time when the Babylonian "schools" were world famous and the major activities of a Babylonian intellectual were astronomy, astrology, mathematics, historiography and the recovery of archaic ritual lore. These Babylonian intellectuals, for all the novelty of their speculation which would culminate in the rich literature of Greco-Egyptian astronomy and astrology and the rich philosophic school of Stoicism, stood in continuity with ancient Babylonian scribalism, an unbroken tradition from the Sumerian period to the sages of the Babylonian Talmud. It is to this scribalism that Berossus directs us for our first clue as to the interrelationship of wisdom and apocalyptic.

Scribalism an unbroken tradition

The scribes were an elite group of learned, literate men, an intellectual aristocracy which played an invaluable role in the administration of their people in both religious and political affairs. They were dedicated to a variety of roles: guardians of their cultural heritage, intellectual innovators, world travellers who brought about a cross-cultural flow of wisdom, lawyers, doctors, astrologers, diviners, magicians, scientists, court functionaries, linguists, exegetes, etc. Their greatest love was the study of themselves, and they guarded and transmitted their teaching, wrote biographies and hagiographies of their lives and their ancestral prototypes, preserved and annotated one another's labours. They projected their scribal activities on high, on a god who created by law according to a written plan, on a god who was a teacher in his heavenly court. They hypostatized the scribe and scribal activities in the figure of Divine Wisdom. They speculated about hidden heavenly tablets, about creation by divine word, about the beginning and the end and thereby claimed to possess the secrets of creation. Above all, they talked, they memorized and remembered, they wrote.

SCRIBES

The essence of scribal knowledge was its character as *Listen-*

Jonathan Z. Smith

wissenschaft, to use A. Alt's useful term.[12] It depends upon catalogues and classification; it progresses by establishing precedents, by observing patterns, similarities and conjunctions and by noting their repetitions. As such their basic faith was in the relevance of a limited number of paradigms to every new situation. Their goal – whether the scribe be called *dubshar, sopher*, "Chaldean" or *rabbi* – was nothing less than absolute perfection, the inclusion of everything within their categories. In the quest of this perfection, they developed complex hermeneutic and exegetical techniques to bridge the gap between paradigm and particular instance, between past and present.

This faith of the scribe may be most clearly seen in the great Babylonian omen series which are the major intellectual achievement of archaic Babylonia.[13] It permeates every other genre of literature as well, including the historigraphic. (Let me note as an aside that I have no intention of opening the old question of Ancient Near Eastern cyclical, mythic thought versus Israelitic linear, historical thought. Recent research by Gese, Goossens, Albrektson, Barr and others have demonstrated that the two are thoroughly comparable and that the dichotomy, linear-cyclical, is inadequate.)[14] For the scribe, if events have significance largely in terms of their precedent, then the same text may be used to describe two widely separated historical events so long as their pattern, their "value" was perceived to be the same. For example, one of the great monuments of Sumerian literary composition is the "Lament over the Destruction of Sumer and Ur," a work composed c. 2100 B.C. bewailing the invasion of the Guti in 2500 B.C.

> For the misfortunes of Uruk, for the misfortunes of Agade, I am stricken.
> The Lady of Uruk wept, that departed was her might.
> The Lady of Agade wept, that departed was her glory ...
> Weep for Uruk, ravaging and shame has she received ...
> The throne of thy glory has been caused to pass away from me.
> The bridegroom, the husband of my well being, Marduk,
> has been taken away from me.

The same text was recopied in 287–286 B.C. bewailing the destructive acts of the Hellenistic monarch, Antigonus.[15] The same text is, at one and the same time, a Sumerian "original" religious expression and a Hellenistic Babylonian "original" religious expression. (The notion of "late copy" must be abandoned in such instances.) The Guti invasion provided a pattern for interpreting all acts of foreign invasion and domination in Babylonia in the same way as the Hyksos invasion provided a pattern for the Egyptian.

This paradigmatic (or, if you prefer, typological) ideology leads

104

to what I would term an *apocalyptic situation*, though not necessarily to apocalyptic literature. While many examples may be furnished from the so-called historical omens and from the various patterns in historiographic literature,[16] I prefer to call attention to a better known example – the Babylonian *Akitu* festival and its relation to the creation epic, *Enuma elish*.

As *Enuma elish* has been dated by some as early as 1600 B.C. (although a date around 1200 B.C. is more likely) and as there are early mentions of *Akitu* festivals, it has been almost universally assumed that the New Year festival which we reconstruct from Akkadian texts with its reading of *Enuma elish* and its ritual humiliation of the king is equally archaic (even though the ritual events in no way resemble the events described in the myth). It has rarely been observed that the Akkadian ritual texts, on which the Myth-Ritual School based their pattern of a Dying-Rising God and a Dying-Rising King (a pattern which, in fact, never existed in the Near East with the possible, but doubtful, exception of Dumuzi)[17] are not from the archaic period. Rather, they are Hellenistic Babylonian documents written during the period of Seleucid domination. They are clear witness to Hellenistic Babylonian religiosity and only possibly witness to earlier practice. The Hellenistic Babylonian New Year festival is either a repetition of an earlier ritual typologically understood to describe the current situation of foreign domination, to have contemporary political as well as religious implications; or the text is a new, Hellenistic composition.

The ritual text begins by reminding the Lord Marduk of his protection of his sacred city and prays that he may return to his city and "establish the liberty of the peoples of Babylon." The priest then prays: "To your city, Babylon, grant release." It is impossible not to read contemporary nationalistic propaganda here – whatever may have been the original ritualistic understanding of the phrases. The king is then "dragged by the ears" before the statue of Marduk by the priest, struck on the cheek and stripped of his royal garments. He then offers a negative confession to the deity ("I have not sinned . . .") and his insignia are restored. Is this the "ritual slaying" of a pious Babylonian king, or is this a threat (if you prefer, a nationalistic phantasy) of what will happen to the impious, foreign, Seleucid monarch? The confession of the king is decisive:

> I was not neglectful of the requirements of your lordship,
> I did not destroy Babylon;
> I did not command its overthrow.
> I [did not destroy] the temple Esagila,

I did not forget its rites ...
[I watched over] Babylon,
I did not smash its walls.

What native Babylonian king ever did? These were all acts committed by foreign rulers: during the period of Assyrian domination from 1360–1200 and 1116–990, under Sennacharib in 689, under Xerxes in 480–476 and finally under Antigonus in 316. As with Cyrus among the Israelites (whose promise to rebuild Jerusalem and its Temple concludes the Jewish version of the Hebrew Scriptures, 2 Chr. 36:23) so too for the Babylonians – foreign kings could be pointed to who restored Esagila and Babylon: Tiglat Pileser III, Sargon II, Ashurbanipal, Nebuchadnezzar, Cyrus, Alexander, Seleukos I and Antiochus I and IV. The implication of the New Year's text is clear. If you act as the evil foreign kings have acted, you will be stripped of your kingship by the gods; if you act in the opposite manner, "the sceptre, and crown and the sword shall be restored to the king."[18]

This religious and nationalistic polemic is placed within a cosmic setting by the reading of *Enuma elish*. For this text is not simply a cosmogony. It is preeminently a myth of the creation of Marduk's city Babylon and his temple, Esagila. Originally composed during the first period of Assyrian domination it correlates Marduk's kingship with kingship in Babylon, the creation of the world with the building of Esagila. The opposite is likewise the case. Destroy Babylon or Esagila, neglect Marduk, and the world will be decreated, will return to its primeval watery chaos.

Examples such as this are what I have termed apocalyptic situations. All of the elements are present, but they have not yet been turned to the future orientation of apocalyptic literature. We may find the beginning of this turning in the proto-apocalyptic works of Hellenistic Babylonian authors such as Berossus and Abydenos.[19] But no native Babylonian apocalypse has survived.[20]

I would argue that wisdom and apocalyptic are related in that they are both essentially scribal phenomena. It is the paradigmatic thought of the scribe – a way of thinking that is both pragmatic and speculative – which has given rise to both. This initial perspective may be enlarged by examining Egyptian materials.

II EGYPT

Egypt presents us with a variety of phenomena analogous to those in Babylonia. It is essentially a scribal culture dominated by *Listen-*

wissenschaft.[21] It has a learned historicistic tradition which, when paraphrased into Greek, may be described as proto-apocalyptic (e.g. Manetho).[22] It employs the paradigm of the Hyksos invasion, not only to interpret all acts of invasion and foreign domination, but also in apocalyptic materials.[23] Indeed, it uses this material in a thoroughly mythic fashion by identifying the Hyksos with the deity of confusion and chaos, Seth.[24] It has ritual texts written in a deliberately archaic style which parallel the apocalyptic situation described with respect to the *Akitu* festival (e.g. the *Book of Overthrowing Apophis* in P. Bremmer-Rhind dated 310 B.C.).[25] However, in contradistinction to Babylonia, we have a variety of full-blown apocalypses from Egypt, spanning a period of almost two millennia.[26] Thus it is possible, in the case of Egypt, to investigate not only the apocalyptic form but also the process of apocalypticization.

The materials available for analysis range from the hieratic apocalypse of Neferti (c.1900 B.C.)[27] through demotic texts such as the so-called *Demotic Chronicle* (second century B.C.)[28] and the *Curse of the Lamb* (beginning of the first century A.D.)[29] to first-century Greek materials such as the *Potter's Oracle*,[30] the apocalypse preserved in *Asclepius* (IX) 24–26 (now recovered in a Coptic recension from Nag Hammadi)[31] as well as the older Ptolemaic materials recoverable from the *Sibylline Oracles* III:350–61, 367–80 (cf. III:46–54, 75–92; V:512–32; XI:245–314).[32] In spite of the chronological range of some two thousand years which separate these texts, their varying language and situation, it is possible to construct a model Egyptian apocalypse by comparing these various documents.

(A) (1) The prophet came before the king and proclaimed to him all that he had asked concerning that which was to come. (2) And these are the words which he spoke on that occasion.

(B) (3) Behold the people are in confusion because there is disorder in the land. (4) Social relations have become reversed. (5) Religious obligations are ignored. (6) The natural cycle is overthrown. (7) Foreigners have appeared and are acting as if they were Egyptians. (8) The whole world is upside down, even the gods are affected. (9) The gods have abandoned Egypt. (10) The land of life has become a land of death.

(C) (11) But then shall come forth a great king sent by the gods. (12) The foreigners shall be driven out. (13) All relations will be restored. (14) All that is good will return to the people, the land and the gods and Egypt will again be a land of life.

(D) (15) Thus the prophet finished speaking before the king and was greatly renowned for the wisdom which he had spoken.

The overall structure is basically that of *Heils- und Unheilsescha-*

tologie which shifts between a present and future set of woes and a future promise. There is an introduction (A) which serves as a narrative framework for the prophecy, usually an encounter between prophet and king. (B) The woes are perceived as a set of reverses affecting the people (3–5), the cosmos (6, 8, 10) and the gods (8–9) – the cause being identified as the intrusion of foreigners (7) who are homologized to the Hyksos pattern and interpreted in a mythical manner – parallel to the Old Testament's "enemies from the North."[33] This is followed by (C), a promise of restoration by a divine king (11) who will expel chaos, i.e., the foreigners (12), and restore good order (13–14) and (D) a narrative conclusion.

It would be tempting to study all of these texts in detail noting their kinship with archaic Egyptian cosmogonies and kinship ideologies. Of particular relevance to our theme are the close parallels between the "woes" in these texts and social teachings which may be found in the rich Egyptian prophetic[34] and wisdom[35] traditions. As "woes" they resemble materials in such well-known texts as *The Lamentations of Khakheperre-Soabe, The Admonitions of Ipu-Wer* and *The Dispute of a Man with his Ba* (esp. lines 103b–130a).[36] They reverse the instructions found in the widespread "Admonitions" and "Teachings" literature as well as in the well-known "Negative Confession" from the *Book of the Dead*, chapter 125 – a text which, by the way, was translated into Greek.[37] However, I should like to focus attention on another set of problems, in consonance with my suggestion as to the centrality of scribalism for an understanding of the relationship of Wisdom and Apocalyptic.

The paradigmatic concerns of the scribes, whether expressed in the interpretation of oracles and omens, in legal rulings, in the hermeneutics of sacred texts or in their other manifold functions, led to the development of complex exegetical techniques devoted to the task of discovering the ever-changing relevance of ancient precedents and archetypes. (These concerns also led, at times, to the fabrication of ancient precedents and archetypes.) These exegetical techniques were international, being diffused throughout scribal centres in the Eastern Mediterranean world.[38] Texts are used and reused, glossed, interpreted and reinterpreted in a continual process of "updating" the materials.

This process of "updating" was particularly acute in prophetic oracular and apocalyptic traditions with their ambiguous messages and unfulfilled predictions. The various techniques of interpretations have been well explored for Jewish apocalyptic literature.[39] Each one of these has clear Egyptian parallels which demand close comparative investigation. For example, the *pesher* technique em-

precedents
archetypes
paradigms

reuse; gloss; updating

Egyptian parallels to pesher

ployed in the Qumran materials (1QpHab, 1QpMic, 4QpNah, 4QpPs 37, 1QpPs 68, 1QpZeph, etc.) finds an almost exact counterpart in the exegetical procedures of the *Demotic Chronicle.*[40]

The clarification of this process of "updating" is more difficult for us to accomplish in the Egyptian materials than it is in the Jewish and Christian because, in most instances, we do not have the various recensions of a tradition to compare (e.g. 4 Ezra 12 with Daniel 7). In the main we must rest content with the analysis of isolated motifs such as Hans Dieter Betz's intricate and convincing discussion of the tradition of the elements addressing the creator deity with prayer.[41] However there is one Egyptian text, the "Potter's Oracle" as interpreted in the pioneering researches of Ludwig Koenen,[42] that provides the possibility of perceiving the dynamics of tradition at work.

Koenen's work depends upon the fact that while the narrative framework of the prophecy is found in only one papyrus (P. Graf 29787), the actual prophecy is preserved in two recensions: P. Ranier 19813 and P. Oxyrhynchus 2332. This makes it possible to compare variants of the same tradition and determine redactional elements and interpolations.[43] Several further papyrus fragments have been tentatively identified as belonging to the "Potter" tradition.[44] While Koenen does not provide any detailed discussion of these, one (P.S.I. 982) demonstrates additional interpretive possibilities by identifying the foreign, chaotic invaders as the Jews.[45]

The major discovery of archaic Wisdom was the paradigmatic figure of the sacred king. In the employ of the royal courts of shrines (whether in Babylonia, Egypt or Judea) the scribe discerned, developed, articulated and created the various ideologies and mythologies in which the king, through divine wisdom, was the centre of social and cosmic order. In the archaic "proto-apocalyptic situation," the saving power of the king, his destruction of his enemies, the establishment of his rule and law were correlated with mythic traditions of the creation of cosmic and social order by a god in the beginning through his defeat of chaos. This pattern underlies a wide variety of materials from cosmogonies to New Year festivals, from royal praise hymns and chronicles to coronation rituals. In Egypt it is expressed in the two great patterns of kingship: the solar cycle of Amon-Re and the essentially chthonic cycle of Osiris-Horus. The former pattern, which depicts the new Pharaoh as the son of the deity, conceived by the Sun god who assumes the form of the ruling Pharaoh and has intercourse with the new Pharaoh's mother, presents a cosmogony where the Sun god is born on a primordial island, defeats the powers of chaos and establishes order and the cosmos.

The Osiris pattern, which depicts every living Pharaoh as Horus, the son of Osiris, and every dead Pharaoh as Osiris, Lord of the Underworld, presents the primordial struggle as that between Osiris' brother, Seth and Osiris-Horus. Seth revolted against Osiris and slew him with cosmic and social consequences. Horus avenges his father's death by slaying Seth and restoring order.[46] In the complex royal ideologies, these two patterns are frequently combined. In "proto-apocalyptic" materials, these two kingship patterns yield corresponding patterns of woes. The Amon-Re ideology expresses chaos as an eclipse of the sun and violent storms; the Osiris pattern, while having signs of cosmic chaos such as the flooding of the Nile, expresses the chaotic primarily as rebellion or the invasion of foreigners. These two series of woes are likewise combined.

Archaic examples of these traditions in what I have termed "proto-apocalyptic situations" abound (e.g. the Hymns of Merneptah[47] and Ramses IV[48]) and these elements persist into the Ptolemaic period. Perhaps the best-known example is the Rosetta Stone decree of March 27, 196 B.C., celebrating the performance of the Djed festival for Ptolemy V:

> In the reign of the young one – who has received his royalty from his father – lord of crowns, glorious, *who has established Egypt* and is pious towards the gods, superior to his foes, *who has restored the civilized life of men ... a king like the Sun ... son of the Sun ... being a god sprung from a god and goddess (like Horus the son of Isis and Osiris who avenged his father Osiris) ...*

After these introductory praises, the text goes on to describe in paradigmatic fashion the central political and cosmic act of the foreign Ptolemaic king: the defeat of the rebels of Lycopolis. The king was first prevented from this by an inundation of the Nile, but this he controlled by "having dammed at many points the outlets of the streams" and having accomplished this strategic (and cosmogonic) deed, he marched against Lycopolis, a city of "impious men ... who had done great harm to the temples and all the dwellers in Egypt," and "took the town by storm, and destroyed all the impious men in it, *even as Hermes and Horus, the son of Isis and Osiris formerly subdued the rebels in the same district.*"[49]

Texts such as these, associated with coronation, renewal of kingship or celebrating a victory, must be interpreted as political propaganda created by the scribe in service of his king. They represent the use of paradigms for typological ends – the presentation of a specific king as the fulfillment (or repetition) of the ancient patterns. These same propagandistic concerns, as Georges Posener has brilliantly demonstrated, yield the oldest surviving "apocalypse," that of Neferti in 1991 B.C. The narrative is cast in the form of a prophecy by the sage Neferti before King Snefru of the Fourth Dynasty; it is actually a piece of blatant propaganda in favour of the legitimacy of King Ammenemes I, the founder of the Twelfth Dynasty.

> Re must begin by creating the land, which is utterly ruined, and nothing remains ... The sun is veiled and will not shine ... none will live when the (sun) is veiled (by) cloud ... Enemies have come into being in the east, Asiatics have come down into Egypt ... I will show you the land in calamity, for what has never happened before has now happened ... Re has separated himself from mankind ... A king of the South will come, Ameny by name ...[50]

Chaos will be subdued; Re's recreation of the world will have begun with his reign.

Such texts may be found in Egypt over a period of close to two millennia. Employing *vaticinia ex eventu*, the prophet describes the ascendancy of a specific king as overcoming chaos (represented by eclipses, rebellions and foreigners) and establishing a new order, a new creation. While such texts "tend towards" apocalypticism, one does not find a full-blown apocalypse until the prophecies and propaganda are disassociated from a specific king. This becomes possible for Egypt (as well as for Babylonia and, perhaps Judea) only in the Greco-Roman period when native kingship ceases. I am tempted to describe apocalypticism as *wisdom lacking a royal patron*. (A definition which will serve at least to question both the "lachrymose theory" of apocalypticism as growing out of a situation of general persecution and the popular recent theory that it reflects lower-class interests.) In such contexts, the older models may become xenophobic nationalistic propaganda as in the case of some fragments of the "Potter's Oracle" where the woes have been reduced to anti-Hellenistic or anti-Jewish polemics – a prophecy against foreigners rather than in favour of a specific king. Or the king may be utterly cosmicized (a tendency always present in the various ideologies of divine kingship) in a thoroughgoing apocalypse. I find Koenen's work most interesting because he attempts to identify the various stages of this process at work in the different redactions of the "Potter's Oracle."

The narrative frame of the story (extant only in P. Graf 29787 – second century A.D.) is pregnant with archaic significance:

> During the reign of king Amenhotep (18th Dynasty), a potter, at the command of Hermes-Thot, goes to the island of Helios-Re where he practices his art. But the people are upset by this sacrilegious action. They pull

the pottery out of the oven, break it and drag the potter before the king. The potter defends himself by interpreting this action as a prophetic sign. Just as the pottery has been destroyed, so Egypt, and finally the city of the followers of the evil god Typhon-Set will be destroyed. [51]

The prophecies which then follow speak of the breakdown of cosmic and social order and the return of chaos. A saviour-king (described in extraordinarily vague language) will come "from the sun" and reestablish order, Egypt and the cosmos.

The "Potter" is an epiphany of the ancient ram-headed deity Chnum, who created the sun, the gods and man on his potter's wheel. [52] He is a traditional giver of royal oracles, including a number from the Hellenistic period that bear a close resemblance to themes in the "Potter's Oracle." [53] Thus his apocalyptic interpretation of the broken pottery goes far beyond the prophetic, symbolic actions of Jeremiah 19. For Chnum to have his pots broken is to plunge the world into total decreation and chaos. But the theme of recreation is likewise suggested by the setting. The island of Helios-Re (in Egyptian, the Island of Flames) is the traditional birthplace of the solar deity and the scene of his defeat of the powers of chaos and darkness. [54] Thus the prophecy which predicts a destruction and restoration plays on a setting and a prophet who are inextricably related to both themes in archaic Egyptian mythology.

The frame story could have originally led to a set of historically identifiable woes and the prediction of a specific king who would set things right. If the text as we now have it is a translation of an Egyptian original and if (on the basis of the alleged similarity of P. Trinity College Dublin 192b) the original composition can be dated to the fourth or middle third centuries B.C. – this would be likely. [55] But I consider both of these suggestions to be extremely dubious. More likely is the suggestion that the text may have originally been produced at the time of the revolt of Harsiesis, c. 130 B.C. and promised his successful restoration of native rule. [56] However, this revolt was quickly crushed, and no native king did rise to overthrow the Ptolemies.

The text describes in vague terms (following the old Osiris-Horus pattern) the desolation of Egypt by the "Typhonians" and the eventual salvation (now combining both Solar and Horus patterns) brought by a king "who shall appear from the sun, established by the most great goddess Isis." But, as Koenen has remarked, this is divorced totally from any individual features and testifies to the Egyptians' awareness of their own weakness: "It is not he (the promised saviour-king) who defeats the Greeks; the Ptolemies will destroy each other. Nor is he the destroyer of Alexandria; the destruction will result from the departure of the protective deity. And finally, he is not the one who recovers the statues of the gods which had been carried off; they will come back on their own ... The prophecies of the potter are not so much propaganda in favour of a specific king as propaganda directed against the Greeks."[57] The "Oracle" represents a characteristic apocalyptic shift necessitated by the cessation of native divine kingship—all decisive historical action and initiative has been transferred from the human to the divine realm.

However even this most general hope did not come true. The Ptolemies and Selucids did not destroy each other; Alexandria endured. Hence the elite, scribal clergy of Chnum (to whom authorship of this oracle must be traced), introduced a learned set of interpolations designed to "update" the predictions. These may be isolated by the fortunate chance that P. Ranier 19813 (third century A.D.) and P. Oxyrhynchus 2332 (late third century A.D.) contain some forty-five lines of closely parallel material as well as many lines which reveal striking variations and interpolations.

The most significant of these interpolations for our purposes occurs in P. Oxyrhynchus 2332, lines 31–34. The prophecy, in both recensions, has assigned a reign of fifty-five years to the promised king. The later gloss now declares (if the editor's proposed reconstruction be accepted) that the fifty-five years do not refer to the good king's reign but rather to the period of evil which the Greeks will bring "as predicted by Bokcharis the Lamb."

The Prophecy of Bokcharis the Lamb (which is likewise a prophecy of the ram-headed potter deity Chnum) is extant both in a demotic papyrus from the first decade of the first century A.D. and is alluded to in Greco-Egyptian and Greco-Roman literature from Manetho to pseudo-Plutarch, Aelian and the *Suda*.[58] It predicts nine hundred years of woes for Egypt from the time of King Bokcharis, before the promised restoration will begin. This period roughly corresponds to 709 B.C.–192 A.D. If one subtracts the fifty-five years from this date by assuming that it refers to the last period of evil, one gets a date for the beginning of the turning towards a new world at 137 A.D. This date has already passed by the writing of P. Oxyrhynchus and hence the prophecy at first glance is a failure. However the date 137 is remarkably close to the beginning of the new Sothis cycle in 139 A.D. and thus Koenen argues, the prophecy is, in fact, greatly extended. The promised restoration will come at some point in the next cycle – a period which stretches from 139–1599 A.D.! "The potter's prophecy ... in which the idea of the concrete saviour-king had virtually disappeared, was reshaped by historical reality. It became something new, namely, a prophecy of a new world cycle. What was originally a prophecy based upon the Egyptian concept of kingship was in the process of being transformed into an apocalypse."[59]

The fact that our surviving papyri indicate that the Oracle was circulated during the late third century and the fact that our latest copy (P. Oxyrhynchus) lacks both a narrative beginning and end suggests that the text had been divorced from all historical context and was being understood as a portrait of cosmic renewal rather than nationalistic restoration. In short, the "Potter's Oracle" by means of learned, scribal reinterpretation had become severed from its original Egyptian genre and had become an apocalypse. As in the case of the Babylonian Berossus, so in Egypt, the historical patterns of the scribal tradent were converted into a paradigm of cosmic history, a recurrent cycle of world creation, destruction and recreation. (One might compare Manetho's *Aegyptiaka* with the epistle of pseudo-Manetho accompanying the *Book of Sothis* for a close Egyptian analogue to Berossus).[60] In both the case of Babylonian and Egyptian tradition (and I would want to argue the same for the Jewish) it is necessary to see this development as an internal "trajectory" within Near Eastern scribalism for which it is unnecessary to postulate either Stoic or Iranian influence.

The pure apocalypse is, perhaps, best represented by the well-known apocalypse preserved in the Hermetic *Asclepius* 24–26 whose kinship with the "Potter's Oracle," especially with the woes, has long been recognized.[61] In *Asclepius* the woes are cosmicized and there is no longer any hint of salvation through a king. Rather the woes are characteristic of the "old age" of the world and when this has run its course at some unspecified time, God shall "recall the earth to its primeval form" and there shall be a "rebirth of the cosmos." The renewal of Egypt which was correlated with the Sothic cycle in the "Potter's Oracle" has become, in the *Asclepius*, a cosmic cycle correlated with the great World Year. In the Coptic recension from Nag Hammadi (which Doresse has suggested represents a more archaic form of the apocalypse than the Latin *Asclepius*) the cyclical character is more pronounced and the futuristic nature of the promised recreation is more heavily emphasized.[62] A final transformation of the Potter tradition is represented by Book VII of Lactanius, *Divine Institutes*. Blending together quotations from the *Sibylline Oracles*,[63] the *Asclepius* apocalypse and the *Oracles of Hystaspes* – the cyclical character of destruction and recreation has been altered, in a characteristically Christian redaction, into an eschatological vision of a final destruction, judgement and salvation.[64]

III

In this paper I have suggested that Wisdom and Apocalyptic are interrelated in that both are essentially scribal phenomena. They both depend on the relentless quest for paradigms, the problematics of applying these paradigms to new situations and the *Listenwissenschaft* which are the characteristic activities of the Near Eastern scribe. When these are applied to historiographic materials one may frequently discern proto-apocalyptic elements, though the genre apocalpyse is lacking. When the historical patterns are correlated with cosmogonic and kingship traditions and when the attendant structures of woes and promises are directed towards a condition of foreign domination, there is an apocalyptic situation – though again lacking the literary form of the apocalypse. Both proto-apocalyptic literature and apocalyptic situations were present in Babylonian materials from the Hellenistic period and these materials stand in close continuity with archaic scribal traditions and activities.

In Egypt, these same elements were found to be present, intertwined with and alongside of literary apocalypses which bore close kinship to other Egyptian wisdom materials. Following Koenen's work on the "Potter's Oracle," we explored the twenty-five-hundred-year "trajectory" from Neferti to Lactantius, from political propaganda and prophecy to apocalypticism and eschatology emphasizing those techniques of interpretation and reinterpretation which provide the dynamics of scribal tradition.

In the course of this investigation, several characteristics of apocalypticism emerged on which I would insist. Apocalypticism is Wisdom lacking a royal court and patron and therefore it surfaces during the period of Late Antiquity not as a response to religious persecution but as an expression of the trauma of the cessation of native kingship. Apocalypticism is a learned rather than a popular religious phenomenon. It is widely distributed throughout the Mediterranean world and is best understood as part of the inner history of the tradition within which it occurs rather than as a syncretism with foreign (most usually held to be Iranian) influences.

It is tempting to continue in this vein, illustrating the movement within Near Eastern scribal tradition from historical precedent and propaganda to apocalypticism and exploring the variety of genres in which a single tradition may be found.[65] More research needs to be undertaken on the relationship of apocalypticism to archaic wisdom forms such as omens and Hellenistic wisdom forms such as astrology. Or we might press on to examine the radical interiorization of apocalyptic motifs in non-Christian Gnostic and alchemical texts such as the *Hymn of the Pearl* and the *Visions of Zosimos*. But there is, within the world of academic discourse, a more definite and final *Endzeit* than has ever been dreamed of by the apocalypticist.

In this paper I have tried to illustrate the implications of adopting the perspective advanced by Peter Brown:

> There are two ways of approaching the way in which Manichaeism spread within the Roman Empire: the jig-saw puzzle and the Chinese boxes. The approach of the jig-saw puzzle sees Manichaeism exclusively as a product of religious syncretism. The scholar asks what pieces in the jig-saw of Manichaean beliefs appealed to what religious groups in the Roman world ... This approach has severe limitations. I would prefer the approach of the Chinese boxes. To become a Manichee or to favour the Manichee meant favouring a group. This group had a distinctive and complex structure.[66]

In a sense this is to return to the older social-functional understanding of syncretism as *syn-krētidzeiv* and to abandon the more recent biological interpretation of syncretism as *syn-kerannymi*.[67]

NOTES

1   See J. Z. Smith, "Native Cults in the Hellenistic Period," *HR* 11 (1971) esp. 236–9.

2   H. D. Betz, "Zum Problem des religionsgeschichtlichen Verstandnisses der Apokalyptik," *ZTK* 63 (1966) 409; ET in *JTC* 6 (1969) 155.

3   Smith, "Native Cults."

4   Compare G. Widengren, *The Ascension of the Apostle and the Heavenly Book* (1950) with G. von Rad, *Theologie des Alten Testaments* (1965) II:327, and Betz, "Problem der Apokalyptik," 392f (*JTC*, 135f).

5   See the edition of the fragments of Berossus in F. Jacoby, *Die Fragmente der griechischen Historiker* (1923) IIIC; n. 680, 364–97 and the older edition by P. Schnabel, *Berossos und die babylonisch-hellenistiche Literatur* (1923) 250–75; Schnabel's work is the only substantial monograph on Berossus.

6   See, in general, A. Pieretti, *la sibilla babilonese nella propaganda hellenistica* (1943) esp. 215–301. For special studies, see J. Geffcken, "Die babylonische Sibylle," *Nachrichten von der Akademie der Wissenschaften zu Göttingen*, Phil-hist. Kl. (1900) 88–102; W. Bousset, "Die Beziehungen der ältesten jüdischen Sibylle zur chaldäischen Sibylle," *ZNW* 3 (1902) 23–49; K. Mras, "'Babylonische' und 'ertryäische' Sibylle," *Weiner Studien* 29 (1907) 25–49; E. Schürer, *Geschichte der jüdischen Volkes im Zeitalter Jesu Christi* (1909), III: 563–7; P. Schnabel,

Berossos, 69–93; H. C. Youtie, "Sambathis," *HTR* 37 (1944) esp. 213–7; V. Tcherikover, et al., *Corpus Papyrorum Judaicarum* (1964) III:47–52; A. M. Denis, *Introduction aux pseudépigraphes grecs d'Ancien Testament* (1970) esp. 113f. I regret that I have not seen V. Nikiprovetsky, *La troisième Sibylle* (1970).

7 For a recent example of such inquiries, see W. Spaerri, *Untersuchung zur babylonische Urgeschichte* (1961).

8 While I reject genetic arguments as methodologically unsound when dealing with international religious phenomena such as apocalypticism, see H. Ludin Jansen, *Die Henoch-Gestalt* (1939) 74–81, who claims Berossus as "das Vorbild der henochitischen Geschichtsübersicht," and compare M. Hengel, *Judentum und Hellenismus* (1969) 348–52.

9 It may be noted that a major crux, the identification of the figure of Oannes, has been resolved by the discovery of his name on cuneiform lists as the "first, primeval sage." See W. C. Lambert, "Catalogues of Texts and Authors," *JCS* 11 (1957) 73f.

10 On this apocalyptic fragment, see J. Bidez, "Bérose et la grande année," in *Mélanges P. Fredericq* (1904) 9–19. P. Schnabel, "Apokalyptische Berechnung der Endzeiten bei Berossos," *Orientalische Literaturzeitung* (1910) 401f; Schnabel, *Berossos*, 94–109; W. Gundel in F. Boll-C. Bezold, *Sternglaube und Sterndeutung* (1931⁴) 200–205 (compare the note in W. and H. G. Gundel, *Astrologumena* (1966) 45–6, n. 14) and B. L. van Waerden, "Das grosse Jahr und die ewige Wiederkehr," *Hermes* 80 (1952) 129–55.

11 As has been by members of the classical pan-Babylonian School such as A. Jeremias and as may be found in attenuated form in Gunkel and Bousset. See above, n. 8.

12 See A. Alt, "Die Weisheit Salomos," *Theologische Literatur Zeitung* 76 (1951) 139–44 and note the comments by von Rad, *Theologie* II:317f. See further, W. von Dosen, "Leistung und Grenze sumerischer und babylonischer Wissenschaft," *Welt als Geschichte* 2 (1936) 411–64, 509–57.

13 On omens and oracles, see J. Nougayrol, et. al., *La divination en Mesopotamie* (1966); A. L. Oppenheim, *Ancient Mesopotamia* (1964) 206–27.

14 See especially, H. Gese, "Geschichtliches Denken im alten Orient," *ZTK* 55 (1958) 127–45; B. Albrektson, *History and the Gods* (1967).

15 T. Pinches, *Historical Records and Legends of Assyria and Babylonia* (1902) 477f. See now the translation of the Sumerian by S. N. Kraemer in the *Supplement* to J. B. Pritchard's *Ancient Near Eastern Texts Relating to the Old Testament* (1969³) 611–19.

16 See J. Nougayrol, "Note sur la place des 'présages historiques' dans extispicine babylonienne," *Annuaire de l'École pratique des Hautes Études* (1944–1945) 5–41 and the classic study by H. G. Güterbock, "Die historische Tradition und ihre literarische Gestaltung bei Babyloniern und Hethitern bis 1200," *ZA* (1934) 1–91; 44 (1939) 45–149.

17 This is not the context for an exhaustive bibliography on this growing consensus; see especially W. von Soden, "Gibt es ein Zeugnis dafür, dass die Babylonier an die Wiederauferstehung Marduks geglaubt haben?" *ZA* N.S.17 (1955) 130–66.

18 I cannot here argue the thesis that the texts of the New Year ceremony break into two groups – an older, ambiguous collection which focuses on the absence

of Marduk from Babylon, all of which are of an Assyrian provenance and seem to be a parody on Babylonian ritual and belief; and the Hellenistic series which I have interpreted as reflecting anti-Seleucid propaganda.

19 On Abydenos, see Jacoby, *Fragmente* IIIC: no. 685.

20 I am discounting the Akkadian "prophecies" interpreted by Hallo as apocalypses, W. W. Hallo, "Akkadian Apocalypses," *Israel Exploration Journal* 16 (1966) 231–42; cf. A. K. Gregson-W. C. Lambert, "Akkadian Prophecies," *JCS* 18 (1964) 7–30. Nor am I including Babylonian material preserved in other apocalyptic works from *Sibylline Oracles III* and *Revelation* to Mani.

21 See, for example, G. Maspero, "Manuel d'hiérarchie égyptienne," *Journal asiatique*, Ser. VIII. 11 (1888) 25–280.

22 See the Loeb Classical Library edition of *Manetho* by W. G. Waddell (1940).

23 On the Hyksos pattern, see the classic work by R. Weill, *La fin du moyen empire égyptien* (1918) esp. 22–68, 76–83, 605–23 and the recent study by J. Yoyette, "L'Égypte ancienne et les origines de l'antijudaïsme," *Revue d'histoire des religions* 163 (1963) 133–43.

24 J. G. Griffiths, "The Interpretation of the Horus-Myth of Edfu," *JEA* 44 (1958) 75–85.

25 See the translation by R. O. Faulkner in *JEA* 22 (1936) 121–40; 23 (1937) 10–16, 166–85; 24 (1938) 41–53.

26 See the comprehensive treatment by C. C. McCown, "Egyptian Apocalyptic Literature," *HTR* 18 (1925) 357–411, and J. Doresse, "Apocalypses égyptiennes," *La Table ronde* 110 (1957) 29–39. The treatment by H. Gressmann, *Der Messias* (1929) 417–45 should also be noted. For extremely archaic elements, which fall outside the scope of this paper, see S. Schott, "Altägyptische Vorstellungen vom Weltende," *Analecta Biblica* 12:3 (1959) [= *Studia Biblica et Orientalia* III:319–30] and G. Lanczkowski, "Eschatology in Ancient Egyptian Religion," *Proceedings of the IX International Congress for the History of Religions* (1960) 129–34.

27 See the translations of this text in Pritchard, *ANET* (1955²) 444–6 (to be cited as *ANET²*) and R. O. Faulkner, et al., *The Literature of Ancient Egypt* (1972) 234–40. See the study by G. Posener, *Littérature et politique dans l'Égypte de la XIIᵉdynastie* (1956) 21–60, 145–57 for an argument as to the propagandistic character of this work. Cf. W. Helck, *Die Prophezieung des Nfr.tj* (1970).

28 W. Spiegelberg, *Die sogenannte demotische Chronik des Pap. 215 der Bibliotheque Nationale zu Paris* (1914). There is a recent Italian translation in E. Bresciani, *Letteratura poesia dell'antico egitto* (1969) 551–60. The classic study remains E. Meyer, "Ägyptische Dokumente aus der Perserzeit, I: Eine eschatologische Prophetie über die Geschichte Ägyptens in persischer und griechischer Zeit," *Sitzungs-berichte der Preussischen Akademie der Wissenschaften*, Phil-hist. K1. (1915) 287–304.

29 J. Krall, "Vom König Bokchoris," *Festgaben zu Ehren Max Büdingers* (1898) 1–11; A. Moret, *De Bocchori Rege* (1903) 35–49; J. M. A. Janssen, "Over Farao Bocchoris," in *Varia Historica aangelborden aan A. W. Byvanck* (1954), 17–29.

30 See now the edition by L. Koenen, "Die Prophezeiungen des 'Töpfers'," *Zeitschrift für Papyrologie und Epigraphik* 2 (1968) 178–209, which supersedes all previous editions and cites all important secondary literature.

31 See A. D. Nock-A. J. Festugière, *Corpus Hermeticum* (1960²) II:322–35. On the

Coptic Text (Nag Hammadi, VI:8), see M. Krause and P. Labib, *Gnostische und hermetische Schriften aus Codex II und Codex VI* (Glücksfadt, 1971); J. Doresse, "Hermes et la gnose: À propos de l'Asclépius copte," *NovT* 1 (1956) 54–69, and M. Krause, "Ägyptisches Gedenkengut in der Apokalypse Asclepius," in *XVII Deutscher Orientalistentag, Vorträge* (1969; = *Zeitschrift der Deutschen Morganländischen Gesellschaft,* Supplement 1:48–57).

32 See esp. W. W. Tarn, "Alexander Helios and the Golden Age," *Journal of Hellenic Studies* 22 (1932) 135–60 for a study of this example of Ptolemaic propaganda.

33 Jer. 4:6f, 6:22f. See B. Childs, "The Enemy from the North and the Chaos Tradition," *JBL* 78 (1959) 187–98.

34 See the comprehensive survey by G. Lanczkowski, *Altägyptischer Prophetismus* (1960).

35 See the rich bibliographical essay by J. Leclant, "Documents nouveaux et points du vue récents sur les sagesses de l'Égypte ancienne," in *La Sagesse du proche-orient ancien: Colloqué du Strasbourg, 17–19 mai, 1962* (1963) 5–26.

36 For the most recent translation of these three texts, see Faulkner, *The Literature of Ancient Egypt*, 230–33, 210–29, 201–9.

37 *ANET*², 34–6 and Ch. Maystre, *Les declarations d'innocence: Livre des morts, chapitre 125* (1937). See the Greek translation by Euphantus, quoted in Porphyry, *De Abstinentia*, IV.10. For the possibility that the *Book of the Dead*, including ch. 125, was translated into Greek by Eudoxus, see J. G. Griffiths, "A Translation from the Egyptian by Eudoxus," *Classical Quarterly* 15 (1965) 75–8.

38 For an archaic example, see the wide diffusion of omen series and commentaries which have been found in Akkadian in such widely dispersed sites as Susa, Nuzi, Hattusha, Qatna and Hazor and translated into Elamite and Hittite (see A. L. Oppenheim, *Ancient Mesopotamia*, 206). For a Hellenistic example, see the fundamental work of D. Daube, "Rabbinic Methods of Interpretation and Hellenistic Rhetoric," *Hebrew Union College Annual* 22 (1949) 239–64.

39 E.g., D. S. Russell, *The Method and Message of Jewish Apocalyptic* (1964) 183–7 *et passim.*

40 I know of only one scholar who has studied these parallels: F. Daumas, "Littérature prophétique et exégétique égyptienne et commentaires esséniens," *Memorial A. Gélin* (1961) 203–211.

41 Betz, "Problem der Apokalyptik," 398–409 (= *JTC* [1969] 138–54).

42 L. Koenen, "Die Prophezeiungen des 'Töpfers'" (above n. 30); "The Prophecies of a Potter: A Prophecy of World Renewal Becomes an Apocalypse," in D. H. Samuel, ed., *Proceedings of the Twelfth International Congress of Papyrology* (1970) 249–54.

43 See the detailed discussion in Koenen, "Die Prophezeiungen," 187–93. See the summary in E. Loebel-C. H. Roberts, *The Oxyrhynchus Papyri* (1954) XII:89.

44 See R. A. Pack, *The Greek and Latin Literary Texts from Greco-Roman Egypt* (1967²) nos. 2488, 2639 and n. 45, below.

45 See the full discussion in V. Tcherikover et al., *Corpus Papyrorum Judaicarum* (1964) III: no. 520 (pages 119–21).

46 There is no "tradition-history" of the Amon-Re cycle comparable to J. G. Griffiths, *The Conflict of Horus and Seth* (1960).

47 *ANET*², 58, 377.

48 *ANET*², 378f.

49 I have followed the translation by E. Bevan, *A History of Egypt Under the Ptolemaic Dynasty* (1927) 263–8.

50 I have followed the translation in W. K. Simpson, *The Literature of Ancient Egypt*, 234–40. See the literature cited above, n. 27, and further, A. Volten, *Zwei altägyptische politische Schriften* (1945).

51 Koenen, "The Prophecies of a Potter," 249.

52 The identification of the Potter and Chnum was first proposed by W. Struve, "Zum Töpferorakel," in *Raccolta G. Lumbroso* (1925) 274, and has been followed by all subsequent commentators.

53 See the examples in L. Kakosy, "Prophecies of Ram Gods," *Acta Orientalia Hungaricae* 19 (1966) 341–58, esp. 343f.

54 See the argument and the literature cited in Koenen, "Die Prophezeiungen," 184f and esp. n. 12.

55 Loebel-Roberts, *Oxyrhynchus Papyri* XII:92f.

56 Koenen, "Die Prophezeiungen," 191.

57 Koenen, "The Prophecies of a Potter," 252.

58 See the literature cited above, n. 29.

59 Koenen, "The Prophecies of a Potter," 253; compare the fuller discussion in Koenen, "Die Prophezeiungen," 189f. The Sothic element was perceived, but wrongly interpreted, by U. Wilckens, "Zur Ägyptischen Prophetie," *Hermes* 40 (1905) esp. 558f and W. Struve "Zum Töpferorakel," 279. Cf. R. Reitzenstein-H. Schaeder, *Studien zum antiken Synkretismus* (1926) 42.

60 On pseudo-Manetho, W. G. Waddell, *Manetho*, 208–11, and compare the parallels in W. Scott, *Hermetica* (1926) III:491–3.

61 Reitzenstein-Schaeder, *Studien*, 38–40; Nock-Festugière, *Hermès Trismegiste* II:288, 379–81. See above, n. 31.

62 J. Doresse, *The Secret Books of the Egyptian Gnostics* (1960) 245–8; Doresse, "Apocalypses égyptiens," 34f.

63 Note the parallels between elements in the *Sibylline Oracles* and the "Potter's Oracle" in E. Norden, *Die Geburt des Kindes* (1924) 55 and the discussion of parallels between the *Sibylline Oracles* and the *Asclepius* apocalypse, see H. Windisch, *Die Orakel des Hystaspes* (1929) esp. 26–33, 44, 89.

65 An excellent example would be the complex Egyptian and Greco-Egyptian traditions surrounding Nectanebo, the last native king of Egypt, to which I shall devote a further study.

66 P. Brown, *Religion and Society in the Age of Saint Augustine* (1972) 108.

67 This paper was prepared under the auspices of the Rosenstiel Fellowship at the University of Notre Dame. I am grateful for the assistance and courtesies extended by the Notre Dame theological faculty.

7

Apocalyptic Christianity

The Synoptic Source "Q"
The Apocalyptic Discourses
The Book of Revelation*

NORMAN PERRIN

We have claimed elsewhere that Christianity began as an apocalyptic sect within ancient Judaism and that apocalypticism was a constant element of much of New Testament Christianity, resurging especially at times of catastrophe or persecution. We must now go into greater detail, but first an explanation of the terms *apocalyptic* and *eschatology* is in order. *Apocalyptic* is from the Greek *apocalypsis*, "an uncovering," and it describes a movement in Judaism and Christianity that characteristically claimed that God had revealed to the writer the secrets of the imminent end of the world and so had given him a message for his people. It features a distinctive view of the end of the world, described in the next section of this chapter. Though this kind of thinking was not confined to Jews and Christians in the Hellenistic world, being found for example also in Babylonia, we are concerned only with its Jewish-Christian manifestation. *Eschatology* is from the Greek *eschatos*, "furthest," and *logos*, "word" or "teaching," and it therefore means "teaching concerning the end of things." This teaching can take any form, and the end can be conceived in any manner. Some modern scholars tend to use the term for a decisive transformation of life, thinking in existentialist terms, but this is a metaphorical usage. In considering the world of the New Testament, *apocalyptic* is a particular form of *eschatology*.

Characteristics of Jewish-Christian Apocalyptic

In ancient Judaism and early Christianity, apocalyptic was a child of hope and despair: hope in the invincible power of God in the

*First published in *The New Testament: An Introduction* by N. Perrin (1974) 65–85.

121

world he created, despair of the present course of human history in that world. God was the creator of the world and the ruler of all within it: that was the primary tenet of Jewish faith. At the same time the actual experience of the people of God in the world was catastrophic: the Babylonians conquered them; they returned to the Holy Land at the pleasure of the Persian kings; the brief period of independence under the Maccabeans was followed by Roman conquest, by the establishment of the half-breed Idumean rule over them, and by direct Roman control of the Holy City and the Temple with its Holy of Holies. This situation was intolerable, and it could mean only that human history was a descent into hell. But God was the ruler of all things and, therefore, the tragic events of human history must have been foreordained by him. Thus, there was some divine plan through which the horrors of history would reach a climax and everything would then change. In the meantime the people of God must prepare themselves for the change and watch for the signs of its coming.

These are the characteristics of apocalyptic: a sense of despair about history that bred the belief that it was rushing to a fore-ordained tragic climax; a hope in God that fostered the conviction that he would act in that climatic moment to change things utterly and forever; and a conviction that it would be possible to recognize the signs of the coming of that climactic moment.

"And when you hear of wars and rumors of wars, do not be alarmed; this must take place, but the end is not yet. For nation will rise against nation, and kingdom against kingdom; there will be earthquakes in various places, there will be famines; this is but the beginning of the birth-pangs ...

But in those days, after that tribulation, the sun will be darkened, and the moon will not give its light, and the stars will be falling from heaven, and the powers in the heavens will be shaken."

Mark 13:7–8, 24–25

This is the language of Jewish apocalyptic looking for the signs of the coming of the End.

Ideas about the form of the End varied tremendously. The passage from Mark 13 continues:

And then they will see the Son of man coming in clouds with great power and glory. And then he will send out the angels, and gather his elect from the four winds, from the ends of the earth to the ends of heaven.

Mark 13:26–27

This is the characteristic Christian form of the apocalyptic hope, derived ultimately from Dan. 7:13–14:

> I saw in the night visions,
>> and behold, with the clouds of heaven
>>> there came one like a son of man,
>> and he came to the Ancient of Days
>>> and was presented before him.
>> And to him was given dominion
>>> and glory and kingdom,
>> that all peoples, nations, and languages
>>> should serve him;
>> his dominion is an everlasting dominion,
>>> which shall not pass away,
>> and his kingdom one
>>> that shall not be destroyed.

The literature of a Jewish apocalyptic sect that reached a similar form of the hope is preserved in a work known as *1 Enoch* (sometimes called Ethiopic Enoch). This group focused their hope on the figure of Enoch who, according to Gen. 5:24, "walked with God; and he was not, for God took him." They interpreted these words to mean that Enoch had been transported to heaven whence he would come as Son of man to judge the world. Whether this sect influenced the Christians or the Christians influenced this sect is a matter of dispute. Our opinion is that both reached a similar position independently, and that the similarity is explained by three factors the Christians and the sect that produced *1 Enoch* have in common: they are Jewish apocalyptic sects, they have a hero translated to heaven, and they use Dan. 7:13.

There are many other forms of the apocalyptic hope. The *Assumption of Moses*, a work contemporary with the New Testament, is particularly interesting because of its use of "Kingdom of God," a key concept in the teaching of Jesus.

And then his [God's] kingdom shall appear throughout all his creation,
And then Satan shall be no more.
And sorrow shall depart with him.
Then the hands of the angel shall be filled
Who has been appointed chief,
And he shall forthwith avenge them of their enemies.
For the Heavenly One will arise from his royal throne,
And he will go forth from his holy habitation
With indignation and wrath on account of his sons.

And the earth shall tremble: to its confines shall it be shaken:
And the high mountains shall be made low
And the hills shall be shaken and fall.
And the horns of the sun shall be broken and he shall be turned into
    darkness;
And the moon shall not give her light, and be turned wholly into blood.
And the circle of the stars shall be disturbed.
And the sea shall retire into the abyss,
And the fountains of waters shall fail,
And the rivers shall dry up.
For the Most High will arise, the Eternal God alone,
And he will appear to punish the Gentiles,
And he will destroy all their idols.
Then thou, O Israel, shalt be happy,
And thou shalt mount upon the necks and wings of the eagle,
And they shall be ended.
And God will exalt thee,
And he will cause thee to approach to the heaven of the stars,
In the place of their habitation.
And thou shalt look from on high and shalt see thy enemies in Gehenna,
And thou shalt recognize them and rejoice,
And thou shalt give thanks and confess thy Creator.

Assumption of Moses 10

Another form of the hope is associated with the coming of a Son
of David, here expressed in the *Psalms of Solomon*, a work slightly
earlier than the New Testament.

Behold, O Lord, and raise up unto them their king, the son of David,
At the time in the which thou seest, O God, that he may reign over
    Israel thy servant.
And gird him with strength, that he may shatter unrighteous rulers,
And that he may purge Jerusalem from nations that trample her down
    to destruction.
Wisely, righteously he shall thrust out sinners from the inheritance,
He shall destroy the godless nations with the word of his mouth;
At his rebuke nations shall flee before him,
    And he shall reprove sinners for the thoughts of their heart.
And he shall gather together a holy people, whom he shall lead in
    righteousness,
    And he shall judge the tribes of the people that has been sanctified
      by the Lord his God.
And he shall not suffer unrighteousness to lodge any more in their
    midst,

Nor shall there dwell with them any man that knoweth wickedness,
For he shall know them, that they are all sons of their God.
And he shall divide them according to their tribes upon the land,
And neither sojourner nor alien shall sojourn with them any more.
He shall judge peoples and nations in the wisdom of his righteousness.
And he shall have the heathen nations to serve him under his yoke;
And he shall glorify the Lord in a place to be seen of all the earth;
And he shall purge Jerusalem, making it holy as of old:
So that nations shall come from the ends of the earth to see his glory,
Bringing as gifts her sons who had fainted,
And to see the glory of the Lord, wherewith God hath glorified her.

Psalms of Solomon 17

Despite the variety of the forms of expression, the hope itself is constant for a climatic series of events that will lead to the final, eschatological intervention of God into human history, directly or through intermediary figures. Through these events the world would be forever changed, transformed into a perfect world in which the people of God would be forever blessed for their fidelity, and their enemies and God's forever punished.

This hope is called the "apocalyptic" hope because the characteristic claim of the literature that expresses it is that God has uncovered or revealed to the writer or seer his plan for the further course of history and the coming of the End. This revelation frequently takes the form of dreams or visions, which are then interpreted by a heavenly figure. The dreams or visions generally use symbols to recount the history of the Jewish (or Christian) people and to express the hope for the immediate future. So, for example, Daniel 7 tells in symbols the history of the Near Eastern world from the Babylonian Empire through the Persian Empire to the conquests of Alexander the Great and his ten successors as kings of the Macedonian Seleucid Kingdom of Syria. The final symbol used to represent a king is the "little horn" (Dan. 7:8), which represents Antiochus IV Epiphanes, who began persecuting the Jews in 168 B.C. in an attempt to consolidate his empire. The result was the Jewish revolt against Syrian overlordship, led first by Judas Maccabeus (i.e., Judas the "hammerer" of his enemies), which achieved religious and ultimately political independence for the Jews – an independence that lasted almost exactly a hundred years, until the coming of the Romans in the person of Pompey in 63 B.C. The author of Daniel 7 is living at the time of the Maccabean revolt, writing to inspire his people with confidence that the war is the beginning of the End, that it will shortly be ended by the coming of the Son of man as judge and ruler of the world.

Literary Characteristics of Apocalyptic

From the standpoint of literary form the apocalyptic movement has a number of interesting features. In the first place its writers make extensive use of symbols, necessary in attempting to depict the final, eschatological intervention of God in human history and the subsequent judging of nations and transformation of the world. How else could one depict these events except in symbols? But symbols were not only used in depicting the End, they were also used in giving an account of the events of past and present that preceded, in the apocalyptic view, the coming of the End. So though in Daniel 11 the history of the Jewish people is sketched in direct language – the "Kings of Persia," the "King of the South" (the Egyptian king), the "King of the North" (the Syrian king), the "ships of the Kittim" (the Romans) – in Daniel 7 the same story is told in terms of beasts and horns.

A second literary characteristic of the movement is pseudonymity. Apocalyptic writers regularly wrote under the pseudonym of a distinguished figure of the past. The unknown author of the book of Daniel, for example, writing at the time of the Maccabean revolt, wrote in the name of Daniel, a legendary hero of the Jews from an earlier age. Others wrote in the guise of other Jewish heroic figures: the Enoch group wrote in the name of their hero, Enoch; the Christians in the name of theirs, Jesus. The Book of Revelation is a remarkable exception to this tendency in that the author used his own name: "The revelation of Jesus Christ ... to his servant John" (Rev. 1:1).

A third literary characteristic of apocalyptic is the extensive quotation of previously existing texts. The apocalyptic writers constantly used and reused, interpreted and reinterpreted, the sacred texts of their tradition, especially earlier apocalyptic texts. We illustrate this facet of apocalyptic later in our analysis of Mark 13.

The Influence of Apocalyptic

Apocalyptic passages appear in earlier prophetic works (e.g., Isaiah 24—27), but the first major apocalyptic text known to us is the Book of Daniel, a product of the Maccabean revolt. Apocalyptic texts can be dated according to the last historical event detectable in their review of history. Daniel 8—12 bewails the desecration of the Jerusalem Temple by Antiochus IV Epiphanes in 168 B.C.. but does not mention its cleansing and rededication by the Maccabees in

165 B.C., so the work is normally dated between those years. From this first full flowering, apocalyptic came to be a major influence in Judaism and later in Christianity, producing a flood of works, many now lost to us. The period of its major influence lasted approximately three centuries. The reason for the decline of apocalyptic is largely that it tended to foster a spirit of revolt against Rome, a passion to begin the war that God would end. After the failure of the bar Cochba rising in A.D. 135, it fell into disrepute in what was becoming mainstream Judaism, and of the many Jewish apocalyptic works, only the Book of Daniel found its way into the Jewish canon. Among the Christians its influence also dwindled. The delay of the parousia (the particularly Christian form of the apocalyptic hope), the necessity of coming to terms with the Roman world rather than constantly hoping for its destruction, the fact that apocalyptic visionaries were free spirits essentially resistant to the growing institutionalization of the church – all this combined to bring about a decline of Christian apocalyptic, and only one of the many Christian apocalyptic works is in the Christian canon, the book of Revelation. But during the three centuries or so of its flowering, apocalyptic was a profound influence in both Judaism and Christianity.

After the return from their exile in Babylonia the Jews experienced a decline of prophecy, and apocalyptic replaced it as the means whereby God still spoke directly to his people. It was the claim of early Christianity that prophecy had returned to them as an eschatological gift, but that prophecy largely took the form of apocalyptic. A major contribution of apocalyptic was that in Judaism it provided the successor to prophecy and in Christianity the vehicle for the return of prophecy. Strange as the characteristic visions of the apocalyptic seers may appear to us today, they were the means whereby the Jews after their return from Exile in Babylonia were convinced that God was still revealing his will and purpose directly to his people. With the decline of apocalyptic, the rabbi interpreting the Law revealed God's will, a process already begun during the period of the ascendancy of apocalyptic. But between the decline of prophecy and the coming of rabbinic Judaism it was apocalyptic, itself a child of prophecy, that fulfilled this essential function and convinced the people that God was still addressing them directly.

Another contribution was apocalyptic's intensive concern for the sacred texts of its tradition and its conviction that these texts could and should be reinterpreted according to changing circumstances. Later the rabbis were to see the scriptures as essentially deposits of God's eternal truth, which could and should be distilled and

127

applied to the current situation by the proper interpretative method, the proper hermeneutics, and the Jewish scribes of the New Testament period were well on their way to this view of the text as fixed and immutable. Apocalyptic, however, envisaged a more dynamic interaction between the past text and the present situation, whereby the text interpreted the situation and the situation interpreted the text, so that the text itself could be modified and rewritten. Ultimately, of course, both these ways of looking at a sacred text are important, and it is not the least contribution of apocalyptic to the future of Judaism, as well as of Christianity, that it developed one of them as extensively as it did.

Apocalyptic contributed to the field of theology and doctrine. It was the vehicle for bringing into Judaism a developed *dualism*, a concept of reality divided into two antithetical forces – good and evil, darkness and light, angels and demons – and of the arena of human history and experience as a battleground where these forces were at war with one another. Further, apocalyptic brought into Judaism the concept of a resurrection, in the form of an expectation of the general resurrection of the dead: "And many of those who sleep in the dust of the earth shall awake, some to everlasting life, and some to shame and everlasting contempt" (Dan. 12:2). It also developed within Judaism the concept of a redeemer figure who would act as God's intermediary and whose coming would be the central act of the apocalyptic dramas: Messiah, Son of David, Son of man, Elect One, the archangel Michael, a prophet like Moses, a Restorer – the possibilities were endless. Sometimes God was conceived of as acting directly rather than through a redeemer figure, as in *Assumption of Moses* 10 where "And then his (God's) kingdom shall appear throughout all his creation" and "For the Heavenly One will arise from his royal throne" are two different ways of saying the same thing. The Kingdom of God is God acting as King; to use the expression is a way of talking about the direct and unmediated eschatological activity of God.

It is obvious even from this short list, which could be considerably extended, that apocalyptic had much influence on ancient Judaism and still more on the movement that began as an apocalyptic sect within ancient Judaism – earliest Christianity.

The Qumran Community

It is not our purpose here to present still another brief account of the community whose writings were discovered in 1947 in some caves near the Dead Sea (and hence were called "Dead Sea Scrolls") and whose headquarters were in what the Arabs call Wadi Qumran, which empties into the northwest corner of the Dead Sea. To be of any value, such an account would have to go beyond the confines permissible in an introductory book, and excellent accounts are readily available in our resource materials, especially the *Interpreter's Dictionary of the Bible* and the *Jerome Biblical Commentary*. But we do want to call attention to the existence of this community and to how being aware of it has increased our understanding of New Testament Christianity.

To begin with the obvious point, both the Qumran community and earliest Christianity were apocalyptic sects within ancient Judaism. The last days of the Qumran community and the first of the Christian coincided, for Qumran perished in the Jewish War of A.D. 66–70. There were many differences between the two communities, the chief being that Qumran was a monastic community that waited for the world to come to it, whereas Christianity went out into the world as a missionary community – but then Qumran numbered no "Hellenists" in its midst. But both communities shared the apocalyptic hope: the men at Qumran expected two Messiahs – a Messiah of Aaron, a priest who would sanctify them, and the Messiah of Israel, a warrior who would lead them in the battle against the Gentiles that would mark the beginning of the End. Indeed one of their texts, 1QM, the War Scroll ("War of the Son of Light and the Son of Darkness') is a battle plan for this war, which they would begin and God would end. The Christians expected the Messiah Jesus to come as eschatological judge and redeemer, but they seem to have abandoned the concept of a Holy War, perhaps under the influence of Jesus himself. The Qumran community ate their communal meals in anticipation of the day when they would eat with the Messiahs, as the Christians ate theirs in anticipation of the Kingdom of God (Mark 14:25). Qumran had an initiatory baptism and subsequent ceremonial lustrations, and great pains were taken to ensure an adequate water supply for these rites. Christianity had an initiatory baptism, but no subsequent ceremonial lustrations. The reason for the difference lay in the fact that the Christians were mostly laymen, but Qumran was essentially a community of priests. Both communities reached the point of sharing their goods in common, Qumran rigidly so, Christianity at the beginning according to the tradition of the "voluntary communism" in Acts 2:43–47. Both communities came to be headed by an individual whose office was described by the same term, the Christian Greek *episkopos* ("bishop," literally "overseer"), an equivalent for the Qumran Hebrew *paqid* or *mebaqqer*. Moreover, the "overseers" in both communities had the same responsibilities: the instruction of initiates and the control of the material resources.

But the most important commonality was their method of interpreting scripture – the common hermeneutics. At Qumran the scribes of the community developed a special form of the method of interpretation whereby the text and the circumstances of the interpreter were brought into a dynamic relationship with one another and the one interpreted in light of the other. This is the *pesher* method, so called because the form is that of a quotation of the passage of scripture followed by the word *pishro* ("its interpretation is" from *pesher*, "interpretation") and then the interpretation itself. It was based on an understanding of the relationship among God, scripture, and community that is indicated in one of the texts, the *pesher* on Habakkuk (1QpHab) 2:8–10 (Vermes' translation):

> They, the men of violence and breakers of the Covenant, will not believe when they hear all that [is to happen to] the final generation from the Priest [in whose heart] God set [understanding] that he might interpret all the words of His servants the Prophets, through whom he foretold all that would happen to His people [and His land].

This method of interpretation exercised great freedom in regard to the text of the scripture concerned. Let us take an example from the *pesher* on Psalm 37 (4QpPs37). Psalm 37:20 reads in part, "the enemies of the Lord are like the glory of the pastures," where the Hebrew represented by "the glory of the pastures" is very difficult and can also be translated "the fat of lambs" (English Revised Version). Clearly, however, either the pastures or the lambs is a good thing to be, and the puzzle has always been why it is that "the enemies of the Lord" should be likened to something good. The New English Bible conjectures a reading, "like fuel in a furnace." The rabbis interpreted the passage, "like the fat of lambs being fattened for a sacrifice." The priests of Qumran read the passage as referring to themselves, not as "the enemies of the Lord" but as "those who love the Lord," a change involving the substitution of one letter for another in the Hebrew, and then interpreted the passage as referring to their eschatological function in the purpose of God.

> And those who love the Lord shall be like the pride of pastures. Interpreted [this concerns] the congregation of His elect, who shall be leaders and prince ... of the flock among their herds.
>
> 4QpPs37 3:4–6 (Vermes' translation)

The Christians certainly shared this freedom in interpreting scripture in terms of themselves and their circumstances. A good example is the quotation from Joel in Acts 2.[1] Joel 2:30 reads, "And I will give portents in the heavens and on the earth, blood and fire and columns of smoke." There is here only one set of portents and signs; the reference to both the heavens and the earth simply means something we would express by an adjective like "cosmic." Now the same is true of the Greek version of the text, the Septuagint, which Acts is using. However, Acts 2:19 adds some words to read, "I will show wonders in the heavens *above* and *signs* on the earth *beneath*." Now we have two sets of portents, and when we get to verse 22 we can see why: the signs on the earth beneath are interpreted as referring to Jesus. "Jesus of Nazareth, a man attested to you by God with mighty works and wonders *and signs* which God did through him in your midst." Many more examples of this *pesher* use of scripture in the New Testament could be given, and it is a major element in the development of New Testament theology.

Apocalyptic Christianity

The Source Q

The first literary evidence in the New Testament for the existence of Christian apocalyptic is the source Q, used by the evangelists Matthew and Luke. Q is not itself an apocalypse, but it is dominated by eschatology and by a particular form of the apocalyptic hope. As reconstructed and thematically arranged by Howard Kee, *Jesus in History*, pp. 71–3, the source contained the following material. (All the references given are to the Gospel of Luke, because it is generally accepted that Luke edited the Q material to a lesser extent than Matthew, who had a special interest in teaching material.)

NARRATIVE MATERIAL

Healing the Centurion's Slave (Luke 7:2, 6b–10)

PARENETIC MATERIAL

Serving Two Masters (16:13)
On Light or Darkness Within (11:34–36)
On Faith and Forgiveness (17:3b–4, 6)

ESCHATOLOGICAL MATERIAL

Eschatological Warning
Preaching Judgement (3:7–9)
Baptism with Spirit and Fire (3:16–17)
Judging and Eschatological Judgement (6:37–42)

Woes on the Cities Where Jesus Performed Mighty Works (10:13–15)
Judgement on the Scribes and Pharisees (11:39–52)
Fire, Baptism, Sword, and Division (12:49–53)
Inability to Interpret the Signs of this Time (12:54–56)
Repent in View of the Impending Crisis (12:57–58)
Prepare for the Crisis (13:24–29)
Lament over Jerusalem's Impending Doom (13:34–35)
Judgement on the Careless and Preoccupied (17:24, 26–27, 33–37)

Eschatological Conflict
Contest with the Devil (4:2–12)
Defeating the Prince of Demons (11:14–22)
Dispelling the Unclean Spirits (11:23–26)

Eschatological Promise
The Beatitudes (6:20b–23)
Love of Enemies (6:27–36)
Eschatological Prayer (11:2–4)
What God Will Give (11:9–13)
Seek the Kingdom (12:22–31)
Treasures in Heaven (12:33–34)
A Role in the Kingdom (22:28–30)

Eschatological Knowledge
Gratitude for What God Has Revealed (10:21–24)

Eschatological Discipleship
Fitness for the Kingdom (9:57–60)
The Kingdom Has Drawn Near (10:2–12)
Fearless Confession (12:2–12)
Bearing the Cross (14:26–27)

Eschatological Parables
Three Parables of Watchfulness (12:39–40, 42–46)
Kingdom Compared with Leaven (13:20–21)
The Great Supper (14:16–23)
The Joyous Shepherd (15:4–7)
Investing the Pounds (19:11–27)
The Threatened House (6:47–49)

Jesus as Eschatological Messenger and Salvation-Bringer
Jesus' Ministry Fulfills Scripture (7:18–23)
John Is the Forerunner; Jesus Brings the Kingdom (7:24–35)

Law and Prophets Give Way to the Kingdom (16:16–17)
To Receive Jesus Is to Receive God (10:16)
Jesus = The Sign of Jonah: Prophet and Wise Man (11:29b–32)
Sitting at Jesus' Table in the Kingdom (14:15; 22:28–30)
Lament over Jerusalem Ends in Promise of Messiah's Coming (13:34–35; 19:41–44)

It can be seen at a glance that Q is indeed dominated by eschatology. The form of apocalyptic hope that it exhibits is the expectation of Jesus coming from heaven as Son of man: Luke 11:30; 12:8–9; 12:40; 17:24; 17:26, 30 (each time with a parallel in Matthew). Richard Edwards has shown[2] that of these six sayings four were created by prophets within the Q community itself (the community that produced the source Q): Luke 11:30; 17:24; 17:26, 30. These four he calls "eschatological correlatives." Käsemann had already shown that Luke 12:8–9 is a product of early Christian prophecy; it is one of what he calls "sentences of holy law" and we would prefer to call "eschatological judgement pronouncements." Under these conditions it is more than likely that the sixth, Luke 12:40 ("You also must be ready for the Son of man is coming at an unexpected hour"), is also early Christian prophetic exhortation. The importance of Jesus as Son of man to the Q community can be seen in the fact that it refers to Jesus as Son of man not only in connection with his eschatological judgement, but also in his earthly ministry: Luke 7:34; 9:58; 12:10; and their parallels in Matthew.

The origin of the expectation of Jesus coming from heaven as Son of man is disputed. It is clear that the ultimate origin is Dan. 7:13–14:

> I saw in the night visions,
>   and behold, with the clouds of heaven
>   there came one like a son of man,
>   and he came to the Ancient of Days
>   and was presented before him.
> And to him was given dominion
>   and glory and kingdom,
>   that all peoples, nations, and languages
>   should serve him;
> his dominion is an everlasting dominion,
>   which shall not pass away,
> and his kingdom one
>   that shall not be destroyed.

But how we got from that to the sayings in Q is a matter of dispute. There are two possibilities. Either (a) Jesus proclaimed the coming of the Son of man as eschatological judge without identifying himself with that figure, and then the early church made the identification: Jesus is that Son of man.[3] Or (b) the early church arrived at the expectation by interpreting the resurrection of Jesus in light of Psalm 110:1 and Dan. 7:13–14, and Jesus himself did not speak of the Son of man as eschatological judge at all. I myself hold the latter view[4] on the grounds that the expectation did not exist as a firm conception for Jesus to use in his message and that, furthermore, all apocalyptic Son of man sayings fail the test of the criteria for authenticity of sayings of Jesus (these criteria are discussed in [Perrin's] chapter 12), while at the same time exhibiting typical characteristics of early Christian prophecy.

The Q community expected the return of Jesus from heaven as Son of Man with power to execute the eschatological judgement (Luke 12:8–9). He would come suddenly and unexpectedly, but he would most certainly come (Luke 12:40). Faced with the need to give form and content to this expectation, prophets in the community reached back into the history of the Jews and claimed that it would be like Jonah's coming to the Ninevites (Luke 11:30), like lightning striking (Luke 17:24), or like the judgemental catastrophes associated with Noah and Lot (Luke 17:26, 30). Then, with this expectation and with the conviction that the coming was imminent, they set out to instruct and exhort, to challenge and teach people to prepare themselves for it. This dominance of an apocalyptic expectation and the subordination of other activities to the urgency of proclamation and instruction, so much so that almost everything is oriented towards eschatology, justifies us in calling the Q source a document of apocalyptic Christianity. Moreover, the prophets interpret Jesus in categories or texts given to them by the apocalyptic movement, and they regard their sacred meal as an anticipation of that which they will eat with Jesus "in the kingdom of God" (Luke 14:15; 22:28–30).

A very similar orientation is to be found in 1 and 2 Thessalonians, and we could certainly adduce those letters as texts produced by apocalyptic Christianity, but we shall defer that aspect of them until we discuss Paul and deutero-Pauline Christianity.

The Apocalyptic Discourses: Mark 13 and Its Parallels

We come nearer to the actual literary forms of apocalyptic in Mark 13 and in its parallels in Matthew 24 and Luke 21. Apocalyptic discourses, speeches detailing the events to be expected when the End actually comes, are a feature of apocalyptic literature in general. *Assumption of Moses* 10, which we gave earlier in our description of the apocalyptic hope, is such a discourse, and other examples are *1 Enoch* 1:3–9; *1 Enoch* 46:1–8; 4 Ezra 6:13–28. These discourses follow the pattern of apocalyptic expectation concerning the End, with variations depending on the particular form of the expectation held by the writer. There is usually a description of the "woes," the climactic catastrophes marking the death throes of human history as now known. This is followed by an account of the form of God's eschatological intervention, either directly or through an eschatological redeemer figure. Then there is an account of the final judgement itself and a description of the punishment of the wicked and the eternal blessedness of the people of God that will follow.

Such discourses were written in a certain way. The particular form of the apocalyptic hope held by the writer gave the overall pattern, but the actual content came from two sources: the scripture, that is, the writings held by the writer to be sacred, and the experience of the writer and the group he represented. The scriptures themselves were used in two ways: they were either directly quoted, or they were alluded to. Sometimes the writer wished to reinterpret an existing text; sometimes he reached his texts by association of ideas, of words, or even of the *sounds* of words (in the ancient world reading usually meant reading aloud, even to oneself, as in Acts 8:30 when Philip *hears* the Ethiopian reading Isaiah 53). So an apocalyptic discourse is usually a mosaic of scriptural quotations and allusions, together perhaps with some reference to the experience of the writer and his community, generally couched in scriptural language.

The Christian apocalyptic discourses vary from this general pattern in that they include sections of parenesis in which the writer exhorts his readers directly out of his text. In this respect the discourses follow the Christian practice of combining parenesis with proclamation.

We now offer an analysis of Mark 13, following in the main that offered by Lars Hartman in *Prophecy Interpreted.*[5]

13:1–5a

An introduction to the discourse, composed by the evangelist Mark to give the discourse its present setting in the gospel as a whole

13:5b–8

The first section of the discourse proper. It quotes Dan. 2:28–29, 45 (LXX: "this must take place"), 2 Chr. 15:6; Isa. 19:2 (the references to nation against nation and kingdom against kingdom), and alludes to Dan. 7:21; 9:26; 11:4–27; and perhaps 2:40 at various places.

13:9–13

The first parenetical section. It couches references to the actual and anticipated sufferings of Christians in language deliberately reminiscent of the sufferings of Jesus during his passion but also allusive of various scriptural passages (Dan. 7:25; Psalm 119:46; Dan. 6:13–24). Verse 11b alludes to Exod. 4:11–17, and verse 12 quotes Mic. 7:2, 6.

13:14–20
The second section of the discourse. It quotes and reinterprets Dan. 11:31 and 12:11 in the reference to the "desolating sacrilege" (in Daniel this is the altar to Zeus set up in the Jerusalem Temple by the Syrians). The command to "flee to the mountains" is a quote from Gen. 19:16, as is the command for the man in the field not to turn back in verse 16. In verse 19 the description of the tribulation quotes Dan. 12:1.

13:21–23
The second parenetical section. The references to the false prophets uses language taken from Deut. 13:1–5, but the whole addresses itself to concrete problems faced by the Christian church in a period of intense apocalyptic expectation.

13:24–27
The third section of the discourse. Here the quotations are frequent. Verse 24 quotes Joel 2:10 (the sun being darkened) and Isa. 13:10 (the moon not giving its light). Verse 25 has the stars falling and the powers of heaven being shaken (from Isa. 34:4). The Son of Man reference in verse 26 is from Dan. 7:13, and verse 27 is a mosaic of Deut. 30:3–4 and Zech. 2:10 (in the LXX version). There are allusions to Isa. 11:10–12; 27:13; and Dan. 7:14 at various places.

Verse 27 ends the apocalyptic discourse proper. The remaining verses 28–37 form a loose-knit, final parenetical section that does not contain a single scriptural quotation but does show a good deal of Christian traditional material. It was almost certainly added to the original discourse by Mark himself.

It is not our purpose here to analyse in any detail the parallel discourses in Matthew and Luke; we are not offering a detailed commentary on these passages but only introducing to the reader this particular early Christian literary form. Briefly, Matt. 24:4–31 follows Mark with only minor additions and changes, as does 24:32–36 (= the loose-knit parenesis of Mark 13:28–32). But Matthew then adds a whole series of sayings of various kinds that have parallels in Luke in a different context; i.e., they are from Q – Matt. 24:37–51. The Lukan context is the more original, since it is Matthew who arranges teaching material in long discourses. Then Matthew further adds a chapter of eschatological parables (Matthew 25). Luke 21:8–28 is close to Mark's discourse, yet sufficiently different from it to make it possible that he may be following a version of the discourse different from what Mark has. But it is in any case fundamentally the same discourse.

What the original date of this discourse might have been, or what its original form might have been, it is equally impossible to say. It is the nature of apocalyptic writers to interpret and reinterpret texts, even their own, so that any discourse text we have represents the version of it that came from the hand of the particular evangelist concerned. Matthew is conservative in his treatment of Mark's discourse, but then Matthew is no longer an apocalyptic writer; he is on the way to becoming a rabbi, as will appear evident when we discuss him in a later chapter. Luke, on the other hand, has a version so different from Mark's and yet so closely related to it that he may be following a different version of the discourse in the tradition of the church, as noted earlier. But it may also be that Luke, who is by no means becoming in any respect a rabbi, is simply exercising the traditional freedom of a writer dealing with an apocalyptic text. Mark is also an apocalyptic writer, and he must certainly have reworked the discourse he presents. Mark 13:5b–27 is a product of the evangelist Mark, and we shall treat it as such when we come to discuss the gospel of Mark later. Yet apocalyptic discourses are such that so complex a discourse could not have been created by one man at one time in one place, but must have grown and developed over a considerable time. As they stand, then, the apocalyptic discourses in the New Testament are testimony to the continuing element of the apocalyptic Christianity and should be read as such. But they are also evidence of the particular concerns of the individual evangelists, and they need also be read in this way.

The Book of Revelation

The one complete apocalyptic text in the New Testament is the Book of Revelation. It is a thoroughly apocalyptic work, and yet in two respects it differs from the usual apocalyptic texts: it is not pseudonymous, and it contains letters to churches located in Asia Minor.

The author identifies himself as "John" and describes himself as having been exiled to Patmos, a small, rocky island in the Aegean Sea about thirty-seven miles southwest of Miletus. Such islands were often used as places of banishment by the Romans, and Christian tradition has it that John was banished there by the emperor Domitian in A.D. 95 and was released some eighteen months later when Nerva became emperor. We have no way of knowing whether this tradition is historically accurate – but surely such a procedure would be entirely normal in the Greco-Roman world. John himself tells us that he was exiled "on account of the word of God and the testimony of Jesus" (Rev. 1:9), that is, as a result of persecution of the Christians. The work itself bears out this claim for it is self-evidently written to encourage Christians in a situation of persecution.

The possibility and fact of the persecution of Christians in the Roman Empire during New Testament times is important enough to warrant spending a moment on it. The Roman government was tolerant of local religions but at the same time anxious to guarantee overall loyalty to the Empire. A polytheistic society presented no problems; local inhabitants were asked to formally acknowledge the gods of Rome, and having done so, they were free to continue their local religious beliefs and practices. As monotheists, the Jews could not acknowledge the gods of Rome; yet their special position was recognized, their religion was accepted by the Roman authorities as a legal religion, and they were freed from the requirement. The Christians, however, were no longer Jews, and were therefore in the position of having to refuse to acknowledge the gods of Rome while lacking the protection of a recognized legal religion. Thus, they were liable to persecution at any time: the local Roman official could demand that they acknowledge the gods of Rome; they would have to refuse and be liable to banishment, torture, or even death. This ever present possibility hung over the church from the moment it severed its ties with Judaism and is reflected constantly in the New Testament itself. Moreover, New Testament Christians lived with the memory of the sudden persecution of the Christians in Rome under the emperor Nero, at which time tradition has it that both Peter and Paul perished. John's exile to Patmos was the result of a local persecution, but he clearly anticipated that it could spread to engulf all the churches to which and for which he wrote.

Another element in the persecution of Christians in New Testament times was the widespread tendency for the Roman emperor to be worshipped as a god. This had spread from the East to the West in the Hellenistic world and was more accepted in some places than in others: some emperors demanded it, while others deplored it; similarly, some local Roman authorities pressed for it while others did not. Again, the Jews were in a privileged position the Christians could not share, in that such worship was not required of them.

There was, furthermore, hostility from and possible persecution by the Jews themselves. Jewish communities tended to be tightly knit, with a certain authority over their own members. Paul says that "five times I have received at the hands of the Jews the forty lashes less one" (2 Cor. 11:24), which was a Jewish punishment, just as the reference "three times I have been beaten with rods" (2 Cor. 11:25) was a Roman one. Similarly, Mark 13:9 speaks of

Christians being "beaten in synagogues" and of standing "before governors and kings for my sake"; these, again, are references respectively to Jewish and to Roman persecution of Christians.

Persecution from Jews and Romans was, then, always a possibility for the men and women of the New Testament. John reports that the blood of martyrs had already flowed (2:13; 6:9); the "hour of trial" was threatening all Christendom (3:10); the emperor would demand divine worship (13:4, 12–17; 16:2; 19:20), which Christians would have to refuse (14:9–12). This impending persecution inspires John's apocalyptic vision. We cannot be sure when or where the particular persecution spoken of took place, but most modern scholars incline to the time of the emperor Domitian (A.D. 81–96) and the locale of Asia Minor. This is where early Christian tradition locates John and his book, for he writes his letters to the churches of Asia Minor. The normal practice of dating an apocalyptic work by its recital of recent history in symbols fails in this instance. The clearest reference is to the "Kings" in 17:10, and the writer appears to have lived under the sixth of these. If these were six Roman emperors, beginning with Augustus and omitting the short reigns of Galbo, Otho, and Vitellius, the sixth would be Vespasian, emperor from A.D. 70–79. But Vespasian did not demand worship of himself as a god, and there is no knowledge of a persecution of Christians in Asia Minor during his reign. The conditions implied by the book as a whole simply do not fit. Either the author is reusing an earlier text, or he does not know his emperors.

More important than the date of the work, however, is the fact that the author identifies himself: moreover, he identifies himself as a prophet by describing his work as a prophecy (Rev. 1:3). We pointed out earlier that a distinguishing feature of earliest Christianity was the consciousness of the return of prophecy to the community. John of Patmos is such an early Christian prophet, and he describes the ecstatic vision that qualifies him: "I was in the Spirit on the Lord's day ..." (1:10). The vision itself is an interesting combination of the kind of experience the classical Hebrew prophets claimed as validating their message (for example, Isaiah 6) and the typical visions of apocalyptic writers. John's vision is characteristically apocalyptic; yet at the same time it is shaped by the characteristics of classical Hebrew prophecy. John is an apocalyptic seer, but he is also a prophet, and this "also" is very important to him, just as the possession of the spirit of prophecy was to early Christianity in general.

That John of Patmos can be identified as a prophet is more important to understanding his work than identifying him with some other individual named John in the New Testament. Traditionally it has been claimed that he is the John, son of Zebedee, known to us from the gospel stories, but this is most unlikely. It has also been claimed that he is the "John" of the fourth gospel, but the difference in style alone makes this identification quite impossible. However, that he is able to identify himself, and as a prophet (in sharp contrast to the pseudonymity and practice of apocalyptic writers in general), speaks volumes for the vitality, power, and self-confidence of New Testament Christianity.

Another most unusual aspect of the book of Revelation is its letters to seven churches in Asia Minor: Ephesus, Smyrna, Pergamum, Thyatira, Sardis, Philadelphia, and Laodicea (see [Perrin's] Chapters 2 and 3). This is unparalleled in apocalyptic writing and has to be due ultimately to the impact that Paul's letter writing made on the New Testament church. Paul's letters had become so important that the literary form was imitated even by an apocalyptic writer. The Book of Revelation as a whole has the external form of a letter in that it begins with an opening salutation (1:4–6) and closes with a benediction (22:21). The contrast in literary form between the direct address of the letters and the symbolic drama of the remainder of the book is startling, but no more so than the fact that an apocalyptic writer identifies himself and calls his work a prophecy.

The fact that we have here the outward form of a Pauline letter helps us to grasp the essential thrust of the work. It begins with a salutation in the Pauline style: "To him who loves us and has freed us from our sins by his blood and made us a kingdom, priests to his God and Father, to him be glory and dominion for ever and ever. Amen" (Rev. 1:5b–6; compare Gal. 1:3–5). But then it continues: "Behold, he is coming with the clouds, and every eye will see him, every one who pierced him; and all tribes of the earth will wail on account of him. Even so. Amen" (1:7). This is a classic statement of the early Christian hope for the return of Jesus as apocalyptic judge and redeemer. Similarly, the closing benediction, "The grace of the Lord Jesus be with all the saints. Amen" (22:21), is in the Pauline style, but it is preceded by a prayer for the coming of the Lord, "Come, Lord Jesus" (22:20). However, this is the early Palestinian Christian Eucharistic prayer *Maranatha*, which Paul himself used at the end of a letter: "Our Lord, come! The grace of the Lord Jesus be with you. My love be with you all in Christ Jesus. Amen" (1 Cor. 16:22–24). It is a reminder that for all its surface strangeness, the Book of Revelation is not to be separated from the rest of the New Testament. The hope it represents is a fundamental feature of a major part of the New Testament.

The nature of an apocalyptic work is such that it necessarily defies exact analysis and a precise outline. Rather it offers a series of dramatic presentations of the author's hope for the future, at the same time reflecting the author's understanding of the past and his reinterpretation of texts he accepts as sacred. The result is that any detailed analysis of the Book of Revelation is somewhat arbitrary and in a sense a denial of its very quality as a literary text. An apocalyptic work seeks to stun its readers by the power of its visions so that the reader loses his fear of the present and is caught up in the hope for the future it presents. Nevertheless, as an aid to understanding and appreciating the book as a whole, the following broad analysis of its contents is offered.

1:1–3
Opening address.

1:4–20
The prophet's vision validating his authority to write to the seven churches.

2:1–3:22
The letters to the seven churches.

4:1–5:14
The prophet's further vision, validating his message as an apocalyptic seer (this vision shows the influence of Ezekiel 1 and 2).

6:1–7:17
The necessary first stages, the overture to the coming of the End itself.

8:1–14:13
The preparation for the End, including an explanation of the status of Christian martyrs.

14:14–20
Interjected prospect of the final judgement.

15:1–22:5
Visions of the coming of the End itself.

22:6–21
Concluding postscript.

The Visions and Symbols of Apocalyptic

The visions of the Book of Revelation and of apocalyptic in general are strange and arbitrary to the modern reader. But remember that visions play a real part in the general history of religion. A vivid example from recent North American culture is the "great vision" of Black Elk, a holy man of the Oglala Sioux, as reported by him to John G. Neihardt.[6] Here is a scene taken at random from that vision:

And as I looked and wept, I saw that there stood on the north side of the starving camp a sacred man who was painted red all over his body, and he held a spear as he walked into the center of the people, and there he lay down and rolled. And when he got up, it was a fat bison standing there, and where the bison stood a sacred herb sprang up right where the tree had been in the center of the nation's hoop. The herb grew and bore four blossoms on a single stem while I was looking – a blue, a white, a scarlet, and a yellow – and the bright rays of these flashed to the heavens. I know now what this meant, that the bison were the gift of a good spirit and were our strength, but we should lose them, and from the same good spirit we must find another strength.[7]

Like John of Patmos, Black Elk is given to understanding the past and to interpreting the future by means of a vision.

The component parts of a vision are conveyed to the seer by his own culture. John of Patmos meditated on the scriptures he inherited from his tradition, and Black Elk on the stories told to him; both were surrounded by the artifacts and sacred elements of their people. The differences between the visions are, therefore, easy to understand; what should be taken seriously is their similarity as visions.

An important element in the visions of John of Patmos is their relationship to early Christian worship. His authenticating vision comes to him while he is "in the Spirit on the Lord's day" (Rev. 1:10), and he constantly quotes what on form-critical grounds can be recognized as fragments of confessions, prayers, and hymns, which must come from the liturgy of his church or be modelled on it: Rev. 1:5–6; 4:8, 11; 5:9–10; 7:10, 12; 11:15, 17–18; 12:10–12; 15:3–4; 19:1–2, 5–8; 22:13. Both the fact of John's visions and the reality of the form they take for him are not to be denied. As we have said, such visions are well known in the general history of religion, and the particular form of John's vision came from the culture he inherited, the scriptures on which he meditated, and the liturgy of the church whose worship was a central aspect of his life.

Another aspect of apocalyptic to be taken seriously is its symbolism. We may perhaps illustrate this best with reference to one symbol common to all New Testament apocalyptic, the "son of man" from Dan. 7:13. We have already noted that the Q community turned to Dan. 7:13, that prophets in that community produced Son of man sayings to put on the lips of Jesus, and that the apocalyptic discourses also turn to that passage and its central symbol. When one gets to a certain level of experience or expectation, the normal structure of language is simply shattered, and what is experienced or expected can be described only in symbols, often in archetypal symbols that have deep roots in the consciousness of man as man. So it is with the consciousness of evil, sin, and guilt and with the expectation of a cataclysmic, eschatological act whereby evil, sin, and guilt will be no more. The Jewish myth explains the existence of sin as the result of the rebellion of primordial man, Adam, and its natural consequence is the expectation that the act of another representative man would redeem that sin. When Paul says, "as one man's trespass led to condemnation for all men, so one man's act of righteousness leads to acquittal and life for all men" (Rom. 5:18), he is reflecting the natural consequence of accepting the myth that sin resulted from the rebellious act of primordial man. In the language of apocalyptic symbolism, the same natural consequence is the idea of the coming of a redeemer figure "like a son of man," a figure human yet more than human, and it is undoubtedly this fundamental propensity of the human mind to think in such terms that accounts for the prominence of Son of man symbolism in early Christian apocalyptic.

Another example of the human mind's fundamental propensity to embrace myth or symbol when attempting to approach the ultimates of human experience or expectation is Amos Wilder's poetic expression of his experience in the First World War.

> There we marched out on haunted battle-ground,
> There smelled the strife of gods, were brushed against
> By higher beings, and were wrapped around
> With passions not of earth, all dimly sensed.
>
> There saw we demons fighting in the sky
> And battles in aerial mirage,
> The feverish Very lights proclaimed them by,
> Their tramplings woke our panting, fierce barrage.
>
> Their tide of battle, hither, thither, driven
> Filled earth and sky with cataclysmic throes,
> Our strife was but the mimicry of heaven's
> And we the shadows of celestial foes.[8]

We quote Wilder deliberately because he is consciously sensitive to this aspect of apocalyptic, ancient or modern, Christian or secular; but many other examples could be given.

So in thinking of apocalyptic we have to think of the human mind at a level of ultimacy and at that level turning naturally to the use of myth and symbol. In the case of the ancient Jewish and early Christian apocalyptic the ultimacy came from a total despair of the course of human history and an absolute trust in the purpose of God. The result is the visions and symbols we have been discussing.

Norman Perrin

The Enduring Influence of Early
Christian Apocalyptic

The most obvious influence of early Christian apocalyptic is the continuing existence of Christian apocalyptic sects and movements. Throughout Christian history, groups of believers have fed their hopes on New Testament apocalyptic literature and calculated the date of the coming of Jesus as Son of man, as indeed many still do. Similarly, the Beast whose number is six hundred and sixty-six (Rev. 13:18) has been identified with every tyrant in Western history, including Hitler and Stalin. But this is a literalistic and hence necessarily false understanding of the apocalyptic hope.

More important is the enduring influence of the myths and symbols of early Christian apocalyptic itself wherever the New Testament has been read. In modern times historical scholars have had all kinds of problems with the Book of Revelation, but poets and artists have found it an unending source of inspiration precisely because it uses images of immense evocative power. Early Christian apocalyptic does not challenge us to gather together on a hillside to await the coming of Jesus as Son of man, or to identify the Beast; it challenges us to recognize the importance and significance of the myths and symbols it uses so dramatically to express hope in the midst of despair.

NOTES

1 This passage is discussed briefly in ch. 2 [of Perrin's book], 35.

2 R. A. Edwards, *The Sign of Jonah in the Theology of the Evangelists and Q*, Studies in Biblical Theology, Second Series, 10 (London: SCM Press, 1971) 49–58.

3 This view is represented, for example, by H. E. Tödt, *The Son of Man in the Synoptic Tradition* (Philadelphia: Westminster Press, 1965) and R. H. Fuller, *The Foundations of New Testament Christology* (New York: Charles Scribner's Sons, 1965).

4 Norman Perrin, *Rediscovering the Teaching of Jesus* (New York: Harper & Row; London: SCM Press, 1967) 164–99. My views as to the subsequent development of the Son of man Christology in the New Testament are to be found in "The Son of Man in the Synoptic Tradition," *Biblical Research* 13 (1965) 1–23; "The Christology of Mark: A Study in Methodology," *Journal of Religion* (1971) 173–87; "Towards the Interpretation of the Gospel of Mark" in H. D. Betz, ed., *Christology and a Modern Pilgrimage: A Discussion with Norman Perrin* (Claremont, Calif.: Society of Biblical Literature, 1971); *A Modern Pilgrimage in New Testament Christology* (Philadelphia: Fortress Press; London: SCM Press, 1974).

5 Lars Hartman, *Prophecy Interpreted*, Coniectanea biblica, New Testament 1 (Lund: G. W. K. Gleerup, 1966) 145–59.

6   G. Neihardt, *Black Elk Speaks* (Lincoln: University of Nebraska Press, 1960) 20–47.

7   Neihardt, 38–9.

8   Quoted by Amos Wilder in his article "The Rhetoric of Ancient and Modern Apocalyptic," *Int* 25 (1971) 436–53. Originally printed in Amos Wilder, *Battle Retrospect and Other Poems*, copyright 1923, Yale University Press. Reprinted by permission.

8

The Attainment of
Millennial Bliss Through Myth:
The Book of Revelation*

JOHN G. GAGER

Thus far we have followed the lead of recent anthropologists in assuming that millenarian movements fail because they do not achieve their stated goal – the millennium. In an obvious sense, of course, this judgement is true. But at the same time certain aspects of these cults have already suggested that they may indeed reach the millennium in other, less obvious, ways. To begin with, there is the undeniable continuity of the group and its individual members. The failure of fundamental prophecies always produces some defections, but the remarkable fact that the majority remains should prompt us to ask whether the millennium has in some sense come to life in the experience of the community as a whole. Undoubtedly, rationalization and missionary activity are factors that facilitate continued adherence to the group, but insofar as millennial dreams remain alive they are probably understood to have been at least partially fulfilled. What interests us at present is the mode of their fulfillment. Some of the standard forms are sacraments, meditation, asceticism, and mystical visions. In these instances, the attainment of millennial bliss is largely individual. Other forms encompass the entire community. M. Simon remarks of Qumran "that the whole organization of the Essene sect is a prefiguration of the coming kingdom."[1] In similar fashion, we have argued that various elements of early Christian ethics can best be understood as efforts to capture in the present the conditions of the future – the self-designation of Christians as brothers and sisters; the abolition, at least in theory, of pre-millennial distinctions between male and female, Jew and Greek, slave and free; and the denigration in some quarters of marriage

* First published in *Kingdom and Community* by J. G. Gager (1975) 49–57, 64–65 (notes).

and sex. Beyond these modes of apprehending the future, I would contend that the Book of Revelation, as an expression of apocalyptic mythology, offers a third and largely unexamined form of anticipating the End.

In approaching this particular book, however, we must be conscious of its fate in Western history, for it has probably alienated more readers than it has enchanted. One common solution to the enigmatic character of the book has been to treat it as a kind of literary puzzle, either by seeing it as a collage of prophetic sayings drawn from Daniel, Ezekiel, Zechariah, and others, or by attempting to decipher its historical and political code.[2] More recently attention has turned from individual symbols and passages to the structure of the writing as a whole. Here, it is thought, lies the key to its interpretation. The obvious advantage of this approach is that it accepts the work for what it is, an irreducibly mythological and tightly structured product of literary creativity. To be sure, there has been nothing even approaching unanimity on specific details of structure. Austin Farrer's tantalizingly complex analysis in *A Rebirth of Images: The Making of Saint John's Apocalypse*[3] and J. W. Bowman's theatrical interpretation,[4] complete with settings and props borrowed from the Greco-Roman stage, have little in common beyond a sense that the key to understanding lies in structure. Still, this common ground is important and offers the only substantial basis for further work.

My own approach presupposes both the importance of structure and the indispensability of myth in locating the author's method and message. In addition, however, I assign both structure and myth to a specific role in relation to the concrete situation (persecution and martyrdom) and purpose (consolation) of the book as a whole. Whatever its date and location, the writing inescapably presupposes a situation in which believers had experienced suffering and death at the hands of Rome. This is the crisis in which John offers his unique message of consolation – consolation not simply as the promise of a happy fate for the martyr in the near future but through the mythological enactment of that future in the present. In a word, through "the suppression of time." Though the phrase itself is borrowed from Claude Lévi-Strauss's *The Raw and the Cooked*,[5] the idea of overcoming time by various means is by no means a novel one. Both Lévi-Strauss[6] and Mircea Eliade[7] have suggested that psychoanalysis represents a secular counterpart of the same phenomenon. And it is at the point of this analogy between ancient myth and ritual on the one hand and modern psychoanalysis on the other that the structure of the Book or Revelation enters the picture.

John G. Gager

For I intend to argue that the writing is a form of therapy, much like the technique of psychoanalysis, whose ultimate goal is to transcend the time between a real present and a mythical future. In this analogy, the relationship between myth and audience parallels the relationship between analyst and patient; both serve as vehicles for suppressing time. In his essay on "The Effectiveness of Symbols," Lévi-Strauss recognizes the differences between the two cases, but insists on a fundamental similarity: the therapeutic value of myth and psychoanalysis lies in their unique ability to manipulate symbols and in so doing to change reality.

One basic function of myth is to overcome unwelcome contradictions between hope and reality, between what ought to be and what is, between an ideal past or future and a flawed present. Clearly, the hearers (Rev. 1:3) of the book were caught in such a predicament. The occasion was persecution at the hands of the church's enemies, but the real crisis lay in the unbearable and irreconcilable tensions created by persecution. On the one hand was the belief that, as Christians, they were the chosen people of God, protected by him and assured of eternal life in his kingdom. On the other hand was the overwhelming experience of suffering, deprivation, and death at the hands of those whom they most despised. Although the precise date of the book is uncertain,[8] it probably dates from the very end of the first century. We know from one of Pliny's letters to the emperor Trajan (*Epistle* 10, dating from 112 C.E.) that Christian communities in Asia Minor were being persecuted by Roman officials in the years between 90 and 100 C.E.[9] What we learn from the book itself is the depth and intensity of the Christian reaction to persecution.

In speaking of medieval millenarian movements, Cohn likens their view of the world to a form of paranoia:

> The megalomaniac view of oneself as the elect, wholly good, abominably persecuted yet assured of ultimate triumph; the attribution of gigantic and demonic powers to the adversary ... these attitudes are symptoms which together constitute the unmistakable syndrome of paranoia. But a paranoic delusion does not cease to be so because it is shared by so many individuals, nor yet because those individuals have real and ample grounds for regarding themselves as victims of oppression.[10]

Whether or not we accept Cohn's comparison of apocalyptic mentality and group paranoia, his language conveys a sense of the internal crisis that confronted the author and his audience. I emphasize this point because it explains why a simple message of consolation, encouraging believers to stand firm and reiterating

148

earlier promises, would have been inadequate to the needs of the occasion. Indeed, these traditional hopes and promises were very much a part of the crisis, for their credibility had been called into question by the fact of persecution, and simply to repeat them would have been to compound the agony. Instead the writer offers a Christian myth, using as building blocks the full supply of Jewish and Christian symbols. And he structures these symbols so as to reflect the bifurcated experience of believers under persecution. Much attention has been given to the obvious role of the number seven in the framework of the work as a whole: seven sections, each with seven parts; seven opening letters; seven trumpets; seven seals; etc. Equally important, however, because it closely mirrors the crisis to which the book is directed, is the separation of all symbols into two distinct categories: symbols of oppression and despair (beasts, plagues, Babylon, Satan, etc.) *and* symbols of hope and victory (Lamb, elders, book of life, New Jerusalem, etc.). There is no middle ground, no possibility of mediation or reconciliation between the two poles. The absence, even the unacceptability of any common ground between worship of the beast and loyalty to the Lamb, is symbolically represented in the last of the letters to the seven churches:

> I know your works: you are neither cold nor hot. Would that you were cold or hot! So, because you are lukewarm, and neither cold nor hot, I will spew you out of my mouth.
>
> Rev. 3:15–16

As we have seen in our earlier discussion of millenarian movements, the category of lukewarmness has no meaning whatsoever in an apocalyptic setting where good and evil are completely unambiguous and totally opposed. Thus it can only be spit out at the very beginning and eliminated from the subsequent drama.

At this point we must return to the overall structure of the work, for it is here that the two patterns (sevens and twos) meet to create a "machine" for transcending time. Contrary to initial impressions, the distribution of the two groups of symbols is not random; it follows a definite and recurring order from start to finish. There is a clear pattern of alternation between them, like the periodic crests and hollows of a continuous wave. This pattern is initiated in the opening letters (chapters 2—3): in three of the letters the writer follows praise with blame (2:2f.; 2:13; 2:19); in two he creates a dramatic tension between being dead and being alive (2:9; 3:1); and in the final letter he stresses the point through his rejection of those who are lukewarm. But the main force of the movement takes shape in the seven visions that stretch from 4:1 to 22:5. Schematically, these visions can be arranged as follows:

VICTORY/HOPE	OPPRESSION/DESPAIR
4:1—5:14 throne and lamb	
	6:1–17 first six seals
7:1—8:4 multitude of the faithful and seventh seal	
	8:5–9:21 first six trumpets
10:1—11:1 dramatic interlude in heaven	
	11:2–14 attack of the beasts
11:15–19 seventh trumpet	
	12:1–17 the dragon assaults the woman 13:1–18 the beast with horns
14:1–7 Mount Zion and Lamb	
	14:8—15:1 destruction and judgement
15:2–8 martyrs worship God	
	16:1–20 seven bowls of wrath 17:1—18:24 fall of Babylon
19:1–16 worship in heaven	
	19:17—20:15 final judgement
21:1—22:5 new heaven, new earth, new Jerusalem	

Several aspects of this rhythmic oscillation need to be underlined. In the first place, the pattern of recurrent crests and hollows breaks the pattern of sevens at three points: at 6:17 where the opening of

150

the sixth seal is followed not by the seventh seal but rather by a vision of the one hundred and forty-four thousand who bear the seal of God (7:1–17); again at 9:21 where the sixth trumpet gives way not to the seventh but to a dramatic interlude in which the final outcome is revealed to John alone (10:1–11); and, finally, at 15:1 where the seven angels with the seven plagues are introduced but followed immediately by a vision of those who have conquered the beast (15:2–4).[11] In the first two instances, an almost perfect series of seven disasters is broken by a vision of final glory; and in the third, the seven plagues are presented as symbols of penultimate rather than ultimate truth. By thus substituting a dynamic for a static relationship between oppression and hope, these broken series serve to undermine any tendency among the audience to treat them as permanent, unbearable contradictions. The glimpse of final victory in each case shatters the anticipation of perfect despair and points to an experience of exultation not just in the future but in the immediacy of the myth itself. Thus the dominant structural feature of the book is not the pattern of sevens, but the simpler and more immediate pattern of oscillating oppositions. A second observation concerns chapter 10, which falls roughly midway in the book. Properly speaking, chapter 10 ought to be bracketed as a moment of dramatic suspense, for it promises but then withholds the final revelation. At the same time, the scene in 10:8–10 provides an indispensable clue to the author's hidden design. His symbolic gesture of eating the scroll, coming as it does after the dramatic announcement of "the mystery of God" in 10:1–7, intimates that the path to understanding the work lies not in deciphering specific symbols or external events but rather in digesting the myth as a whole. Finally, we should note the relative imbalance between crests and hollows before and after chapter 10. In chapters 4—9 there is a rough equilibrium between symbols of hope (4:1—5:14; 7:1—8:4) and those of despair (6:1–17; 8:5—9:21), whereas after chapter 10 symbols of hope are in relative decline. But within the schema outlined above, this decline may be regarded as a deliberately dramatic preparation for the climactic visions of 21:1—22:5, which crown the story:

> Then I saw a new heaven and a new earth ... And night shall be no more; they need no light of lamp or sun, for the Lord God will be their light, and they shall reign for ever and ever.

To appreciate the therapeutic function of this final episode we must return to Lévi-Strauss's comparison of myth and psychoanalysis. In most cases the key to successful analysis lies in the dynamics of transference, through which the patient comes to experience repressed memories, relationships and instincts from the past – Lévi-Strauss likens them to a myth[12] – as alive in the present.[13] Through transference the therapist becomes a contemporaneous gateway for past events as they are recovered and rehearsed in a series of therapeutic encounters. Similarly, the therapeutic value of the myth rests on its periodic structure.[14] The audience's ability to identify with it depends on its wavelike character, which in turn expresses the contradictory experience of faith under persecution. And if we have sustained our analysis thus far, the triumphant visions of 21:1—22:5 represent both the suppression of time and the dissolution of contradictions. Their role is not just to illustrate what lies in the future but to transcend the time separating present from future, to make possible an experience of millennial bliss as living reality. Just as the therapeutic situation is the machine through which the patient comes to experience the *past* as present, so the myth is the machine through which the believing community comes to experience the *future* as present. In psychoanalytic terms, this appears as the phenomenon of abreaction, in which the patient reacts momentarily – in anger, fear, love, dependence, or whatever – to the therapist as he once related to parents, siblings, etc. The therapeutic function of myth could thus be called a form of abreaction.[15] And what unites the two techniques is a common view – one is tempted to label it as primitive – that knowledge can change the world. In comparing shamanism and psychoanalysis, Lévi-Strauss remarks that,

> in both cases also, the conflicts and resistances are resolved, not because of the knowledge, real or alleged, which the sick woman acquires of them, but because this knowledge makes possible *a specific experience, in the course of which conflicts materialize in an order and on a level permitting their free development and leading to their resolution.*[16]

To be sure, there is one major difference in the forms of this resolution, in that psychoanalysis leads to an integration of the conflicting poles, whereas the apocalyptic solution envisages the complete eradication of one pole. Apart from this difference of form, however, the process is essentially the same. Again in Lévi-Strauss's words,

> the effectiveness of symbols would consist precisely in the "inductive property," by which homologous structures, built out of different materials at different levels of life – organic processes, unconscious mind, rational thought – are related to one another.[17]

If Lévi-Strauss and others are right in proposing that changes at one level of reality or consciousness, say mythological, can induce homologous changes at other levels, say in one's perception of time, then we must revise our earlier assumption that millenarian movements always fail to attain the millennium. This is not to deny that the overcoming of time, whether through myth, abreaction, music, or poetic metaphor, is anything but transitory. The real world, in the form of persecution, reasserted itself with dogged persistence for Christian communities. But in an apocalyptic setting, where the goal is to support the community for a short time before the End, this ephemeral experience of the future might have been sufficient. For hearers of this book, even a fleeting experience of the millennium may have provided the energy needed to withstand the wrath of the beast.

Finally, we must consider the specific setting in which the book would have been able to exercise its therapeutic function. From the opening verse we know that it was meant to be read aloud before a gathered community: "Blessed is he who reads aloud the words of the prophecy, and blessed are those who hear ..." (1:3). We also know that it was customary in communal assemblies to read aloud from early Christian writings (Col. 4:16; 1 Thess. 5:27). Thus the intended setting for reading the book was collective rather than private. Furthermore, to an extent shared by no other primitive Christian document, the book's language, content, and structure is thoroughly liturgical; at one level it is little more than a compilation of prayers, benedictions, and hymns. Whether these liturgical fragments are the creations of the author himself or whether, as seems more likely, they reflect liturgical practice in Asia Minor,[18] they reinforce the view that the book was meant to be read before the community gathered for the purpose of worship. What role it may have played in the liturgy is more difficult to ascertain. The one undeniable fact is that the attention of the community, and thus of its worship, was entirely on the imminent End. "The time is near" (1:3) and "Amen, come Lord Jesus" (22:20) frame the work as a whole as much as they express the mood of its hearers. What other elements entered the liturgy must remain unknown, although it seems probable that the Lord's Supper would have been celebrated. If so, it no doubt took the primitive form of an eschatological sacrament in which, according to Schweitzer and others, the meal anticipated the return of Jesus and the messianic feast with him in the immediate future.[19] More importantly, we do not know whether the reading was completed in a single session, in which case reading the book would have been the chief ritual of the liturgy, or whether it was done in portions over a period of consecutive daily or weekly gatherings. At most, we may assume that the book would have achieved its maximum effectiveness if read in a compressed period of time. In any case, we know that it was not written for posterity nor as a permanent contribution to Christian worship. For it was the fervent hope of writer and hearer alike that there would be no need to hear these words on more than one or two occasions.

NOTES

[The bracketed number indicates the original footnote number in Gager's text.]

1 [121] Marcel Simon, *Jewish Sects at the Time of Jesus* (Philadelphia: Fortress Press, 1967).

2 [122] Both concerns dominate the massive and still indispensable commentary of R. H. Charles, *A Critical and Exegetical Commentary on the Revelation of St. John* (ICC; Edinburgh: T. & T. Clark, 1920), 2 vols.

3 [123] Austin Farrer, *A Rebirth of Images: The Making of Saint John's Apocalypse* (Boston: Beacon Press, 1963).

4 [124] J. W. Bowman, "The Revelation to John: Its Dramatic Structure and Message," *Int* 9 (1955) 436–53. See also his article, "Revelation, Book of," in *IDB* 4 (1962) 58–71.

5 [125] Claude Lévi-Strauss, *The Raw and the Cooked* (New York: Harper & Row, 1969) 16.

6 [126] Lévi-Strauss, especially in his essay, "The Effectiveness of Symbols," in *Structural Anthropology* (Garden City, N.Y.: Anchor Books, 1967) 181–201.

7 [127] Mircea Eliade, "Time Can Be Overcome," in *Myth and Reality* (New York: Harper & Row, 1963) 75–91.

8 [128] It is usually dated under the reign of Domitian, around the years 90–95 C.E.

9 [129] See W. H. C. Frend, *Martyrdom and Persecution in the Early Church: A Study of a Conflict from the Maccabees to Donatus* (Garden City, N.Y.: Anchor Books, 1967) 155–72.

10 [130] Norman Cohn, *The Pursuit of the Millennium: Revolutionary Messianism in Medieval and Reformation Europe and Its Bearing on Modern Totalitarian Movements* (New York: Harper & Row, 1961) 309. It should be noted that this particular passage does not appear in Cohn's second edition (1961) published as a Harper Torchbook by Harper & Row.

11 [132] Note also that the seven angels with the seven baleful trumpets are introduced in 8:2, then disappear in 8:3–5 (vision of the heavenly altar), and do not commence blowing until 8:6!

12 [133] Lévi-Strauss, "Effectiveness of Symbols," 196f.

13 [134] On transference see S. Freud, "The Dynamics of Transference (1912)," in *Collected Papers*, ed. Joan Riviere (2 vols.; New York: International Psycho-Analytical Press, 1959) 2:312–22.

14 [135] The role of repetition or redundancy is stressed by Lévi-Strauss in "Effec-

tiveness of Symbols," 188, 190, and 193f; and by Edmund Leach in *Genesis as Myth and Other Essays* (London: Jonathan Cape, 1969) 8–9.

15   [136] See also Lévi-Strauss, "Effectiveness of Symbols," 193f.

16   [137] Lévi-Strauss, 193f (emphasis added).

17   [138] Lévi-Strauss, 197.

18   [139] So, among others, Oscar Cullmann, *Early Christian Worship* (Philadelphia: Westminster Press, 1978; London: SCM Press, 1953) 7.

19   [140] Albert Schweitzer, *The Mysticism of Paul the Apostle* (New York: Seabury Press, 1968) 239–72. The eschatological character of the Lord's Supper in early Christian tradition is clearly visible in numerous texts: "Truly, I say to you, I shall not drink again of the fruit of the vine until that day when I drink it new in the kingdom of God" (Mark 14:25; cf. Matt. 26:29); and "For as often as you eat this bread and drink this cup, you proclaim the Lord's death until he comes" (1 Cor. 11:26).

Bibliography

Amsler, S. "Zacharie et l'origine de l'apocalyptique." VTSup 22 (1972) 227–31.

Barr, James. "Jewish Apocalyptic in Recent Scholarly Study." BJRL 58 (1975) 9–25.

Bentzen, Aage. Daniel. HAT 19, Tübingen: J. C. B. Mohr (Paul Siebeck), 1952.

Betz, Hans Dieter. "On the Problem of the Religio-historical Under-standing of Apocalypticism." JTC 6 (1969) 134–56.

Block, J. On the Apocalyptic in Judaism. JQRMS 2. Philadelphia: Dropsie College, 1952.

Collins, John J. The Apocalyptic Vision of the Book of Daniel. HSM 16. Missoula, Mont.: Scholars Press, 1977.

—, ed. Apocalypse: The Morphology of a Genre. Semeia 14. Missoula, Mont.: Scholars Press, 1979.

Cross, Frank Moore. "A Note on the Study of Apocalyptic Origins." In Canaanite Myth and Hebrew Epic: Essays in the History of the Religion of Israel, 343–6. Cambridge, Mass.: Harvard Univ. Press, 1973.

Delcor, Mathias. Le livre de Daniel. Sources bibliques Paris: Gabalda, 1971.

Dexinger, Ferdinand. Henochs Zehnwochenapokalypse und offene Probleme der Apokalyptikforschung. Studia Post-Biblica 29. Leiden: E. J. Brill, 1977.

Dingerman, Friedrich. "Die Botschaft vom Vergehen dieser Welt und von den Geheimnissen der Endzeit. Beginnende Apokalyptik im Alten Testament." In Wort und Botschaft, ed. J. Schreiner, 329–42. Wurzburg: Echter, 1967.

Emerton, John A. "The Origin of the Son of Man Imagery." JTS 9 (1958) 225–42.

Flusser, David. s.v. "Apocalypse." Encyclopaedia Judaica, 1971 ed.

Frost, S. B. 'Eschatology and Myth." VT 2 (1952) 70–80.

—Old Testament Apocalyptic: Its Origins and Growth. London: Epworth Press, 1952.

Frye, Richard N. "Reitzenstein and Qumran Revisited by an Iranian." HTR 55 (1962) 261–8.

Gese, Hartmut. "Anfang und Ende der Apokalyptik, dargestellt am Sachar-jabuch." ZTK 70 (1973) 20–49.

Ginsberg, H. L. Studies in Daniel. New York: Jewish Theological Seminary, 1948.

Gressmann, Hugo. Der Ursprung der israelitisch-jüdischen Eschatologie. Göttingen: Vandenhoeck & Ruprecht, 1905.

Gunkel, Hermann. *Schöpfung und Chaos in Urzeit und Endzeit: Eine religionsgeschichtliche Untersuchung über Gen 1 und Ap Joh 12.* Göttingen: Vandenhoeck & Ruprecht, 1895.

Hamerton-Kelly, Robert. "The Temple and the Origins of Jewish Apocalyptic." *VT* 20 (1970) 1–20.

Hammer, Raymond. *The Book of Daniel.* CBC. New York/Cambridge: Cambridge Univ. Press, 1976.

Hanson, Paul D. s.v. "Apocalypse, Genre." IDBSup.

—s.v. "Apocalypticism." IDBSup.

—"Apocalyptic Literature." In *The Old Testament and Its Modern Interpreters.* Forthcoming from Fortress Press/Scholars Press.

—*The Dawn of Apocalyptic: The Historical and Sociological Roots of Jewish Apocalyptic Eschatology.* 2d ed. Philadelphia: Fortress Press, 1979.

—*The Diversity of Scripture.* Philadelphia: Fortress Press, 1982.

—"The Historical Setting of Intertestamental Writings." In *The Cambridge History of Judaism.* Forthcoming from Cambridge Univer. Press.

—"In Defiance of Death: Zechariah's Symbolic Universe." Forthcoming in *Love and Death,* edited by John Marks.

—"Jewish Apocalyptic against its Near Eastern Environment." *RB* 78 (1971) 31–58.

—"Old Testament Apocalyptic Reexamined." *Int* 25 (1971) 454–79 and herein, 37–60.

—"Prolegomena to the Study of Jewish Apocalyptic." In *Magnalia Dei: The Mighty Acts of God. Essays on the Bible and Archaeology in Memory of G. Ernest Wright,* ed. F. M. Cross, 389–413. New York: Doubleday & Co., 1976.

—"Rebellion in Heaven, Azazel, and Euhemeristic Heroes in 1 Enoch 6—11." *JBL* 96 (1977) 195–233.

—"Zechariah 9 and the Recapitulation of an Ancient Ritual Pattern." *JBL* 92 (1973) 37–59.

Hartman, Louis F. and Alexander DiLella. *Daniel.* Anchor Bible. New York: Doubleday & Co., 1978.

Heaton, E. W. *Daniel.* London: SCM Press, 1956.

Jeremias, Christian. *Die Nachgesichte des Sacharja: Untersuchungen zu ihrer Stellung im Zusammenhang der Visionsberichte im Alten Testament und zu ihrem Bildmaterial.* FRLANT 117. Göttingen: Vandenhoeck & Ruprecht, 1977.

Käsemann, Ernst. "On the Subject of Primitive Christian Apocalyptic." In *New Testament Questions of Today,* 108–37. ET, W. J. Montague. Philadelphia: Fortress Press; London: SCM Press, 1969. Original "Die Anfänge christliches Theologie." In *ZTK* 57 (1960) 162–85.

Koch, Klaus, and Johann M. Schmidt, ed. *Apokalyptik.* Wege der Forschung [= *ZTK* 365]. Darmstadt: Wissenschaftliche Buchgesellschaft, 1982.

Koch, Klaus. "Spätisraelitisches Geschichtsdenken am Beispiel des Buches Daniel." *HZ* 193 (1961) 1–32.

—*The Rediscovery of Apocalyptic.* ET, M. Kohl. London: SCM Press, 1972.

Lacocque, André. *The Book of Daniel.* ET, D. Pellauer. Atlanta: John Knox Press, 1979.

Ladd, George E. "Why Not Prophetic Apocalyptic?" *JBL* 76 (1957) 192–200.

Lindblom, Johannes. *Die Jesaja-Apokalypse, Jes. 24—27.* Lund: C. W. K. Gleerup, 1938.

de Manasee, J. *Daniel,* Paris: Cerf, 1958.

Millar, William R. *Isaiah 24—27 and the Origin of Apocalyptic.* HSM 11. Missoula, Mont.: Scholars Press, 1976.

Montgomery, James A. *The Book of Daniel.* ICC. Edinburgh: T. & T. Clark, 1927.

Mowinckel, Sigmund. *He That Cometh.* ET, G. W. Anderson. Nashville: Abingdon Press, 1956.

Müller, Hans-Peter. "Mantische Weisheit und Apokalyptik." VTSup 22 (1972) 268–93.

—"Prophetie und Apokalyptik bei Joel." *Theologia Viatorum* 10, ed. Ulrich Wilckens, 231–52. Berlin: Walter de Gruyter, 1966.

Müller, Karlheinz. "Die Ansätze der Apokalyptik." In *Literatur und Religion des Fruhjudentums,* ed. J. Schreiner and J. Maier, 31–42. Wurzburg: Echter, 1973.

Murdock, William R. "History and Revelation in Jewish Apocalypticism." *Int* 21 (1967) 167–87.

Nickelsburg, George W. E. *Resurrection, Immortality, and Eternal Life in Intertestamental Judaism.* HTS 26. Cambridge, Mass.: Harvard Univ. Press; London: Oxford Univ. Press, 1972.

North, Robert. "Prophecy to Apocalyptic via Zechariah." In Vetus Testamentum's *Congress Volume, Uppsala 1971, 1972,* VTSup 22, 47–72. Leiden: E. J. Brill, 1972.

Noth, Martin. "History in Old Testament Apocalyptic." In *The Laws of the Pentateuch and Other Studies.* ET, D. R. Ap-Thomas. Philadelphia: Fortress Press, 1967; Edinburgh: Oliver & Boyd, 1966.

von der Osten-Sacken, Peter. *Die Apokalyptik in ihrem Verhältnis zu Prophetie und Weisheit.* Munich: Chr. Kaiser, 1969.

Perrin, Norman. *The New Testament: An Introduction.* New York: Harcourt Brace Jovanovich, 1974.

Petersen, David L. *Late Israelite Prophecy: Studies in Deutero-Prophetic Literature and in Chronicles.* SBLMS 23. Missoula, Mont.: Scholars Press, 1977.

Plöger, Otto. *Theocracy and Eschatology.* ET, S. Rudman. Richmond; John Knox Press; Oxford: Basil Blackwell, 1968.

Porteous, Norman W. *Daniel.* OTL. Philadelphia: Westminster Press; London: SCM Press, 1965.

von Rad, Gerhard. *Old Testament Theology*, vol. 2 ET, D. M. G. Stalker. New York: Harper & Row; Edinburgh: Oliver & Boyd, 1965.

—*Wisdom in Israel.* ET, J. D. Martin. Nashville: Abingdon Press; London: SCM Press, 1972.

Rowley, H. H. *The Relevance of Apocalyptic.* 2d ed. London: Lutterworth Press, 1947.

Russell, D. S. *The Method and Message of Jewish Apocalyptic.* OTL. Philadelphia: Westminster Press; London: SCM Press, 1964.

—*Apocalyptic: Ancient and Modern.* Philadelphia: Fortress Press; London: SCM Press, 1978.

Schmidt, Johann M. *Die jüdische Apokalyptik: Die Geschichte ihrer Erforschung von den Anfängen bis zu den Textfunden von Qumran.* Neukirchen-Vluyn: Neukirchener, 1969.

Schmithals, Walter. *The Apocalyptic Movement: Introduction and Interpretation.* ET, J. Steely. Nashville: Abingdon Press, 1973.

Schreiner, Josef. *Alttestamentlich-jüdische Apokalyptik.* Munich: Kösel, 1969.

Schunk, Klaus-Dietrich. "Die Eschatologie der Propheten des Alten Testaments und ihre Wandlung in exilisch-nachexilischer Zeit." In *Studies on Prophecy*, VTSup 26, 116–32. Leiden: E. J. Brill, 1974.

Steinmann, Jean. *Daniel.* Paris: Cerf, 1950.

Stone, Michael E. "Apocalyptic Literature." In *Compendia Rerum Iudaicarum ad Novum Testamentum*, sec. 2, vol. 2. Forthcoming.

Stuhlmueller, Carroll. s.v. "Post-exilic Period: Spirit, Apocalyptic." *The Jerome Biblical Commentary.*

Vawter, Bruce. "Apocalyptic: Its Relation to Prophecy." *CBQ* 22 (1960) 33–46.

Index of Modern Authors

160